DIGITAL CURRENCY
ECONOMICS AND POLICY

DIGITAL CURRENCY
ECONOMICS AND POLICY

Editor
Bernard Yeung
National University of Singapore
Asian Bureau of Finance and Economic Research

World Scientific
NEW JERSEY • LONDON • SINGAPORE • BEIJING • SHANGHAI • HONG KONG • TAIPEI • CHENNAI • TOKYO

Published by

World Scientific Publishing Co. Pte. Ltd.

5 Toh Tuck Link, Singapore 596224

USA office: 27 Warren Street, Suite 401-402, Hackensack, NJ 07601

UK office: 57 Shelton Street, Covent Garden, London WC2H 9HE

Library of Congress Cataloging-in-Publication Data
Names: Yeung, Bernard, 1953– editor.
Title: Digital currency economics and policy / editor, Bernard Yeung,
National University of Singapore, Asian Bureau of Finance and Economic Research.
Description: Hackensack : World Scientific, 2020. | Includes bibliographical references and index.
Identifiers: LCCN 2020028095 | ISBN 9789811223778 (hardcover) | ISBN 9789811223785 (ebook) |
ISBN 9789811223792 (ebook other)
Subjects: LCSH: Digital currency.
Classification: LCC HG1710 .D54 2020 | DDC 332.4--dc23
LC record available at https://lccn.loc.gov/2020028095

British Library Cataloguing-in-Publication Data
A catalogue record for this book is available from the British Library.

For any available supplementary material, please visit
https://www.worldscientific.com/worldscibooks/10.1142/11922#t=suppl

Desk Editor: Ong Shi Min Nicole

Typeset by Stallion Press
Email: enquiries@stallionpress.com

About the Editor

Bernard Yeung is Stephen Riady Distinguished Professor in Finance and Strategic Management at the National University of Singapore (NUS) Business School and President of the Asian Bureau of Finance and Economic Research. He was Dean of NUS Business School from June 2008 to May 2019. Before joining NUS, he was the Abraham Krasnoff Professor in Global Business, Economics, and Management at New York University (NYU) Stern School of Business and the Director of the NYU China House. From 1988 to 1999, he taught at the University of Michigan and at the University of Alberta from 1983 to 1988. He has published widely in top tier academic journals covering topics in Finance, Economics, and Strategy; his writing also appears in important media publications such as the *People's Daily*, *The Financial Times*, *The Economist*, and the *Wall Street Journal*. He won the Public Administration Silver Medal (2018) in Singapore, the Irwin Outstanding Educator Award (2013) from the Academy of Management and is an elected Fellow of the Academy of International Business. He received his Bachelor of Arts in Economics and Mathematics from the University of Western Ontario and his MBA and PhD degrees from the Graduate School of Business at the University of Chicago.

Professor Yeung was a member of the Economic Strategies Committee in Singapore (2009), a member of the Social Science Research Council (SSRC) in Singapore (2016–2018) and a member of the Financial Research Council of the Monetary Authority of Singapore (2010–2013). He sits on the 3rd Advisory Board of the Antai College of Economics and

Management at Shanghai Jiao Tong University, the Advisory Council of the Economics and Management School of Wuhan University and the Advisory Committee of the Institute of Economics, Academia Sinica. Professor Yeung also serves as an independent Non-Executive Director of the Bank of China (BOC) Aviation Limited since 2016.

Contents

Opening Statement Proceedings

Edward Robinson and Bernard Yeung[1]

Workshop on Digital Currency Economics and Policy, 15–16 Nov 2018
Jan 13th, 2020

I. Introduction

In November 2018, the Asian Bureau of Finance and Economic Research (ABFER), the Economic Policy Group (EPG) of the Monetary Authority of Singapore (MAS), and the National University of Singapore (NUS) Business School co-organised a two-day workshop to explore the economics of digital currencies and their implications for monetary and financial regulatory policies. Leading academic researchers in monetary and financial economics were invited to speak at the workshop, which attracted a large number of participants, including central bankers, academics, and practitioners in the financial industry.[2]

---

[1] Edward Robinson is Chief Economist at the Monetary Authority of Singapore. Bernard Yeung is the President of the Asian Bureau of Finance and Economic Research and the Stephan Riady Distinguished Professor of the NUS Business School. This chapter/summary benefitted greatly from the contributions and suggestions of Choy Keen Meng, Ng DingXuan, Xiong Wei from EPG, MAS and from Joseph Cherian of NUS.

[2] The speakers and discussants at the workshop were Franklin Allen (Imperial College London), Robleh Ali (MIT), Markus Brunnermeier (Princeton University), Barry Eichengreen (University of California, Berkeley), Charles Engel (University of Wisconsin-Madison), Gur Huberman (Columbia University), Randall Morck (University of Alberta), Danny Quah (NUS), Kenneth Rogoff (Harvard University), Andrew Rose (National University of Singapore), Prateek Saxena (NUS), Beatrice Weder di Mauro (INSEAD Singapore), David Yermack (New York University) and Bernard Yeung (NUS Business School). Materials from the workshop are available at the ABFER website.

This document distils the key insights generated by the two days of enriching conversations and provides a summary of the authors' and discussants' presentations.

The advent of the distributed ledger technology has facilitated the development of private digital currencies. To appreciate what is new, we need to remind ourselves of the past.

Electronic transaction record keeping has been around for decades and has evolved into convenient payment systems, e.g., telegraphic clearings and transfers, credit card payments, and e-wallets. So far, these systems have been denominated in fiat currencies, each with a controller who enforces compliance with regulations and protocols on permitted member-users to affirm that all entries are credible and valid, i.e., mitigating fraudulent behaviour or double spending. In each system the controller, or an assigned operator, maintains a centralized ledger to keep track of transactions, attains correctness (and thus user trust), and strives for internal cost efficiency in administering the system. However, the cost efficiencies result in significant economies of scale which could deter entry even while the controlling party seeks to exploit the rents.

The distributed ledger technology, on the contrary, does not have a centralized controller. Instead, its built-in regulations and protocols lead to the distribution of all records, time stamped, to all users. The decentralized system allows all users to investigate and verify the integrity of the ledger.[3] Furthermore, this "trust-no-human but just the technology" system does not have to be denominated in any fiat currency. In other words, the system's technology uses intrinsic regulations and protocols to ascertain ***correctness***, allows free entrants and ***decentralized*** record keeping, and its unit of account can be itself, e.g., Bitcoin. In contrast, a centralized system is backed up by a controlling entity and often rested on fiat money which is issued by a monetary authority with mandates specified by the state. However, an open distributed ledger backed system, thus far, incurs

[3] A distributed ledger may be permission free or permission based. In the case of Bitcoin, the distributed ledger is open; an entrant just needs to run the software necessary to conform to the protocol (e.g., to mine a Bitcoin). Currently, some applications of the distributed ledger technology impose a permission requirement.

substantial operation ***costs*** due to the computational requirements to verify that each entry follows the protocols.

The creation of private digital currencies leads to many fundamental questions. The discussions during the two-day conference focused on: (i) whether private digital currencies can be considered "money" and their impact on monetary policy and the international monetary system; (ii) whether central banks would issue their own digital currencies and the impact of such actions; and (iii) the usage of the distributed ledger technology in the financial system.

II. Private digital currencies as money and their impact on monetary policy and international monetary system

Present day monetary systems are already mostly digital with a trusted third-party keeping track of transactions on a centralized ledger. These transactions involve customer deposits held with commercial banks, and bank reserves held by commercial banks with the central bank. The latter, together with cash in circulation, forms the monetary base which is the basis for money creation by commercial banks through lending (and deposit) activities.

As described above, the distributed ledger-based system allows the development of a unit of account and possibly a medium of transaction by-passing any centralized third party, including the government. Naturally, one would question whether this technology-driven digital entity truly constitutes money and how its introduction would impact the monetary system and policy. Currently, private digital currencies, even in aggregate, are fairly insignificant, and they cannot yet be money for a number of reasons.

First, there is an efficiency consideration. Historically, there has been a tendency for currency and coin issuance to be increasingly concentrated in the hands of the central government. Using a uniform stable currency enhances informational efficiency; in contrast, having multiple currencies increases the costs of acquiring information on relative prices and on the credibility of each of the different currency issuers. Currently, high volatility in the prices of private digital currencies impedes their ability to serve as a unit of account and medium of transaction, although a limited few could serve as a store of value.

Second, stable money, serving as a unit of account and medium of transaction, including for taxation and redistribution purposes, is a public good that is too important to be left to a decentralized system. Moreover, publicly used money needs to be managed to secure price and financial stability, and counter business cycles. Currently, it is not clear if private digital currencies can be algorithmically designed to carry out these functions. Price and financial stability is a public good, justifying governments' historical concern with retaining control over monetary management.

Third, there is an issue of mitigating socially undesirable behavior. Private digital currencies allow for anonymous transactions, many of which may arise from socially undesirable or illegal activities. A government may then have to limit the proliferation of private digital currencies which allow anonymous transactions. A state can reduce the liquidity of private digital currencies simply by prohibiting their conversion into legalised currencies. Indeed, if governments can cooperate internationally to make all private digital currencies non-convertible, they can drastically reduce their use in tax evasion and other illegal transactions.

The original motive for developing private digital currencies, e.g., Bitcoin, may include weakening the government's monopoly on seigniorage, but the world's monetary authorities have been successful in keeping prices stable, except in a few countries with political instability or a high level of corruption.[4] Internationally, stable fiat currencies can serve as substitutes to unstable currencies and thus constrain a government's ability to impose a high inflation tax. Finally, while the development of private digital currencies may stem from some people's desire to be independent of centralized control in transactions, this conflicts with the public's preference for stable money.

In summary, the likelihood of private digital currencies, as currently designed, replacing national currencies is likely to be limited at this point. Given that the share of overall transactions involving private digital

---

[4] Currently high inflation countries include Venezuela, Zimbabwe, South Sudan, North Korea, Argentina, Iran, Sudan, Liberia, Haiti, Sierra Leone, Angola, Ethiopia, Turkey, Uzbekistan, and Nigeria ranging from 282,973% to 11%.

currencies also remains relatively small, their effects on monetary policies or the international monetary system are also likely to be insignificant at present, aside from possibly helping to loosen somewhat the effects of capital controls. Last but not least, one should be cautious in using private digital currencies as investment and retirement products because they are unregulated and may not be backed by any underlying asset.

III. Central bank digital currency

Central banks may opt to issue their own digital currency, which is referred to as a Central Bank Digital Currency (CBDC). It can be made accessible throughout the economy or only at the wholesale level. In a 2018 survey of central banks, 69% said they were studying the implications of introducing a CBDC. However, central banks are generally cautious and not many are currently committed to the actual issuance of CBDCs.[5] There are both positive and negative considerations associated with the issuance of a CBDC.

The positive considerations stem from the fact that CBDC accounts provide a useful source of economic data and facilitate effective and flexible monetary policy.

First, CBDC transactions contain detailed microeconomic data and thus convey information on economic trends that may be used to inform monetary policy.

Second, a CBDC can strengthen monetary policy transmission mechanisms, especially if every citizen has a CBDC account. As funds can move expediently between CDBC and bank accounts, banks have to offer deposit rates closely tied with the CBDC interest rate, leading to more immediate monetary policy transmission. A central bank can even perform targeted money creation to stimulate aggregate demand in specific segments of the economy.

[5] See slides 6 and 8 of Dr. Agustín Carstens's presentation during the workshop. These slides indicate that the numbers are drawn from BIS's Committee on Payments and Market Infrastructure central bank survey on CBDC and digital tokens. (Dr. Agustín Carstens is General Manager, Bank for International Settlements.)

Third, CBDC can result in more flexible monetary policy: if cash is abolished, a central bank will then be able to impose negative interest rates on CBDC.

Fourth, CBDC accounts, if made widely accessible, can improve financial inclusion.

However, we do have to be aware that these latter uses of CBDC blur the boundaries between monetary and fiscal policies, including redistribution policy.

Meanwhile, the negative considerations stem from the structural impact that the creation of CBDC may have on the country's financial system.

First, through a CBDC, citizens can hold deposits at the central bank, which raises the number of digital transactions performed at the central bank. This creates concentrated operation risks (e.g., exposure to relentless hacking) and calls for system back-ups in a geographically diverse manner.

Second, central banks would have to absorb the responsibility of "knowing your clients"; that is, safeguarding against money laundering and similar illegal transactions becomes a direct central bank responsibility.

Third, demand for safe assets may lead to depositors reallocating funds from commercial bank deposits to CBDC, eventually leading to what resembles a "narrow banking" system where CBDC becomes "narrow" money. Also, the digital system facilitates savers' fund movements between private sector banks and the central bank. Banks will have to directly source deposits from the central bank or to offer deposit rates very close to the CBDC deposit rate. Further, the system raises the efficiency of fund transmission but reduces banks' potential payment intermediation income. How these changes will impact commercial banks' risk-taking behaviour is unclear. However, the view is that there will be rapid "runs" whenever a bank shows signs of weakness. While this may (or may not) make individual banks more risk-averse, system-wide financial stability may be weakened. A central bank can provide deposits to commercial banks to safeguard against adverse spillovers, but this potentially increases the prominence of the central bank's role as a lender of last resort and gives rise to increased concerns over moral hazards in the commercial banking system.

Fourth, as the potential dominance of the central bank in the payments system could negatively impact banks' and big tech companies' potential earnings from managing payments, there may be strong resistant to the creation of an open CBDC.

These positive and negative considerations clearly justify central banks' exhaustive ongoing work on understanding and exploring CBDCs and the related technology.

IV. The usage of the distributed ledger technology in the financial system

Undeniably, the distributed ledger technology (DLT) that underlies many new private digital currencies could potentially lead to revolutionary changes in the financial system.

A distributed ledger (DL) system is more transparent, auditable and resilient than a centralized ledger system. The DL system records transactions or contracts in a decentralized manner across different locations and people, with each record being time stamped. Hence, the full transaction history is visible to anyone. The open records' reliability and accuracy rest ***not*** on the capability and integrity of a central authority. Rather, information is typically etched on the decentralized ledger using cryptography and can be modified only using keys and cryptographic signatures. The resultant database is harder to modify and more resistant to cyber-attacks than centralized ledgers (because all the distributed copies need to be attacked simultaneously).

Earlier generations of DLT tended to be slow in processing transactions and costly to operate and were thus not very scalable. For example, Bitcoin is based on a type of distributed ledger technology known as the blockchain — a sequence of chained blocks. Acquiring the proof of work to become a part of the chain greatly slows down operation and raises costs. Other decentralized ledgers have resorted to restricting access to only a subset of permissioned users; this prevents fraudulent changes to the ledger while reducing the costs of processing transactions. Indeed, some business-to-business transactions have begun using private permission-based blockchain systems, leading to more efficient and scalable DL record keeping.[6]

---

[6] See Ali, Robleh, (2019). "Cellular Structure for a Digital Fiat Currency," MIT Digital Currency Initiative, paper presented at the workshop.

The resilience, auditability and scalability properties together have led to efficiency enhancing applications in Singapore's financial system. "Project Ubin" allows MAS to offer a central bank digital Singapore dollar on a distributed ledger platform for inter-bank transactions. The platform allows for decentralized netting of payments but preserves privacy, allows tokenization of physical assets, and results in improvements to efficiency, cost, speed and risk management in cross border transactions.[7] Such systems can be extended to increase the efficiency and security of DLT-based payments systems. Likewise, the distributed ledger technology can be expanded to raise efficiency and speed in currently cumbersome trade financing arrangements. Many big-tech companies in Asia and the US are developing such systems, e.g., Libra, that save on payment intermediation costs and expand clients' choices.

Besides the application to payments, DLT has also been increasingly harnessed for another key function of the financial system — borrowing and lending services. However, both regulators and investors need to exercise caution. For example, as discussed in the workshop, initial coin offerings (ICO) allow firms to borrow by issuing coins which can then be traded on cryptocurrency exchanges. This enables firms to raise funds from international investors without having to meet local legal standards of issuing debt or equity. However, the lack of regulatory oversight has led to relatively high instances of scams among ICOs. There is a need to regulate ICOs to ensure that only qualified investors can participate in them. Yet, even seasoned investors need to have the right skills in computer science, law and finance to invest in ICOs.

V. Taking stock

The discussions in the workshop were useful in clarifying the manner in which private digital currencies could prove to be destabilizing. While the jury is still out on this, current private digital currencies do not carry out significant roles as a unit of account and a medium of payment,

---

[7] This project is the collaboration between MAS, the Singapore Exchange, banks, technology companies, and academic institutions. At a later stage, Project Ubin was linked with Project Jasper of the Bank of Canada.

and are a relatively small asset class at this point. They therefore have a negligible impact on monetary policy and the international monetary system. However, they may provide a slight boost in international payment flows, and at present can facilitate the conduct of anonymous transactions, some of which could stem from illegal activities.

The participants also provided a framework to evaluate the prospects of CBDC. A monetary system with CBDC implies a greater degree of movements of deposit funds between CBDC accounts and deposit accounts. It raises the effectiveness of monetary policy as the CBDC interest rate and bank deposit rates will be closely tied because they are close substitutes. If cash is eliminated, central banks can even implement negative interest rate policies. Data from CDBC accounts will also give the central bank potentially valuable information about the economy. Yet, CBDC's potential impact on the structure of a financial system deserves a high level of attention. CBDC deposits may displace traditional bank deposits and may also become narrow money, with the central bank becoming fund provider for commercial sector financial intermediation. Fluid movements of funds between CBDC accounts and bank deposit accounts may increase financial institutions' exposures to runs. Banks may reduce their risk-taking but the overall impact on financial stability is unclear. Clearly, a central bank will have to be more vigilant in safeguarding financial stability and against banks' morally hazardous behavior. Finally, concentrating transactions at the CBDC level may create significant operation risk at the central bank.

The workshop provided greater clarity on the usage of the distributed ledger technology in the financial system. Innovative applications of distributed ledger technology, particularly those that economize on operation cost, can be efficient, resilient and scalable. The key is that the technology, given its distributed record keeping, is more resilient to cyberattacks than centralized record keeping and the "intrinsic to technology" user rules and regulations allow for greater user trust. These innovations have the potential to increase efficiency for within and cross border payments, trade financing, and the like, all of which reduce the reliance of centralized control and transform current practices.

VI. A summary of the presentations and discussions

The following is a summary of the presentations and discussions in the workshop.

Mr. Edward Robinson, Chief Economist, MAS, gave the opening remarks. He pointed out that electronic money and payment systems are not new, with the US Federal Reserve making telegraphic transfers in the 1910s and credit card payments beginning in the 1950s. These innovations have made payments more efficient but have not impacted the monopoly of fiat monies. Supply of private digital currencies, enabled by encryption technology, first appeared around 2008. While this has increased over the years, their share of transactions is currently still limited. A fundamental understanding of the demand side and the underlying technology is called for. In a global environment where central banks have generally managed to keep inflation in check, the demand for private digital currencies does not seem to be driven by the need to mitigate seigniorage. Rather, Mr. Robinson noted that private digital currencies cater to the demand for increased anonymity and privacy in transactions. Nevertheless, such anonymity may also facilitate transactions stemming from illegal activities. Furthermore, the advance of the technology may have other effects on the payments and financial systems. Thus, the distributed-ledger technology behind digital currencies may be a supply-driven innovation shock. He also pointed out that the privilege of currency issuance brings with it an enormous responsibility — in safeguarding the integrity of a country's supply of money.

With these and many other important questions in the minds of academics, practitioners and policymakers, Mr. Robinson encouraged a vigorous intellectual discourse on digital currency based on established paradigms in economics and finance, in order to develop an internally consistent narrative on this fast-moving development. With this objective in mind, MAS, ABFER and NUS collaborated to organize this workshop, gathering globally renowned experts to discuss the implications of new digital currencies from a range of perspectives, including the history of currencies, monetary theory and policy, financial structures, and technological developments in DLT.

In his keynote speech, ***Professor Rogoff of the Harvard Kennedy School***, drew the audience's attention to two issues: digital currencies as a form of money and the implications of using the technology underlying it. He highlighted several important policy concerns.

Private digital currencies allow anonymity in their use. Yet, Prof Rogoff argued that functions such as the unit of account, the medium for final clearing of transactions among financial institutions, and especially the payment of taxes and transfers are simply too vital for modern-day countries to leave in the hands of a decentralized private sector system. He argued that, "The long history of currency innovation teaches us that the private sector innovates, but in due time the government regulates and appropriates. The same will eventually be true for innovations in digital currencies. ... Indeed, governments will surely in due time have the capacity to issue secure digital currencies." He believed that trusted party "permissioned" systems will almost surely dominate "permissionless systems" in which private digital currencies reside. The main issue with central bank digital currencies is disintermediation, similar to having only narrow banks.

Prof. Rogoff explained that, as a technological innovation, blockchain has a vast number of actual and potential applications outside the payments system, ranging from providing faster and better ways to have digital signatures to providing a completely different means for social networking. In terms of applications to payments system, the technology can provide cheaper, faster, and more secure payment rails, reducing the monopoly and related profits captured by credit and debit card clearing systems. Central banks have been perfectly content to allow the development of superior transactions technologies while keeping a watchful eye on price and financial stability. They will also put a significant premium on regulating anonymity. The important regulatory tradeoff is between unleashing the technology's potential for improving efficiency versus safeguarding the security and stability of the financial system.

Prof. Barry Eichengreen of UC Berkeley delivered the first workshop paper, *"From Commodity to Fiat and Now to Crypto: What Does History Tell us?"*. His presentation focused on: (i) providing an historical perspective on the evolution of currency; (ii) using historical records to provide an analysis of stable coins, and; (iii) analyzing the cases for and against central bank digital currency.

History has shown a tendency for currency and coin issuance to be increasingly *concentrated* in the hands of the central or federal government. There are two explanations. First, from the earlier days when the modern state system emerged till the end of the 18th Century, central governments needed to wield control over currency creation (and seigniorage) in order to mobilize resources for national defense and in case of emergencies. Second, with the evolution of modern financial systems since the 19th Century, government monopoly of money issuance, either *de facto* or *de jure*, rests on the economic efficiency of a currency that is both uniform (because there is only one issuer) and stable (because it is issued in economically appropriate amounts, for example, by an independent central bank with a politically-assigned mandate to pursue price stability). A uniform currency reduces information costs because utilizing a reliable issuer's currency makes it unnecessary to have information about the creditworthiness of each and every issuer. By the same token, the digital payment services provided by Visa and Mastercard are attractive because they are information insensitive: the credit card companies protect sellers from buyers' default risk and a dollar on a credit card is convertible into a dollar one-to-one. This consideration implies that the costs of producing and obtaining information about changes in the actual and prospective value of privately issued digital currencies is an obstacle to their wider utilization.

Prof. Eichengreen pointed out that stable coins can be classified into four categories: fiat fully collateralized, crypto collateralized, partially collateralized and uncollateralized. The information efficiency consideration suggests that the first three are all inferior to a central bank cryptocurrency. For example, information asymmetry (between providers of a stable coin and coin-holders) on the value of collateral can lead to wild fluctuations of a coin's market price, speculative "runs," and huge costs and risks (on the part of the providers) to stabilize coin value. Unlike central banks, a stable coin provider cannot stipulate exchange controls (i.e., capital controls) against runs. Similarly, if they change the ratio of stable coin to collateral (when depleted by runs), they undermine the basis of the stable coin. The concept of uncollateralized stable coin appears to be underdeveloped, and Prof. Eichengreen noted, "It is not clear whether the architects of uncollateralized stable coins are conversant in that literature (on speculative attacks on pegged exchange rates)."

According to Prof. Eichengreen, over ninety central banks are exploring the possibility of issuing their own digital currencies, which can take the form of electronic accounts at the central bank. A central bank's digital unit could also circulate in a distributed fashion (held in mobile wallets or on electronic smart cards). The usage could be for wholesale payments only, or it could be extended to other forms of transactions.

Prof. Eichengreen described both negative and positive considerations. First, concentrating all digital currency transactions at the central bank would also concentrate operational risk. Second, CDBCs could induce runs on traditional banks as the public would be able to transfer their deposits at the push of a button. Limiting overall deposit size at the central bank would create a premium on central bank accounts, re-introducing the complexity of non-uniform currencies. Third, a central bank-based digital currency can generate more information for the monetary authority and make monetary policy more direct and effective — central banks can influence market interest rates more effectively and can set the policy interest rate below the zero lower bound; they can even provide targeted helicopter money to specific groups.

Prof. Eichengreen concluded that there is strong economic justification for a uniform digital currency and the national government is the only entity capable of credibly providing for it on a national scale. However, depending on further technological developments, the jury is still out on whether private digital currencies will be adopted more widely.

Prof. Randall Morck (University of Alberta), agreed with Prof. Eichengreen's inferences on the historical experience. He pointed out that the tension between competing versus monopolistic money creation existed at the beginning of written history: ancient Egyptians used competing moneys — metals by weight, oils and grains by volume (Janssen 1975).[8] Private digital currencies so far have not served as an effective medium of exchange, unit of account and store of value because as Prof. Eichengreen

[8] Janssen, Jozef. 1975. *Commodity Prices from the Ramessid Period: An economic study of the village of necropolis workmen at Thebes*. Brill.

explained, they incur high costs and are broadly inferior to fiat money in all three roles. Blockchain allegedly provides anonymity that may compensate for the costs; but at present, it largely facilitates illegal transactions: a study reveals that up to 70% of Bitcoin holdings and up to 60% of Bitcoin transactions are illegal (Foley *et al.* 2019).[9] Furthermore, the energy requirements for maintaining the Bitcoin ledger restrict its scalability. Bitcoin mining already uses enough electricity to power Austria (Krause and Tolaymat 2018) and the environmental cost will only rise if Bitcoin is more widely used.[10]

Prof. Morck concurred with Prof. Eichengreen that central bank digital currencies have their advantages. First, a CBDC would allow central banks to run more effective and direct monetary policy. Currently, central banks stimulate the economy by creating money to buy treasury securities, increasing their prices, lowering debt yields and bank interest rates, so as to encourage borrowing and stimulate aggregate demand. If everyone had a CBDC account, a recession-fighting central bank could directly inject new money into the accounts of low-income people who have higher marginal propensities to consume. Second, CBDC can eliminate the roughly 3% overhead costs in credit card payments or check clearing. The Bank of Canada has successfully tested such a system for buying and selling goods, stocks, and foreign exchange. The trade-off is the cost in building geographically separated backup computers to safeguard against operation risk. Prof. Morck raised the point that commercial banks, credit card companies, securities brokers, stock exchanges, and providers of all manner of back-office settlement services would lobby intensely to prevent such efficiency (Duffie 2019),[11] while Big Finance is also a formidable foe (Johnson and Kwak 2010).[12]

---

[9] Foley, Sean, Jonathan R. Karlsen & Tālis J. Putniņš. 2019. Sex, drugs, and bitcoin: How much illegal activity is financed through cryptocurrencies? *Review of Financial Studies* 32(5)1798–1853.

[10] Krause, Max & Thabet Tolaymat. 2018. Quantification of energy and carbon costs for mining cryptocurrencies. *Nature Sustainability* 1, 711–718.

[11] Duffie, Darrell. 2019. Digital Currencies and Fast Payment Systems: Disruption is Coming." Unpublished manuscript, Stanford University.

[12] Johnson, Simon, and James Kwak. 2010. *13 bankers: The Wall Street takeover and the next financial meltdown*. Pantheon Books, ISBN 978-0-307-37905-4.

Prof. Markus Brunnermeier, Princeton University, presented his thinking (based on his joint work with ***Dr. Dirk Niepelt*** of Study Center Gerzensee and University of Bern) on *"the co-existence of private digital currencies and central bank currencies."* Private sector digital currencies are based on decentralized record keeping while a central bank issued digital currency is based on centralized record keeping. The decentralized approach has rigorous competition in validating an entry, but the proof of work consumes huge energy and effort. (The economic gain to taking stock of records and creating a fake entry can be huge.) In the centralized approach, entries are validated by the issuer which is cost-efficient. However, the issuer can over time be tempted to change the digital currency's value (seigniorage). Prof. Brunnermeier termed the three considerations — degree of centralization, correctness, and cost efficiency — *a digital currency trilemma*. Private digital currencies and central bank digital currency can achieve only two, but not all three, considerations.

Prof. Brunnermeier clarified some important characteristics of CBDCs. CBDCs, if available to all residents, can displace deposits. A concern is whether this triggers runs on banks and disrupts investments. Prof. Brunnermeier pointed out that CBDC is fundamentally equivalent to narrow money and has been proposed both in Continental Europe (Vollgeld) and the US (Chicago plan). First, a central bank can still provide deposits to banks for intermediation. Thus, CDBC would not affect private sector banks' access to deposits and should not reduce private sector investment. Second, while CBDC allows speedy transfer of deposits from banks to a central bank, the same central bank can equally speedily provide liquidity to banks at risk of a run. Third, while widespread reallocation of bank deposits into CBDC can erode bank profits, banks can be compensated if it is deemed desirable by the public.

Prof. Danny Quah, Dean of Lee Kuan Yew School of Public Policy (LKYSPP) at NUS, focused his comments on the potential implications of greater utilization of digital payments platforms in general, rather than addressing DLT. First, he posited that greater utilization of digital payments may lead to information management issues. Digitization in means of payment and store of value calls for strong cyber-security protection. At the same time, there could be tension between the rights to privacy and anonymity vs authorities' rights to know for legitimate purposes and for public policy formation purposes. Digital means also lower information and access barriers, potentially raising financial inclusivity, e.g., in poor rural areas. Data integration can lead to effective dashboards that lower transaction costs, e.g., in matching buyers and sellers, and predictive rather than reactive public policy making. He thought that building trust is a challenge to all of these exciting viable developments but that legal systems are currently ill-equipped to manage the widespread adoption of digital payments. He suggested that the answer may be a private-public partnership on digital currency provision, rather than competition, to alleviate concerns.

Prof. Charles Engel (University of Wisconsin Madison) considered *"Implications of digital currency on the international monetary system and monetary policy,"* conditional on private digital currencies becoming viable and established, even though many uncertainties remain.

Prof. Engel pointed out that the anonymity of private digital currencies makes it much easier to evade capital flows management policies. The "traditional" view of economists (and the IMF) is that free capital flows is desirable for efficiency considerations, and that capital controls are costly to enforce and induce corruption. However, there are situations in which the ability to monitor and manage capital flows is desirable: (i) to stop transactions stemming from illegal activities from crossing borders; (ii) when individual investors do not internalize the externality in home investment; and (iii) when incomplete information can lead to undesirable mismatch in currency exposures of assets and liabilities and in term structure, and may even lead to bubbles. Indeed, countries need to have measures to mitigate volatility in exchange rates or capital flows to maintain price and financial system stability. While preference for anonymity may motivate the development of private digital currencies, the contribution of anonymity to social welfare is questionable.

Prof. Engel believed that private digital currencies are unlikely to replace government currencies for well-managed economies, whose central banks have been successful in maintaining price stability. However, they can be a disciplining force on governments motivated by seigniorage, just like dollarization, or like currency substitution in which unreliable home currencies will be substituted by other currencies or even commodities.

Still, private digital currencies would only present a marginal immediate "threat" to monetary policy and the international financial system, except for facilitating the evasion of capital controls. The challenges for the future depend completely on how the role of digital currencies evolves: how widely they are used in transactions and are held as reserves.

A central bank digital currency, if developed and available to the public, has implications for monetary policy. Prof. Engel's starting point is that central bank digital currency is the ultimate safe asset, for its default risk is lower than bank deposits and its transaction and handling costs are lower than Treasury bills. This leads to two considerations.

First, commercial banks may be concerned about losing deposits. They still have a role in maturity transformation. However, their funding will become more expensive and lending cost will rise. A suggestion is that a central bank can provide funding to commercial banks, but that raises the need for vigilant regulators to safeguard against moral hazard problems.

Second, Prof. Engel raised a conjecture that a reliable central bank's digital currency is a safe asset and an economy may then in aggregate adjust its portfolio towards this safe asset. Greater holdings of this safe asset may encourage more lending and borrowing in local currency. Correspondingly, there will also be less of a need to invoice trade in the US dollar. This may mitigate the international financial system's strong reliance on the US dollar.

Prof. Andrew Rose (Dean NUS Business School 2019) agreed with the main conclusion that private sector digital currencies would have little immediate effect on monetary policy or the international monetary system, except that they facilitate the loosening of capital controls. He added that electronic payment arrangements are already quite prevalent so that "money" is mostly digital, but these technological innovations have not compromised the effectiveness of monetary policy. However, the potential of digital currency to increase capital mobility over time may make the choice between fixed exchange rate and monetary sovereignty sharper.

Prof. Rose commented that private digital currencies, even in aggregate, are fairly small: the total stock of them is less than 2% of worldwide currency and less than 4% of daily foreign exchange transactions. Because of the volatility stemming from their inelastic supply, private digital currencies do not meet the requirements of being money: a medium of exchange, unit of account and store of value. If the objective of creating a private digital currency is to discipline the central bank's monopoly on money supply, most digital currencies fail. More fundamentally, it is not clear if private (decentralized) digital currencies can be algorithmically designed to stabilize prices, counter business cycles and serve as a lender of last resort, all of which are currently functions residing with the monetary authority.

Prof. Rose argued that a central bank digital currency can indeed give a monetary authority the flexibility to offer negative interest rates. A central bank, however, needs to safeguard against hacking and create its own know your client (KYC) protocols and risks substituting practices for commercial banks' deposits. He further pointed out that with or without a central bank digital currency, the monetary authority's policy assignment remains: a society gives its central bank power and independence in return for price and financial stability.

Mr. Robleh Ali (Digital Currency Initiative, MIT Media Lab) gave a presentation based on his work, "*The Structure of Digital Fiat Currencies.*" He suggested that a digital fiat currency, either issued by a central bank or by a private entity, can be provided to the financial system in the future to reduce entry barriers and improve efficiency. Currently, payment systems comprise an operator running the system and members providing services to end-users. This ***centralized*** control of systems deters competing entrants. The control's core function is to prevent double spending (***correctness***), which is accomplished by having well-enforced contractual obligations and regulations extrinsic to technology. The enforcement is that only trusted new entrants are granted permission to join and there will be heavy penalties if rules are not followed.

Bitcoin, using distributed ledger technology, makes rules and enforcement intrinsic to technology. It is a ***decentralized*** system that solves the no double payment problem without the need to screen and monitor trusted participants. The system rejects any transaction that does not follow its rules. Indeed, all participants inside a Bitcoin system have to ***validate*** a record (***confirm correctness***). However, the only requirement for a participant to join the system is running the software necessary to conform to the protocol: it is largely an open system, the integrity of which is based on the system's intrinsic rules and protocol. The distinction between the controlled system and the open system is the extrinsic trust requirement in the former; the higher the requirement, the higher the entry barrier.

Mr. Ali proposed an intermediate system that addresses some of the problems associated with Bitcoin's completely decentralized ledger structure, while retaining some features of distributed ledger technology that allow for greater security and privacy for users relative to the centralized ledgers in the status quo. Essentially, the proposed system is built up from multiple different ledgers recording transactions for the same fiat currency. Each ledger (cell) in the system has its own issuer which holds central bank money equal to the amount of digital fiat currency issued in the cell. This 100 percent backing is vastly different from Bitcoin which has zero backing. In addition to the backing, the issuer is responsible for the software and protocol used to make transactions within its own cell. The cell will also have validators recording and updating copies of its transaction ledger. The validators can use Cryptokernel (a blockchain-based toolkit developed at the *MIT Digital Currency Initiative*) which allows the validators to be separate from the issuer. Transactions among cells are based on a "trustless" arrangement: rules are intrinsic to the technology, e.g., via all cells adopting Hashed Timelock Contracts. This trustless intermediation system lowers barrier to entry.

Besides providing competition to existing payment systems, such an alternative infrastructure also diversifies operational failure risks due to cyberattacks.

Dr Prateek Saxena (NUS School of Computing) commented that decentralization strengthens systems resilience because there will be no single point of failure. He added that tokenization allows fractional ownership and improves liquidity. Overall, blockchain technology has many innovative applications that are scalable and resilient.

Prof. David Yermack (Stern NYU) presented his work on "*How private digital currencies affect government policy*," co-authored with

Max Raskin (NYU Law School) and Fahad Saleh (McGill University). He first presented a simple but useful classification of digital currencies along two axes: state-sponsorship and centralization. A digital currency can be private or state-sponsored, which includes legal enforcement that privileges the digital currency, e.g., legal tender laws or taxation on competing money. Centralization pertains to formal barriers to entry that prevent participation in the writing and validating process of a cryptocurrency network. To illustrate, the authors pointed out that Bitcoin is private and decentralized, digital currencies run by a closely held company (e.g., Google Wallet and Apply Pay) are private and centralized, a central bank digital currency is state sponsored and centralized while no candidate emerges for the state sponsored decentralized category.

The vision is that a private decentralized digital currency, e.g., the Bitcoin, is an "e-currency based on cryptographic proof, without the need to trust a third-party middleman" making money "secure and transactions effortless." The creation of private digital currencies offers an opportunity to examine the impact that alternative digital currencies have on unstable sovereign currencies in countries like Turkey and Argentina, as well as their fiscal and regulatory policies. The authors formalized a simple model comprising several propositions. First, a private sector-created digital currency offers the public the scope to diversify their asset holdings. Second, while a self-interested government would collect returns to assets and hence seigniorage, it cannot collect seigniorage on a private sector digital currency. Thus, the private sector digital currency effectively disciplines the government in collecting seigniorage. Citizens' welfare gain is greater the more the diversification benefit; that is, the more negatively returns to productive assets and to digital currency as an asset class are correlated. The authors conclude that "The history of money … suggests that there will always be a demand for a non-state currency that serves as a check on the inflationary monetary tendencies."

Prof. Gur Huberman of Columbia Business School commented that the typology was useful. He pointed out that Prof. Yermack's analysis is more likely to apply in corrupt regimes. A private decentralized digital currency is owned by no one, rules are fixed by a protocol and participants are price-takers. Thus, there is no issue of rent extraction. Prof. Huberman further raised important questions: who supplies digital currency? How desirable is it to exclude the transfer of illegally obtained wealth? Is a digital currency, which has no underlying value, an asset? Is some flexibility in levying seigniorage desirable?

Mr. Ravi Menon, Managing Director of MAS, moderated a central bankers' panel which comprised **Dr. Agustín Carstens**, General Manager of BIS and **Ms. Cecilia Skingsley**, Deputy Governor of the Sveriges Riksbank. In his opening remarks, Mr. Menon highlighted that practitioners are concerned about the use of private digital currencies as investment and retirement products which bypass the central bank as the settling authority. He also stated that current cross-border payment systems are costly because they utilize old technology and because of the presence of multiple middlemen. However, the application of the blockchain technology has brought down costs (e.g., MAS' project Ubin leverages on blockchain-based transactions to streamline cross-border payments) and CBDCs could be another application of such technology.

Dr. Carstens provided a taxonomy of money, based on the following: issuer (central bank or not); form (digital or physical); accessibility (open or restricted); and technology (account-based or token-based). He further pointed out that while general usage of card payments has gone up, cash in circulation varies a great deal around the world e.g., Japan and India still have significant amounts of cash in circulation while Sweden has seen a significant fall in theirs. Dr. Carstens noted that the current system can already support domestic real-time gross settlement around the clock, though he admitted that there may be issues with cross-border payments as highlighted by Mr. Menon. He therefore did not see an urgent need for a blockchain-based means of payment. On the topic of CBDC, he noted that while a considerable number of central banks were looking into both wholesale and retail digital currencies, not many are committed to the actual development and issuance of CBDCs, as the demand for them is still muted. In terms of financial stability, Dr. Carstens also cautioned that the adoption of digital currencies means that there is an increased risk of technical vulnerabilities stemming from the nature of the technology, on top of the inherent financial market risks that already exist today.

Ms Skingsley highlighted that her country's cash in circulation had dropped by 50 per cent over the past 10 years and is now just 1% of GDP.

Indeed, businesses are now not obliged to accept cash. She said that a CBDC can be account-based or token-based with wide or limited scope. A CBDC with wide accessibility could be a transmission mechanism for interest rates that would facilitate monetary policy. She also discussed Sweden's focus on public-private partnerships to build digital payments systems that can retain widespread use of and public trust in the national currency.

Prof. Franklin Allen (Imperial College, London) discussed "*Digital tokens and financial regulations.*" ICOs are done in a number of ways; a typical sequence of events is that the party making the ICO will issue a "White Paper" describing the nature of the technology being funded and the uses the technology can be put to. Potential investors can raise questions before an initial sale of "coin" is made. Promoters use the funds raised to implement the promised project while coins can be traded on cryptocurrency exchanges.

Prof. Allen referred to Cohney *et al.* (2018), which compared the governance of ICOs and protection of investors through computer code, and found that the ICO code and ICO disclosures often do not match.[13] Kaal (2018) points to several advantages of ICOs compared to conventional ways of raising capital, e.g., ICOs enable borderless online sales enabling promoters to bypass the usual legal and jurisdictional hurdles, continuous access to trade around the clock, and providing liquidity to investors faster than other forms of capital formation, e.g., venture capital funds.[14] However, the lack of regulatory oversight and legal recourse to the promoters is a major drawback.

ICOs raise a whole set of interesting regulation issues but many countries are still silent on their regulatory status. Countries like China and South Korean have banned ICOs outright while the US's SEC Report of Investigation (July 2017) found that a blockchain-based token qualified as a security requiring registration under the Securities Act of 1933. The UK adopts a "regulatory sandbox" approach.

---

[13] See Cohney, S., D. Hoffman, J. Sklaroff and D. Wishnick (2018). "Coin-Operated Capitalism," working paper, University of Pennsylvania, SSRN-id3215345.

[14] See Kaal, W. (2018). "Initial Coin Offerings: The Top 25 Jurisdictions and their Comparative Regulatory Responses," working paper, University of St. Thomas School of Law, SSRN-id3117224.

The dilemma in this area is how to prevent scams without hampering innovation. Unlike other products, relying on investors' due diligence may not sufficiently safeguard against fraud as the required combination of computer science, legal and finance skills needed to understand ICOs are rare.

Prof. Beatrice Weder di Mauro (INSEAD and CEPR) concurred with Prof. Allen's main arguments. She pointed out that only 3.8% of ICOs are traded after launch.[15] While there might be an economic justification for ICOs, e.g., stemming from imperfections of VC, PE, crowdfunding, and seed funding, regulations indeed vary across countries and regulators are wary. Furthermore, there is a lack of clarity on regulatory protection, financial stability, financial center competitiveness and protection of investors against market failure.

VII. Sum-Up

ABFER, MAS, and NUS are grateful to the participants for a holistic research and educational effort into the pertinent aspects of digital currencies. They provided us with a better understanding of the underlying technology, e.g., the fundamental differentiation between the distributed and centralized ledger. Technology has relaxed the constraints, but it has not made time-honored concepts obsolete. Collaborative efforts among policymakers, practitioners and academics can help us to continue to extract positive results from the continuously improving technology and applications in this area.

[15] Source: https://news.bitcoin.com/80-of-icos-are-scams-only-8-reach-an-exchange/

CHAPTER 1

Chapter 1

Opening Remarks for the Workshop on Digital Currency Economics and Policy, 15–16 Nov 2018

Edward Robinson

Chief Economist
Monetary Authority of Singapore

Distinguished speakers, central bank colleagues, ladies and gentlemen, good morning, and welcome to the Workshop on Digital Currency Economics and Policy, jointly organized by the Asian Bureau of Finance and Economic Research (ABFER), the NUS Business School, and the Monetary Authority of Singapore (MAS). The ABFER was founded six years ago and held its fifth annual flagship Conference in May this year. Some of you attended as speakers and participants. We also organize more focused workshops on specialized topics. Today's event falls in this category. I want to acknowledge our co-organizer, Professor Bernard Yeung, Dean of NUS Business School and President of the ABFER, who has put tremendous effort into this workshop.

Amid the frontline innovation of the Fintech festival, we thought it would be important to engage upstream, in an intellectual discourse on Digital Currency, and to anchor it on established paradigms in economics and finance. We need a more formal, internally consistent narrative on what is a fast-evolving development in the marketplace.

In a sense, the concept of electronic money is not new at all. The United States (US) Federal Reserve started making transfers by telegraph in the

1910s. Credit cards that could be used to make payments electronically date back to the 1950s.

However, these technological innovations were, essentially, just new and more efficient ways of effecting traditional payment transactions, but did not encroach on the monopoly of the monies in use.

What is somewhat more novel is the advent of digital assets that use encryption technology to control the *creation* of money and their transfer — the so-called digital currencies. The first of these appeared around 2008, and there are now over a thousand of them. The amounts of each in circulation vary with their fluctuating market values.

Innovation in money and credit goes to the very heart of central banking. Central banks are fundamentally concerned with the link between money of all kinds and inflation, and the ability of the financial system to efficiently and safely fund real economic activity.

At the very outset, we are confronted with the question of what has driven the emergence of digital currencies. According to the United Nations (UN), the world's 195 independent states already have 180 currencies between them. It is not obvious that we have a shortage of currencies.

After all, John Stuart Mills did say that "so much barbarism, however, still remains in the transactions of most civilized nations, that almost all independent countries choose to assert their nationality by having, to their inconvenience and that of their neighbors, a peculiar currency of their own."

Of course, shortage of a specific currency that is used more than others, such as the US dollar, do occur from time to time, as witnessed by the occasional debates on the Triffin Dilemma, but to me that is a separate, allocative issue, perhaps.

A theorist might see the emergence of alternative forms of private sector-created money as an effective way of disciplining governments to preserve the value of official money. Governments may be compelled to ensure they retain at least the lion's share of the market for currency in order to secure their seigniorage revenue, and perhaps to enjoy the less quantifiable benefits of prestige and statehood associated with money issuance.

Indeed, the privilege of currency issuance brings with it an enormous responsibility — in safeguarding the integrity of a country's supply of money.

But it seems hard to argue that concern over a debasement of currencies is behind the rise of digital currencies, given the low inflation record of central banks in the last few decades.

There might be some real underlying demand for a new type of money that allows anonymity, although regulators are mindful that the enabling technology may inadvertently reduce the transaction costs of criminal activities and terrorism-related financing.

Conversely, it may simply be that the distributed-ledger technology behind digital currencies allowed them to take place, and that what we have effectively is a supply-driven shock — or to put it differently as Ken Rogoff does, "a solution in search of a problem."

Whatever the underlying drivers, it appears that digital currencies are probably here to stay. In fact, the evolution of the digital currency phenomenon may have proceeded ahead of academics' and central banks' understanding of the associated issues and implications.

This workshop is an attempt to catch up. To this end, we have gathered here some of the keenest minds in the areas of monetary and financial economics. We have Barry Eichengreen (University of California, Berkeley), who will motivate the issues, from a historical perspective on privately-issued currencies and the tendency for currency issuance to be concentrated in the hands of governments. Markus Brunnermeier (Princeton University), Charles Engel (University of Wisconsin-Madison), David Yermack (New York University) and Franklin Allen (Imperial College London) will help us make sense of how digital currencies could alter the monetary and financial landscape, and what they imply for policies. Robleh Ali (MIT) will educate us on some technical design aspects of digital fiat currencies. General Manager Agustín Carstens (BIS), Managing Director Ravi Menon (MAS) and Deputy Governor Cecilia Skingsley (Sveriges Riksbank) will share with us the key central bank considerations around the advent of digital currencies. So we have a judicious mix of topics and approaches, from the historical to monetary theory, to financial structure, technology and policy, and the right assembly of people to apply the analytical toolkits. In fact, we have a room of academic greats.

We will have the privilege of hearing from all these experts over the next two days including our Opening Speaker, Kenneth Rogoff. He is Professor of Public Policy and Professor of Economics at Harvard University, and served as Chief Economist at the IMF from 2001 to 2003.

Ken has made substantial and seminal contributions to issues closely related to central banking: exchange rates, central bank independence and financial crises. His work with Maurice Obstfeld on developing a unified framework for analyzing policy issues in international macro-economics was path-breaking and had enormous influence on subsequent open economy modelling efforts.

His regular syndicated columns have highlighted the value of the economic perspective on a range of pertinent issues and made them accessible to a broader audience. He is also a member of that pre-eminent Group of Thirty.

Ken is no stranger to Singapore, the MAS, and ABFER, having visited and spoken at our events on several occasions. I have also personally benefitted from the wisdom of his insights. It is a delight to be able to welcome him back again.

Some of us would know that his proposal to scale back on paper money preceded the advent of crypto-/digital currencies by about two decades, and was most recently reinvigorated in his 2016 book, *The Curse of Cash*.

So I think it is most apt that he kicks off the workshop.

May I now invite Professor Kenneth Rogoff to make his presentation, please.

CHAPTER 2

Chapter 2

From the Curse of Cash to the Burden of Digitization

Kenneth S. Rogoff

Harvard University

November 11, 2018

Background paper prepared for Workshop on Digital Currency Economics and Policy, November 15, 2018.

Are cryptocurrencies still an answer in search of a problem? For reasons discussed at length in Rogoff (2016), decentralized "permission-less" blockchain tokens are extremely unlikely to replace centralized government-issued "fiat" money.[1] As the long history of currency illustrates, while it is usually the private sector that is originally responsible for the most important innovations, governments eventually regulate and appropriate. However fervently cryptocurrency evangelists believe that superior private technology must eventually win out in the long run, they do not seem to understand that, when it comes to the core of the monetary system, governments cannot afford to lose, and they will not. Functions such as the unit of account, the medium for final clearing of transactions among financial institutions, and especially the payment of taxes and transfers are simply too vital for modern-day countries to leave in the hands of a decentralized private sector system. History shows that governments always have the capacity to keep changing the rules of the game until fiat money wins out.

[1] Later discussions by Bank for International Settlements (2018) and the International Monetary Fund (2018) echo very similar arguments.

This is not to deny the fertile opportunities that blockchain affords in making all kinds of transactions and record-keeping safer while (in theory) dramatically reducing transactions costs. Blockchain also offers the potential for engaging in much more complex state-contingent contracts than would be feasible with existing technologies. To the extent that blockchain technologies eventually supplant existing banking services such as credit cards and debit cards, or reduce the need for legal services, they are simply a new generation of efficiency-enhancing technology, raising only the normal regulatory concerns for central banks. New fintech technologies that do not depend on any form of anonymity for their value and purpose offer vast potential.

However, those that rely on a form of anonymity (or difficult to penetrate pseudonymity) for their value are likely to fall by the wayside. Governments simply cannot allow untraceable payments on a large scale if they hope to collect taxes at the level needed to support basic government activity. Widespread tax evasion also undermines "horizontal equity," the principle that citizens with similar income streams should pay similar taxes.

Yes, it is true that transactions in the leading cryptocurrency, Bitcoin, can in theory be traced, though if it were simple, it is highly unlikely Bitcoin would be worth much today. Tracing Bitcoin (or any cryptocurrency) is fairly easy if someone uses an "exchange" (an intermediary that makes transaction much simpler for ordinary individuals but typically forces them to reveal their identity in the same manner as a bank account). Tracing is generally still possible even for transactions done outside exchanges, provided a government is motivated enough, as it would be, for example, if trying to track terrorists or election hackers. But at present, unravelling Bitcoin transactions is far too costly to be done on a routine basis, and each week the cryptocurrency community is coming up with new cryptocurrencies that are far more robust to detection than Bitcoin.

Even if Bitcoin falls by the wayside, won't more robustly untraceable coins just replace it, making it virtually impossible for governments to stop their spread? That perspective is stupefyingly naïve (Rogoff, 2016). Governments may not be able to eliminate cryptocurrencies, but they have tremendous latitude to undermine their liquidity, If a government can make it very hard to launder a coin into the legal economy, its value will plummet. And governments have many tools at their disposal. For example, they can ban financial institutions from accepting cryptocurrencies for use at financial institutions, and they can also ban their use for payments in the legal, tax-compliant economy. The fact that this has not happened on wide scale yet is mainly because, so far, actual use of cryptocurrencies is transactions has been extremely limited.

Of course, even radical steps to make cryptocurrencies illiquid will not stop mutually agreeable parties from using cryptocurrencies to transact in the underground economy. However, by making it expensive to convert cryptocurrencies into mainstream economy goods — by making the currencies highly illiquid — their value can be greatly reduced. The fact that hundred-dollar bills can still be used to buy most ordinary goods, and that there is no law against holding them, makes $100 a vastly more valuable asset than if they could only be used for purchases in the underground economy.

I want to be careful not to side with those who confidently predict that Bitcoin is a pure bubble and the value must eventually fall to zero. That is far from obvious. There are at least three important channels through which Bitcoin can retain value, one quite plausible but only consistent with a much lower value of Bitcoin than today, and two rather speculative possibilities nevertheless consistent with potentially a much higher price for cryptocurrencies in general and Bitcoin in particular.

First, there may be "rogue" governments that do not completely prohibit pseudonymous currencies (or networks layered on Bitcoin) for use within their own borders. Why would any government do this if it created huge difficulties in tax collection and law enforcement? For one thing, there are some governments that have so many ways of monitoring their citizens (though surveillance cameras, internet and telephone monitoring, digital exhaust and active centralized information gathering), that they are less reliant on financial receipts. Moreover, United States (US) policy over the past decade has pushed many countries to actively seek ways to process transactions completely outside the mainstream global networks. Consider the fact that, at present, the US is imposing financial sanctions on a dozen countries including Belarus, Cuba, the Democratic Republic of the Congo, Iran, Libya, North Korea, Somalia,

Sudan/Darfur, Syria, Russia, Ukraine, and Venezuela.[2] Even countries that are not being actively disintermediated chafe under the fact that most of the major financial transactions processing systems are cleared through the US, so even countries such as Great Britain are effectively forced to allow US authorities to have extensive information about their business and financial systems.

In this situation, it is hardly surprising that countries such as Venezuela have attempted to foster their own cryptocurrencies, currencies that could potentially be used anywhere. (Venezuela is increasingly a failed state and its cryptocurrency has little chance of wide acceptance even within its own borders, but that would not be the case for some of the others on the US sanctions list.) By providing a pathway to spend cryptocurrencies in the legal economy — akin to using a $100 bill in a retail store — rogue states can provide final demand and potentially, give long-term value to cryptocurrencies everywhere. But just because a cryptocurrency can be used for transaction in, say, North Korea, does not mean it will have great value outside it. On the other hand, if an economy the size of Japan were to sustain its embrace of cryptocurrencies, that would be a different matter. Even if Japanese authorities maintain a tight regulatory grip on local cryptocurrencies exchanges — and therefore be able to expose the identities of Japanese holders — it is important they also have thorough information on coins laundered into Japan, and be willing to share that information with foreign counterparts. Japan's early embrace of cryptocurrencies likely did much to drive up their value in 2017. Over time, as other advanced economies perceive the effects of Japan's policies on their own underground economies, there will surely be enormous pushback, probably forcing Japan to reverse course. In the long run, no advanced economy is likely be allowing widespread use of nearly anonymous transactions vehicles.

What about the argument that even if there is no underlying transaction use whatsoever, Bitcoin might still have monetary value as "digital gold," valuable simply because investors believe it should have value? Bitcoin evangelists frequently opine that this is what the long

[2] Ahn, Daniel P. and Rodney Ludema, "The Sword and the Shield: The Economics of Targeted Sanctions," Georgetown Center for Economic Research Working Paper (2018).

run will look like. It is unlikely that such an equilibrium will prevail. Pure speculative bubbles have been widely studied in economics, both theoretically and empirically, and the overwhelming conclusion is that they are not sustainable.

True, there are exceptional circumstances where speculative bubbles can flourish and assets with no intrinsic value can be highly valued. The canonical case is where the steady state global real return on wealth is less than the economy's growth rate, a situation that can occur in a world where there is chronic (not just cyclical) overinvestment. If this were the case, however, then one would expect rampant bubbles around the economy, and not an isolated case. In sum, it is extremely unlikely that any cryptocurrency, and Bitcoin in particular, can sustain a positive price indefinitely without the bubble eventually bursting.

But wait, isn't the price of gold itself a bubble, and if so how can we be so sure Bitcoin won't end up in a similar equilibrium? Indeed, some economists have argued that the value of gold is a 6,000-year bubble (e.g, Buiter, 2014) and if they are right there can be others. But the bubble interpretation of the gold price is overblown and not really all that parallel with Bitcoin. It is true that gold derives some of its value from its history of use as a monetary instrument, but this misses the point that the use of gold is not by random chance. Gold has a number of properties that make it a strong candidate to use as a monetary instrument, including its durability, its balance between hardness and malleability, the fact that it is the most non-reactive of all metals and does not rust or tarnish and, above all, the fact that it is scarce (ignoring the vast deposits of molten gold in the earth's core that are not likely to be mined for millennia to come) but not too scarce. Since the invention of standardized coins in Lydia in 7th century BC, it is no surprise that gold has a unique role. Of course, today, the fact that the global gold supply cannot easily be manipulated by the state, and that it provides a means for anonymous payment, means that if anything its value is likely to rise in a future world of digital payments. Moreover, many of its special properties are precisely the reason that NASA uses it to protect parts in space, and why it is a component found in electric cars and all kinds of electronics, as Rogoff (2016) emphasizes.

Bitcoin proponents will argue that supply of their currency is far more tightly fixed than gold, which is continually mined, even if the annual percentage increase in supply is small. Famously, the supply of Bitcoin is fixed by design, reaching about 21 million by the year 2041 at which point the supply will be capped. But the "fixity" of Bitcoin supply is a tenuous one. Silver is hardly a perfect substitute for gold, but nearly perfect Bitcoin clones are easy to create. After all, Bitcoin is an open source program, so it is possible to produce nearly identical (but better) variants almost without limit. Many of the over 1,500 coins now in existence do exactly this, and of course there are have already been "forks" on the Bitcoin chain that adopt different variants (for example "Bitcoin cash"), although so far none of these has reached anywhere near the market capitalization of bitcoin.

Granted, the predominance of Bitcoin to date has been quite remarkable. Its leadership position owes to many factors, including especially the high credibility it has achieved by proving relatively tamper-proof to date. Bitcoin has developed a large community around it and has proven robust for over nine years now. At the same time, new coins are subject to huge regulatory uncertainty, such as on whether they will be treated as securities, a fate that Bitcoin has so far avoided even in the United States; being treated as a security risks a regulatory nightmare for new entrants. Nevertheless, the assumption that no substitute can ever substantially supplant Bitcoin is very likely wrong, particularly if a major state actor were to stand behind another challenger, if not directly then through regulatory policy. (I will abstract from an important limitation of Bitcoin, which is the large amount of energy it dissipates.)

Nevertheless, even absent a challenger, it is hard to sustain a high value for Bitcoin in the case once regulatory policy has stripped away a large portion of its transactions value. In this sense Bitcoin is different from gold.

Much the stronger case for a high value of Bitcoin comes because of the belief that it is likely to be an integral part of very useful blockchain applications in the future. Although a digital cryptocurrency is the original concept raised by the mythical Satoshi Nakamoto in his 2009 paper, it is now well understood that the potential applications are vast, ranging from providing faster and better ways to have digital signatures to providing a completely different framework for social networking, using a decentralized information system to strip away, for example, Facebook's monopoly. Blockchain technologies certainly will eventually eat away the monopoly held by credit and debit card clearing systems; the main reason why transactions costs remain high is that these networks are dominated by just a couple of monopoly systems. Blockchain technology offers promise to provide much cheaper, faster and more secure "rails" and drastically compete down transactions costs, particularly in international transactions.

Although the Bitcoin network itself has many well-known limitations (such as speed of processing), these can be mitigated by layering on other networks, using Bitcoin only a digital gold clearinghouse. What is far from clear, however, is whether Bitcoin is a help or a hindrance to these other applications, which in some cases would be much easier to run with a centralized clearing house, and in some cases where it would be vastly more efficient to use a different token system entirely. Although one often sees the analogy between Beta and VHS video technologies (where the inferior VHS technology defeated Beta thanks to network effects), the differences between the two technologies was really second-order compared to the differences between energy-intensive, slow-footed Bitcoin and new superior technologies that are faster, consume less energy, and offer richer options for how anonymous to make the tokens, and therefore are more regulatory friendly.

In currency use, it is almost certain that central bank digital currencies will eventually supplant private ones, for reasons given by Rogoff (2016), and later by the by Bank for International Settlements (BIS) (2018) and the International Monetary Fund (IMF) (2018). In the case of broader blockchain applications, it is less obvious how the regulatory environment will evolve. Central banks have been perfectly content to allow the development of superior transactions technologies, as long as they maintain control of stabilizing the unit of account, and have access to printing currencies in a crisis situation. Governments do not have nearly as pressing reasons to interfere with other applications of blockchain. But in any world, they will put a huge premium on regulating anonymity. For example, in major cities around the world today, one will often see real estate transactions done in currency, transactions that almost always involve money laundering, capital flight or tax evasion. If some future token application involves clearing real estate transactions, authorities will surely insist (eventually) on being able to trace the underlying entities that are engaged in the transaction.

In sum, although the blockchain community is understandably very excited about potential applications, it remains very hard to put a value on the first generation of digital assets including especially Bitcoin, despite the enormous attention and popularity it receives. Bitcoin devotees tend to overrate the first-mover advantage, and underrate the power of states to overturn the status quo, as they have with earlier innovations in transaction technologies. Nevertheless, from a policy perspective, the interesting issues have little to do with the value of individual cryptocurrencies, and far more to do with how to regulate this fast-evolving world in order to unleash its potential for improving the efficiency and security of the financial system.

References

Bank for International Settlements, 2018. "Bitcoin: Looking Beyond the Hype." *BIS Annual Report*, Chapter 5. BIS, Zurich, June.

Buiter, Willem H., 2014. "Gold, A Six Thousand Year Bubble Revisited." *Citi Economics Research* paper (November). https://willembuiter.com/gold2.pdf.

International Monetary Fund, 2018. Global Financial Stability Report, Washington: IMF, April.

Rogoff, Kenneth, 2016. *The Curse of Cash*. New York: Princeton University Press.

From the Curse of Cash to the Burden of Digitization

Kenneth S. Rogoff, Harvard University

Workshop on Digital Currency Economics and Policy,
Asian Bureau of Finance and Economic Research,
Monetary Authority of Singapore,
National University of Singapore Business School
Singapore, November 15, 2018

Based on book the *Curse of Cash*, Princeton University Press, 2016

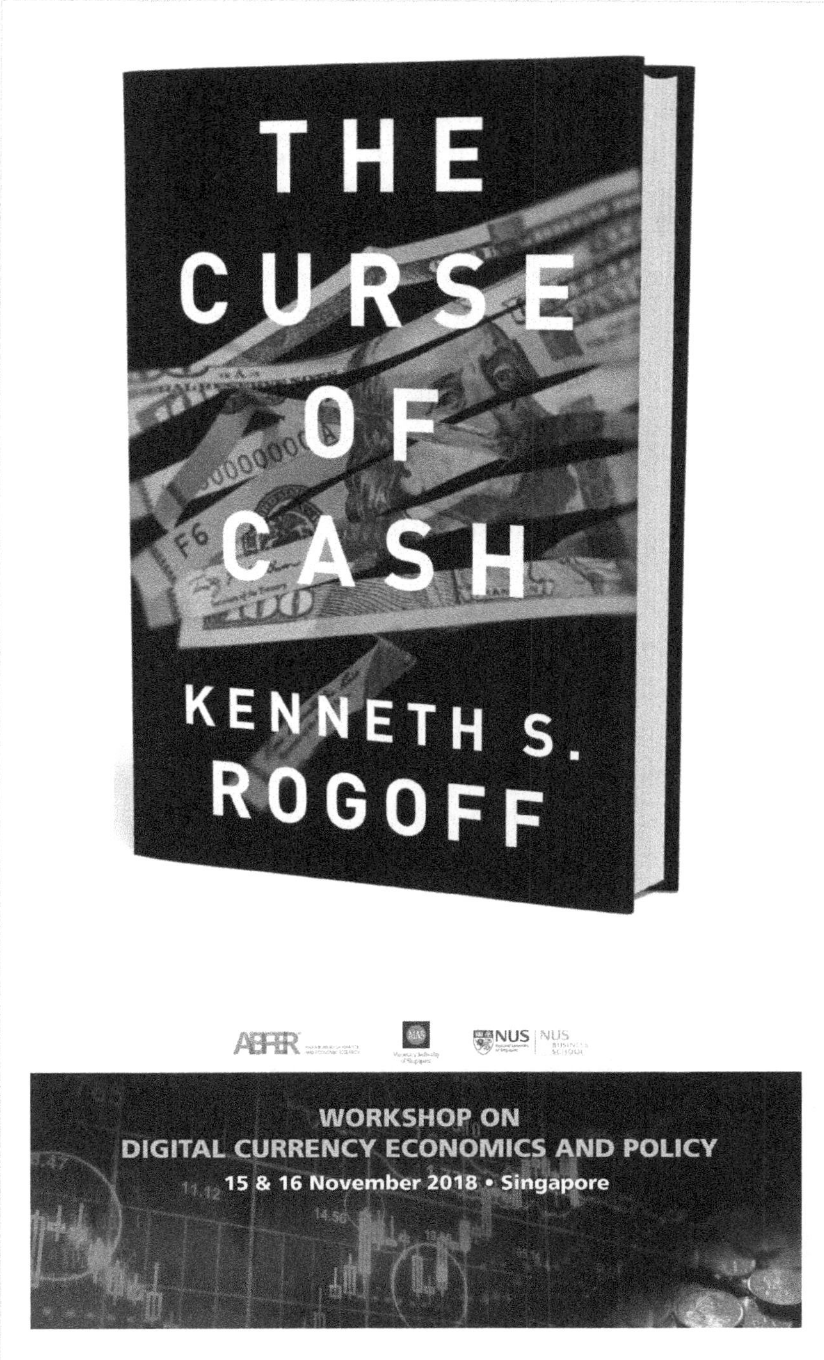
THE
CURSE
OF
CASH
KENNETH S.
ROGOFF
WORKSHOP ON
DIGITAL CURRENCY ECONOMICS AND POLICY
15 & 16 November 2018 • Singapore

Book has four distinct parts (perhaps more accurate title: *The Past, Present and Future of Currency*)

- Chapter 1 is a history of currency.
  - Electrum coins of 7th Century Lydia (Western Turkey).
  - The tree bark currency of Kublai Khan (grandson Genghis, made famous by chapter in Marco Polo).
  - Ben Franklin's book *A modest inquiry into the nature and necessity of paper currency.*
  - The gold standard era.
  - The modern fiat currency era.
- A key point for today's digital currency debate: The history of currency tells us that the private sector innovates, but governments invariably regulate and appropriate.
- Section I looks the public finance case for rethinking the issuance of large-denomination notes, and for possibly restricting large-scale cash purchases.
  - It follows closely Rogoff (1998); the vast bulk of cash holdings in advanced economies are due to tax evasion and crime. Employs a broad range of cross-country data, including surveys.
  - Make the case for a "less cash" society but NOT a cashless society, Sweden not Orwell.

- Part II of the book looks at a related, but different, topic: How should central banks deal with the zero bound in future systemic financial crises or deep recessions.
  - Look at all the options that central banks have tried (quantitative easing, forward guidance, etc.) also options that have not (raising inflation targets, helicopter money).
  - The myriad of counterintuitive suggestions that fill the leading journals.
  - It is as if the economics literature has insisted on positing "assume we don't have a can opener" (Rogoff JEP 2017).
- Part III of the book looks at international aspects, cryptocurrencies, gold and the future of currencies.
  - Argues that governments can and will ultimately restrict options for conducting anonymous transactions.
  - Refers back to historical experience in evaluating likely future.

Appendices and Afterward

- Appendix addressing the "Wallace conjecture" (which might seem to imply that if all currency becomes electronic, central banks will no longer be able to stabilize prices and the world will be forced to commodity-backed currency as under the gold standard.)
- Afterward to paperback covering Indian demonetization.

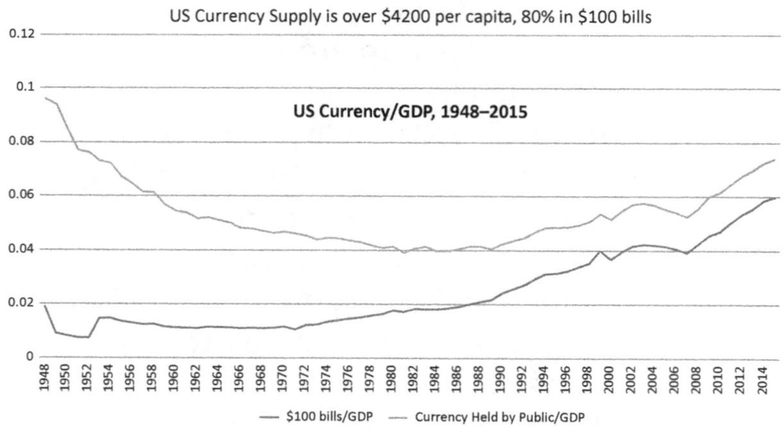

US is not so Different: Currency to GDP Selected Countries

	Currency to GDP (% end 2015)
Norway	1.45%
Nigeria	1.53%
Sweden	1.80%
Argentina	2.09%
Canada	3.74%
United States	7.38%
Eurozone	10.09%
India	12.51%
Japan	18.61%

Source**: Kenneth Rogoff, *****The Curse of Cash*****, 2016**

Proportion large notes by value, selected countries

	Proportion of Large Notes (by Value)	Local Currency Threshold used to define large note
Australia	92.2%	50 Australian dollar
Japan	91.1%	5000 yen
Eurozone	90.7%	50 Euro
India (Nov 7 2016)	86.0%	500 Rupee
United States	84.2%	50 dollars
Hong Kong	84.2%	500 Hong Kong Dollars
Sweden	79.2%	500 Kroner
New Zealand	70.7%	50 NZ dollar

Source**: Kenneth Rogoff, *****The Curse of Cash*****, 2016**

Not much in wallets, or (reported) on property

Table 4.1 Average cash balances in wallet (converted to US dollars by PPP adjusted exchange rates)

	Australia	Austria	Canada	France	Germany	Netherlands	US
mean	59	148	64	70	123	51	74
median	32	114	38	30	94	28	37

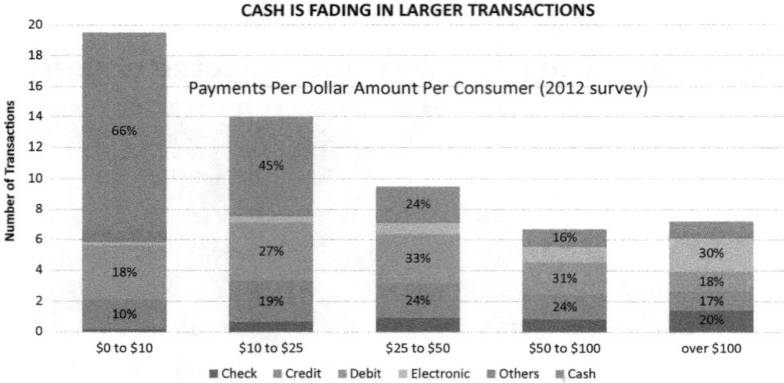

There are many different approaches to restricting use of cash

- Restricting size of cash payments (Italy, Spain, France).
- Taking cash out of banks and wiring cash registers to Treasury (Sweden).
- Restricting size of notes Henry (1976), (Rogoff, 1998, 2016), Summers and Sands (2016).
  - Rogoff plan takes large bills out gradually over several years.
  - Has a financial inclusion piece.
- NOT MUTUALLY EXCLUSIVE.

November 8 2016: Prime Minister Modi announces "demonetization" of India's two largest notes

India demonetization might yield long-run benefits but also shows things to avoid

- In *The Curse of Cash*, I essentially argue "If you are a developing economy, do not try this at home". Cost of providing financial inclusion, small in advanced economies, is too great.
- *TCOC* argues for taking five to seven years to phase out big bills. India did this almost overnight.
- *TCOC* argues only for taking LARGE BILLS out of Circulation. But 500 rupees is only $7.
- Few people realize that it takes six months to one year to print a new currency supply due to technical difficulties in producing counterfeit resistant currency. India's biggest problem was that it did not have nearly enough new notes on hand to exchange for the old ones.

No government can sit by and allow large anonymous payments to avoid taxes, regulations, and laws;

- Of course, this is exactly the role cash performs, but digital currencies potentially perform the same function on a massive scale.
- (Caveat: Eventually, there may be some countries where authorities have so much granular information on citizens' activities that they can tolerate crypto with out the same risks as today's democracies.)

Authorities have ability to make any difficult to trace (pseudonymous) currencies illiquid

- If (say) Bitcoin can never be spent at retail stores or traded in for fiat currencies at financial institutions, it becomes very illiquid and value collapses.
- However, international cooperation is important. If a large country (say Japan) makes it relatively easy to spend Bitcoin, it risks providing a way for the entire world to launder crypto.
- Regulators can also reduce value through treating coins as securities and through tax rules.

Ways Bitcoin might retain value

- Even if most countries take measures to completely strip pseudonymity, a few countries might make it legal and provide a place to spend (launder) coins. Could be rogue states (e.g. North Korea) or countries that have been shut out of important financial markets by US financial sanctions (or threat thereof).
- US presently has sanctions on Belarus, Cuba, the Democratic Republic of the Congo, Iran, Libya, North Korea, Somalia, Sudan/Darfur, Syria, Russia, Ukraine, and Venezuela
- If Bitcoin can only be spent on ordinary goods and services in some subset of these states, its value would not go to zero but be far below todays value.
- Despite having no practical use, it retains value as a pure speculative bubble, valuable because enough people think it is valuable "digital gold"
- Economic theorists have extensively analyzed this kind of bubble, it is only a theoretical possibility in the case where the rate of return on wealth is less than the growth rate.
  - Does not seem to be the case empirically on several levels.
  - In this case, the economy would be replete with speculative bubbles.

Ways Bitcoin might retain value (continued)

- Bitcoin is useful because other functions build around it ("layers above and layers below") solving all the various problems such as energy consumption.
  - Possible, but then there are so many superior approaches.
  - Nevertheless, Bitcoin does have important advantages in having developed a large community, and having proven resilient, properties that other currencies would have to prove.
- Bitcoin is finite, but nearly perfect substitutes can be made "Bitcoin + epsilon".
- Some have argued that gold itself is a bubble, so why not Bitcoin? In fact, gold has a number of unique properties that made it a very natural monetary asset historically, and still give it value in making anonymous transactions after paper currency is gone.
  - Gold also has important uses, for example across many modern electronics.

It is folly to think that government regulation policy is going to be passive

- The long history of currency innovation teaches us that the private sector innovates, but in due time the government regulates and appropropriates.
- The same will eventually be true for innovations in digital currencies
- Indeed, governments will surely in due time have the capacity to issue secure digital currencies.
  - Trusted party "permissioned" system will almost surely dominate "permissionless systems".
- The main issue with central bank digital currencies is disintermediation, (similar to having only narrow banks).

CHAPTER 3

Chapter 3

From Commodity to Fiat and Now to Crypto: What Does History Tell Us?[1]

Barry Eichengreen

University of California, Berkeley

December 2018

1. Introduction

Money makes the world go round. More concretely, it greases the wheels of commerce and finance. The adequacy of the supply of currency and coin, and of their financial derivatives, has long been a preoccupation of governments, since the stability of the economy and hence of the state itself rides upon it.

Now the monetary landscape is being turned upside down by the digital revolution: by the issuance and circulation of private-label cryptocurrencies and the prospect of central bank digital currencies. These new units, it is said, will transform the monetary world as we know it. But just saying so does not make it true. The challenge is separating the facts from the hype.

This paper is an effort to get my mind and those of readers around the issue by placing it in historical perspective. I start with a brief review of the relevant European and United States (US) history, starting with commodity money and moving to bank money and fiat currency. Digital

---

[1] Revision of a paper prepared for the Digital Currency Economics and Policy Workshop of National University of Singapore, November 2018. For comments I am grateful to Nadar Al-Jaji, Randall Morck and David Wen.

currencies can be seen as the next step in this evolution, where advances in technology, first the substitution of currency notes for metal discs and now the substitution of bits for paper, allow means of payment, store of value and unit of account services to be provided more widely at lower cost. But at another level, digital currencies run counter to the prevailing historical trend, which has been in the direction of the state assuming control of the money supply and inhabitants of a common economic space converging on a common unit. The question is: when these two trends collide, which monetary unit survives?

2. Before digital

Once upon a time, many polities meant many currencies. Early modern polities were fragmented. Europe, for example, was divided into more than 500 polities prior to the Peace of Westphalia in 1648. It was difficult, given the technological conditions of the time, for rulers to control large swathes of territory. Medieval France, for instance, was ruled by scores of feudal lords, each of whom operated his own mint.[2] It was hard for those rulers even to control their borders. As a result, monies issued — that is to say, minted — in different jurisdictions circulated across borders. Since those coins varied in purity (or fineness), they traded against one another at variable rates.

After 1648, the modern state system emerged. Rulers were able to control larger swathes of land with the help of modern military means, which is what the economic historian Philip Hoffman refers to as "gunpowder technology."[3] Standing armies became more important and also more expensive. It now became imperative for these centralized states to control the mint (or to grant it a royal monopoly in return for income) in order to be able to raise extraordinary resources in an emergency. The state or monarch used its brand name (that is to say, its reputation) to signal, hopefully credibly, that coins minted under its imprint were full bodied — that they contained precious metal of the specified purity in

---

[2] Successive French monarchs took control of these feudal mints starting in the 13th century as part of their ongoing consolidation of power.

[3] See Hoffman (2013).

advertised amounts. As owner of the mint, the monarch or magnate enjoyed the advantages of monopoly, notably the largest possible stream of seigniorage revenue. Entry was deterred by the fact that mints were capital and skilled-labor intensive, immobile, and required publicity in order to attract business, characteristics that rendered start-ups vulnerable to discovery and expropriation by the crown.

Under exceptional circumstances, such as an existential threat from a rival power, the monarch had the option of reducing the metallic content of the unit in order to temporarily boost seigniorage revenues when these were needed to mobilize resources for the national defense and to ensure state survival.[4] The dilemma was that the monarch might also be tempted to debase the currency and temporarily increase seigniorage for other less legitimate reasons, abusing his monopoly power. In the absence of competition, there might be little to restrain this temptation.[5]

Limits on such practices derived from the aforementioned tendency for coins minted in different jurisdictions to circulate across borders.[6] The state monopoly of money, in other words, was still less than complete. Gold coin was the main means of payment used in long-distance trade; it followed that gold coin migrated across borders and that different coins circulated side by side. The same could be true of silver and even copper coin, depending on circumstances. Thus, the newly independent US established a mint in 1792 and began striking US silver dollars in 1894, but Spanish silver dollars (the basis for the famous "pieces of eight") minted in Spanish America continued to circulate until they were demonetized by an act of Congress in 1857. Gresham's Law suggests that debased coins should have driven full-bodied coins out of circulation, but in practice traders capable of assaying and weighing coins bearing different imprints

---

[4] This is the explanation for the state monopoly of money advanced by Glasner (1989).

[5] The classic analysis of the problem is Cipolla (1963). Munro (2012) argues that debasement might reflect not just national defense imperatives but also be a response to a deterioration of coins in circulation.

[6] The modern analog to this tendency is known as "currency substitution" or "dollarization," where residents of a country subject to high inflation, presumably reflecting the government's financing needs, substitute dollars or another foreign currency for the local money (see Alesina and Barro 2001 and below).

could determine what they were getting and demand an appropriate premium when accepting debased money.

The advent of bank money, first bills of exchange (promissory notes connected to a specific transactions but often guaranteed and/or discounted by a bank) and then bank notes (claims backed not by specific transactions or collateral but by the reserves of the bank itself), added an additional layer of complexity.[7] Now the state, in its capacity as regulator, had to decide whether this note-issuing privilege should remain a state monopoly and assign it to a favored agent (the central bank, which acted as its fiscal agent), or else to permit competition subject to restrictions. Typically, the state monopoly was incomplete (Selgin 2008). Scottish banks issued notes alongside the Bank of England, for example.[8] Until 1897, Swedish commercial banks were allowed to issue notes alongside the Riksbank. But banks that competed with the government or with its privileged fiscal agent did so subject to restrictions on the volume of private money they could issue, the collateral they had to hold, and the circumstances under which issuance could occur.

With the evolution of modern financial systems, governments developed additional means, aside from debasing the coinage or printing currency, of financing expensive wars.[9] They could issue bonds, which they serviced and then retired following the conclusion of hostilities. The three most expensive wars of the 19th century, the Napoleonic Wars, the US Civil War and the Franco-Prussian War, were heavily financed in this manner.[10] The argument for concentrating issuance in the hands of a central or federal government now rested not so much on national defense imperatives as on economic efficiency arguments. A uniform currency minimized transaction costs. It substituted for information in that it was not necessary to have information about the creditworthiness of each and every issuer, since there was only one. Information being costly to produce, the information insensitivity of government money

[7] The modern bank note grew out of the notes issued by early modern goldsmiths (effectively goldsmith bankers) as receipts for the gold they held on behalf of their customers circulated hand to hand. See Quinn (1997).

[8] Under different rules before and after the adoption of Peel's Act in 1844.

[9] As emphasized by Glasner (1989).

[10] Details are in Eichengreen, El-Ganainy, Esteves and Michener (2018).

minimized these costs (Dang, Gordon and Holmstrom 2015, Berentsen and Schar 2018).

US experience illustrates the range of alternative arrangements and consequences. In the newly independent US, a mélange of foreign monies circulated (such as the famous Spanish pieces of eight, noted above). Prior to 1836, the paper money circulation was made up of the notes issued by state-chartered banks, whose number varied across states, plus one federally chartered bank, the Bank of the United States. State regulation, notably regulations specifying the obligation of the issuer to redeem its liabilities in specie at par, determined the conditions under which state-chartered banks could emit notes, together with corresponding limits. Importantly, the Bank of the United States with its nationwide branch network acted as enforcer of those regulations, returning notes to the issuing banks and demanding specie, especially when the notes in question showed signs of circulating at a discount.

For many bankers, this discipline was less than welcome, and their objections resonated with deep-seated American suspicion of concentrated power, leading President Andrew Jackson to veto the bill re-chartering the Bank of the United States when it reached his desk in 1832. Jackson's decision opened the door to the free banking era. To ensure an adequate supply of money and credit to the local economy, state legislatures liberalized licensing requirements for banks. No longer was it necessary to obtain a legislative charter, although some bankers still proceeded in this way. Banks could enter and operate without a charter so long as they met minimum capital requirements and held specie or financial assets readily convertible into specie in amounts sufficient to redeem their notes at par. Throughout the period, which ended with the Civil War, multiple competing private currencies circulated side by side, often trading at different prices. That these currencies were multiple, private and variable in price suggests a parallel with cryptocurrencies. The difference is that there was regulation of the market from the start.

Efforts to evaluate the efficiency of that regulation and of the resulting market are controversial. Classic indictments like that of Hammond (1957) dismiss regulation as inadequate and bankers as opportunistic and duplicitous. Regulators allowed bankers to value discounted state government and railway bonds at par when reporting their capital and reserves. So-called wildcat bankers purchased bonds "with their own circulating notes and disappeared in order to avoid having to redeem the notes. They had to be hunted for in the woods...their cash reserves were sometimes kegs of nails and broken glass with a layer of coin on top" (Hammond 1957, p. 601). By implication, these private currencies were not reliable units of account, means of payment, and stores of value.

Subsequent revisionism (Rockoff 1975, Rolnik and Weber 1983) insists that the situation was not so bad. Regulation was not uniformly incompetent. In some jurisdictions, such as New York State, it was in fact quite rigorous. Bank notes issued in New York traded at little if any discount, and losses to noteholders were slight. Where discounts were larger and more variable, the market policed and disciplined issuers through commercial note reporters that listed prevailing discounts on the notes issued by individual banks and prevented the latter from passing these off for more than they were worth. Still, it inconvenienced a storekeeper to have to consult a note reporter each time a customer presented him with a currency note. In other words, information alone was not enough to subdue dissatisfaction with the operation of the prevailing system.

This account begs the question of why regulatory enforcement differed so dramatically across jurisdictions. The answer is that the line between monetary and fiscal policy was blurred and, consequently, motives were mixed under this regime of private competing currencies. State governments with pressing fiscal needs and few alternative sources of finance, generally states on the frontier, saw state banks as a source of demand for their bonds, and generous regulatory treatment of those bonds was a way of augmenting that demand. The relationship became clear during the Civil War, when the Congress passed the National Banking Act, creating a system of nationally-chartered banks required to hold their reserves in US government bonds issued to finance the war effort, and then after the war when progressively higher taxes were levied on state bank note issuance, ultimately taxing the latter out of existence.[11] Federally-chartered banks were required to deposit US government bonds with the Treasury and permitted to issue bank notes equal to 90 per cent

[11] The tax in question was raised from 2 per cent to 10 per cent and then ultimately to 20 per cent.

of the value of the bonds. The Treasury stood ready to redeem those bonds or their currency equivalent in gold in fixed amounts on demand. Bank notes bore two serial numbers, that of the Treasury and that of the issuing bank. Notes traded at fixed prices relative to one another. That the federal budget was in surplus for much of the period removed the pressure to relax regulation.

But just because the currency was now uniform did not mean that it operated to everyone's satisfaction. Populist politicians complained of the system's deflationary bias, due to the fact that the volume of transactions and economic activity expanded more rapidly than the supply of monetary gold (recall William Jennings Bryan's "Cross of Gold" speech at the 1896 Democratic National Convention). Economic specialists warned of the destabilizing consequences of volatile spikes in interest rates (Kemmerer 1911). Following the crisis of 1907 they worried about the country's dependence for stabilizing intervention on the good offices of one exceedingly wealthy individual, J.P. Morgan, and on the emission of clearinghouse certificates, in effect multiple private monies that circulated at discounts and premia against one another (Gorton 2009). The result, to cut a long story short, was the Federal Reserve Act of 1913 to create an "elastic currency," supplies of which expanded and contracted with the seasons.

Even then, however, multiple (semi-) private currencies — national bank notes with two serial numbers — continued to circulate. This changed with passage of the Gold Reserve Act of 1934, under which remaining national bank notes were retired. This change occurred in the throes of the Great Depression, when the federal government was mobilizing resources to fight the slump and fund its budget deficit (see Jacobson, Leeper and Preston 2017), again highlighting the fuzzy line between monetary and fiscal policies. The result was to give the United States the monetary system and federal government monopoly of money it has today — or that it has had until recently.

In sum, history shows a tendency for currency and coin issuance to be increasingly concentrated in the hands of the central or federal government. The national defense rationale for this centralization has if anything weakened over time. Modern economies, unlike their predecessors, accumulate the resources needed to defend themselves and prosecute military campaigns already during peacetime. Modern financial systems give their governments means other than debasing the coinage or printing currency to finance those operations. It is sometimes argued that the Vietnam War was a source of inflation in the United States in the 1960s, because it created pressure for the Federal Reserve to help finance federal government deficits.[12] Perhaps this may be so.[13] But the general point remains: seigniorage, whether ongoing or on an exceptional basis, is a less important source of public-sector resources than in the past.

If so, then the argument for government monopoly of money issuance must rest on the economic efficiency of a currency that is both uniform (because there is only one issuer) and stable (because it is issued in economically appropriate amounts, for example by an independent central bank with a politically-assigned mandate to pursue price stability). Such a currency minimizes transaction costs. It substitutes for information in the sense that it is not necessary to have information about the creditworthiness of each and every issuer, there being only one.

It follows that the costs of producing and obtaining information about changes in the actual and prospective value of privately-issued digital currencies is an obstacle to their wider utilization. To put the point another way, the digital payment services provided by Visa and Mastercard, albeit at a price and only vis-à-vis certain counterparties, are attractive because they are information insensitive. The credit card companies provide the end user with protection from default. And a dollar credit on one's Visa account is convertible into dollars one-to-one.

Stable coins

From this flows the appeal of so-called stable coins, which are designed to maintain a peg (typically one to one) to an official numeraire (typically the US dollar), and therefore should be information insensitive (assuming the viability of the model).[14] Four types of stable coins can

---

[12] As argued for example by Riddell (1989).

[13] For a skeptical view see Walker and Vatter (1982).

[14] Thus, my focus on whether it may be possible for the private or public sectors to issue a digital coin that is *stable* and *uniform* is why I consciously do not discuss other developments in the crypto space (Bitcoin and its rivals) that do not purport to display this stability and uniformity relative to the established numeraire.

be distinguished, with different implications for the future of money and the future of digital money.[15] Type 1 is the fiat fully collateralized stable coin, which is pegged one-to-one to the US dollar or another existing numeraire. Tether is a leading example of a fully collateralized cryptocurrency pegged one-to-one to the dollar.[16]

More specifically, Tether is a US dollar-linked fiat fully collateralized stable coin.[17] Each coin is collateralized by an equal amount of US dollar deposits held on deposit in commercial bank accounts in Taiwan. Like conventional cash transactions, Tether offers its users the advantage of anonymity, since those transactions can be verified using the Bitcoin blockchain. It displayed the promised degree of stability, with the exception of a brief period in April 2017, for several years.[18]

But this type of stable coin is expensive to operate. The issuer and its investors must commit substantial amounts of collateral in low-yielding liquid form. This makes the resulting "currency" more like the "money" created by commercial banks (see inter alia Tobin 1963 — quotation marks in original), which has to be funded by inter alia deposits, than the currency created by governments and central banks, which doesn't have to be financed in this way. The contract gives reasons for doubting that the model is scalable, since large amounts of additional funding would be required. Assuming that the costs are passed along to the end user, there is no difference between holding a certain number of dollars in one's commercial bank account and using that account to pay bills and receive

[15] I build on Pauw (2018), who lists three of the four categories I distinguish here.

[16] Saga is an example of a collateralized currency pegged to an alternative numeraire, the IMF's Special Drawing Rights (more on this below). Just like pegged exchange rates, none of these coins are actually pegged one-to-one to their numeraire; rather they fluctuate within narrow bands as determined by bid-ask spreads and transactions costs. Saga's is the only white paper I have seen that makes this explicit.

[17] Other examples include Digix, which is supposed to be fully collateralized in gold, and Venezuela's Petro, which purports to be fully collateralized by oil.

[18] One conjecture about the April 2017 episode is that the Taiwanese banks cut off the international wire transfer privileges of Bitfinex, the digital coin trading platform that is Tether's parent, causing Bitfinex to resort to Tether for liquidity. In the second half of 2018 there was then another period when the value of Tether dropped precipitously against the dollar. A full explanation for the unit's behavior in this period is not available at the time of writing.

wire transfers from one's customers, on the one hand, and using Tether for transactions, on the other — aside from the fact that a conventional bank account may permit one to engage in a larger volume of transactions at lower cost, given the current state of blockchain technology.[19] Tether's market capitalization is just a small fraction of that of Bitcoin, which suggests that the means of payment function — as opposed to speculation — is not the principal motive of investors active in the cryptocurrency currency space.[20]

In addition, the search for profitability may encourage issuers to cut corners. Questions have been raised about whether Tether in fact holds all the dollars it claims. It has issued hundreds of millions of additional tokens without allowing its reserves to be audited.[21] One is reminded of Bray Hammond's "kegs of nails and broken glass with a layer of coin on top."[22]

A second category is made up of crypto collateralized stable coins. In this case another cryptocurrency is held as collateral to back the stable coin. This variant frees the issuer from having to deal with, inter alia, Taiwanese banks, which may have qualms about providing services to a platform that can be used for illicit purposes.

The problem in this case is that the value of the collateral will fluctuate, since the collateral is not in the form of a stable coin. Because the value of the collateral can fall, crypto collateralized stable coins, to be credible, must be overcapitalized, potentially making them even more expensive

---

[19] And there is also the fact that bank accounts may be insured by the Federal Deposit Insurance Corporation or another government agency. Working in the other direction, of course, is the fact that the anonymity that fiat collateralized currencies provide will be attractive for entities engaged in money laundering, tax evasion and terrorist finance.

[20] There are now plenty of other fully-collateralized stable coins, such as TrueUSD, which is similarly pegged one-to-one to the US dollar. But it maintains a $10,000 minimum on redemptions and charges 10 basis points on transactions as of the time of writing.

[21] It is sometimes argued that there is a fundamental tension between the need for credible auditing and cryptocurrency holders' desire for anonymity. With effective auditing it becomes easier for governments to locate and freeze assets, which cryptocurrency holders are anxious to avoid, but the worse the auditing the less credible the backing.

[22] A separate allegation is that additional units of Tether have been created to finance purchases of Bitcoin and artificially inflate the market in that unit (see Griffin and Shams 2018). I do not explore that avenue here.

to operate than fiat collateralized stable coins. Dai, the leading crypto collateralized stable coin, has an announced collateralization ratio of 300 per cent. In addition, because nothing in principal prevents the value of the collateral from falling below the par value of the coin issuance, over-collateralization notwithstanding, these coins are vulnerable to bank-run-like problems.

A third category is the partially collateralized stable coin, of which Saga is an example. Saga is interesting in that it is issued by a nonprofit foundation and requires compliance checks so as to avoid facilitating money laundering and similar abuses, while also using blockchain to ensure the anonymity of transactions among approved parties.[23] It promises its users low transactions costs and scalability (time will tell).

Different from the first two categories of stable coins, Saga is only partially collateralized. The platform sells and buys Saga tokens in return for Ethereum (another cryptocurrency) and invests the proceeds, aside from an Ethereum liquidity buffer, in the fiat currencies making up the Special Drawing Rights (SDR) basket. Initially the protocol holds 100 per cent reserves in these currencies, essentially replicating what Tether purports to do (in Tether's case in dollars). Over time, however, Saga's reserve ratio will be reduced. At what rate is not specified in the Saga white paper, which states only that the reserve ratio will decline "as inherent value becomes less volatile." An unpublished paper on Saga's "monetary policy" indicates that the reserve ratio will decline asymptotically to ten per cent (Saga 2018).

Herein lies the problem. As the relevant footnote to the white paper notes, "...inherent value is derived from a combination of factors: market confidence, usefulness as means of exchange, sentiment, and future prospects." Confidence, as any central banker with experience in operating a currency peg can tell you, is fragile. Just because volatility has been declining in the past, whether because of the existence of a larger installed base of users or for other reasons, is no guarantee against it rising in the future. And questions about confidence can become self-fulfilling when the reserves are fractional. If some holders of Saga tokens develop doubts, whether for reasons good or bad, about the convertibility of their

[23] It will be interesting to see how background checks and anonymity fit together in practice.

tokens into fixed numbers of SDRs (more precisely, into units of Etherium currently valued at those fixed numbers of SDRs), they will seek to cash out. Other holders, not wishing to be at the end of the queue, will scramble to do likewise before the reserve cupboard is bare. The platform's fractional reserves could be exhausted by the resulting run.

Central banks faced with this situation generally respond in two ways. First, they devalue the currency, which reduces their ratio of liabilities to reserves. In the present context, this would not be consistent with the stable-coin rationale; it would not be good for confidence and market share. Second, they impose capital controls, effectively limiting the access of investors to their reserves. Limiting the convertibility of the crypto token into fiat currency in this way would again be inconsistent with the rationale for creating a stable coin and therefore for with future prospects.

The fourth variant is the uncollateralized stable coin. Smart contracts are used to manage the supply of the digital coin with the goal of maintaining its value against, inter alia, the dollar. The platform issues both digital coins and digital bonds, and the smart contract sells bonds for coin (coin for bonds) when the price of the latter dips (rises) in terms of dollars. In some variants, bonds are automatically redeemed by the blockchain in the same order in which they were issued, as opposed to being purchased on the open market, when it is necessary to expand the coin supply.

Bonds are less liquid than coin, come in larger denominations, and are less useful for transactions, but investors have an incentive to hold them because bondholders are promised "dividends" in the form of digital coin when additional quantities of the latter are issued (that is, when the price of the token threatens to exceed $1). Dividends are funded out of the commission, or seigniorage, taken by the platform when selling additional coins. In addition, some uncollateralized stable coins issue a third unit, known as shares, whose recipients automatically receive additional coins when additional issuance is required and all bonds have been redeemed.[24]

---

[24] Some uncollateralized cryptocurrencies, such as Carbon, foresee doing away with the bonds, issuing only tokens and "credits" — essentially equities — which, since they are not senior to other claims, are likely to be even more volatile than bonds.

The viability of such schemes depends on success at growing the platform, since without additional stable coin holders/users, there will be no additional issuance with which to pay bondholders.[25] To be sure, when additional bonds are sold to prevent the value of the coin from slipping below par, the platform will then acquire the coin balances taken out of circulation. But those balances have to be retired, or frozen, to maintain the coin's value; they can't be injected back into circulation in order to pay dividends to bondholders without threatening the peg.

And even if the platform is growing, doubts about its future may undermine stability now. Doubts about whether the platform will be able to generate sufficient seigniorage in the future to pay the bondholders may cause investors to reduce their bids for new bonds, making it even more expensive for the platform to take excess coin out of circulation (increasing the value of claims on dividends relative to remaining circulating coin), which will only heighten preexisting doubts — with good reason. It is not hard to imagine a self-reinforcing spiral in which investors are unwilling to purchase additional bonds at any price and the platform is therefore unable to prevent the price of the stable coin from collapsing. Again, the problem will be familiar to anyone conversant in the literature on speculative attacks on pegged exchange rates.

It is not clear whether the architects of uncollateralized stable coins are conversant in that literature. The white paper for Basis (Al-Naji, Chen and Diao 2018), until recently the leading stable coin, cites the existence of a five-year expiration date on its bonds as protection against the danger that the bondholder queue will grow too long to be serviced.[26] This reads like a non sequitur. As the authors write, "We elected a 5-year bond expiration after rigorous simulation showed that this produced a robust system with sufficiently high bond prices even in the face of wild price swings. We save the details for later discussion." Say no more.

---

[25] A less charitable way of putting it would be that this approach smells suspiciously like a Ponzi scheme.

[26] In December, Basis announced that it was returning its remaining capital to its funders, having concluded that its bonds would be treated as securities by the Securities and Exchange Commission and thus be subject to regulation.

Later in their white paper, the authors argue that their system would be robust even if bond prices hit zero because bonds are automatically extinguished on reaching maturity at five years, reducing the dividend liabilities of the platform. Extinguishing old bonds without repaying the principal is akin to a debt default or restructuring, where the sustainability of a sovereign's debt is restored and bond prices rise after the bondholders receive a haircut. But as any student of sovereign debt will know, the promise of a haircut in the future will only make investors demand a larger risk premium ex ante and bring forward the crisis of sustainability ultimately requiring the haircut.[27]

3. Central bank digital currency

It follows that the only reliable way of creating a stable-value digital currency is for the central bank to issue it. The central bank can issue digital currency by fiat, as it were. It can inject it into circulation by purchasing other financial assets. It can retire it by selling those assets. It can ensure parity between its digital and non-digital liabilities by standing ready to exchange them for one another in unlimited amounts, much as it exchanges nickels for dimes. More than 90 central banks are currently studying the possibility (Roland Berger 2016).

A central bank digital currency could be implemented in a number of different ways. The most straightforward is allowing individuals, and not just member banks, to maintain electronic accounts with the central bank. The central bank would be providing the same services as Visa,

[27] A final issue is whether private-label stable coins would in fact be able to efficiently execute the means-of-payment function offered by conventional currency — or, for that matter, by credit card companies like Visa and electronic-payment platforms like Paypal but at a significantly lower price. One problem is the cost, in electricity and computing power, of verifying blockchain-based transactions. Some technologists claim that the efficiency of this process can be significantly enhanced; time will tell. Another problem is simple fraud: googling "Paypal fraud" or "stolen Bitcoin" reveals that this can be a serious problem for electronic payments problems and unstable cryptocoins. Why it should not also be a problem for stable coins is, to put it mildly, unclear. Visa and Mastercard have massive internal divisions whose sole purpose is to detect and deter fraud. Would a stable coin that relied on the digital wallet services of private providers be equally fraud proof and secure?

Paypal or a debit-card issuing commercial bank, with the advantage that access would be universal (Bjerg 2018). Everyone could have an account, just as everyone can carry currency notes in his or her wallet. This might result in social savings if universal coverage translates into additional economies of scale.

Alternatively, the central bank could issue a digital unit that circulates in a distributed fashion — that is held in mobile wallets or on electronic smart cards, between which payments could take place directly. This model would presumably be useful mainly for smaller transactions. It is also conceivable that access to central bank digital currency could be limited to businesses and usable only for wholesale payments (Bech and Garratt 2018).

There is also the issue of the efficiency of public enterprise. Whether private-label digital currencies, and for that matter private mobile-payment platforms like Paypal or Visa, could successfully compete with a central bank offering digital payment services to retail customers is far from clear. Conversely, absent the chill winds of competition, the efficiency of the dominant state-sector producer can be questioned. Granting a monopoly to a public-sector enterprise or positioning it to be the dominant player results in social savings only if that public enterprise is efficient in delivering services. In practice, the efficiency record of public enterprises is far from spotless.

Having the central bank issue the digital currency, much less giving it a monopoly in this space, would not appeal to libertarians who oppose all government involvement, though this would be less bothersome to the rest of us. One can imagine different systems in different countries that attach varying degrees of anonymity to transactions conducted using the central bank digital currency. One can imagine a blockchain-based approach in where all transactions are anonymous, although this might create concerns about tax evasion, money laundering and other criminal activity.[28] Alternatively one can imagine a system in which the central bank sees every resident's balance but not the counterparty in each and

[28] These concerns would be all the greater insofar as it would be easier to engage in large-value surreptitious transactions using digital as opposed to paper currency (Claeys, Demertzis and Efastathiou 2018).

every transaction, just as different countries apply and enforce rules on cash transactions of various degrees of severity (Rogoff 2016).

But concentrating all digital currency transactions at the central bank would also concentrate risk, in much the manner that concentrating the clearing of trades in derivative securities in central clearing houses concentrates failure risk.[29] If the central bank's digital currency network goes down, cash transactions may be halted (all of them if digital currency replaces paper currency *in toto*).[30] For terrorists and hackers, the central bank's digital currency network would be a rich target.[31] Then there are the related problems of counterfeiting digital currency and preventing its theft (stories of private cryptocurrencies being stolen from digital wallets and platforms by hackers exploiting software glitches being legion).[32]

Companies like eCurrency seek to provide central banks with hardware, software and advanced cryptography protecting them against counterfeiting, theft and security threats.[33] Blockchain may be part of the solution, although eCurrency also refers to additional layers of hardware and software encryption (Yang and Hou 2018). Others (e.g. Grym, Heikkinen, Kauto and Takala 2017) argue that blockchain is not suitable for central bank digital currencies and advocate other solutions entirely. Whatever the solution, regulators have an old saying about their relationship with the regulated — regulators are like bloodhounds, always

---

[29] See the discussions in Roe (2013), Yadav (2013) and Peirce (2016).

[30] Recall the brouhaha that resulted on June 1, 2018, when some of Visa's systems went down, preventing its European customers from making purchases. And recall that those were only some systems of one of several competing commercial networks affecting only one part of the world.

[31] It can be argued that a blockchain-based central bank digital currency, because it is distributed, removes this single point of failure and should therefore be more resilient, but it has other costs, such as high energy inputs, and would still be vulnerable to internet and electricity outages (Wadsworth 2018).

[32] Some central banks, the Danish National Bank for example, have provisionally concluded that the benefits are outweighed by the risks (National Bank of Denmark 2017).

[33] It is sometimes said that the costs of issuing a digital currency would be less than those of printing paper currency. Given the costs of ensuring security, the accuracy of this assertion is uncertain.

on the trail, but the regulated are greyhounds; they run very fast — which would also seem to be applicable here.

Another financial-stability concern is the danger of facilitating runs on conventional banks (Tolle 2016). Claims on the central bank, including currency claims, are presumably free of default risk, where this is not necessarily true of claims on commercial banks. Historically, when doubts develop about the stability and solvency of the commercial banking system, depositors have shifted into currency (see e.g. Boughton and Wicker 1979). The danger is that this kind of behavior will become more frequent, it being easier to shift one's digital balances from a commercial bank to the central bank with a mere swipe of the phone — with destabilizing consequences.[34]

Some observers (National Bank of Denmark 2016, Coats 2018) have suggested that this risk could be mitigated by limiting the volume of such transfers or limiting the overall size of central bank digital accounts. But this would presumably give rise to the situation where central bank money traded at a premium relative to accounts held at commercial banks, reintroducing all the complications of a non-uniform currency.

Finally there are the implications of central bank-issued digital currency for the conduct of monetary policy. Monetary policy operates first and foremost by influencing the deposit and lending interest rates of commercial banks. By altering the policy rate, the monetary authority changes the incentive for commercial banks to maintain reserves at or borrow from the central bank, and thereby the volume and price of deposits and loans. Were a central bank-issued digital currency available,

---

[34] Berentsen and Schar (2018) argue that a central-bank-issued digital currency would be stabilizing because commercial banks would respond to this increased danger of runs by de-risking their operations and upgrading their business models. Claeys, Demertzis and Efstathiou (2018) conjecture that they could move to full reserve banking. My own reading is that the connection between run risk and de-risking is tenuous and that the unintended consequences of the former can be costly. For elaboration see Admati and Hellwig (2013). Then there are the implications for commercial bank funding. Wadsworth (2018) conjectures that commercial banks would respond to the availability of retail accounts at the central bank by increasing their reliance on wholesale funding. As demonstrated in the 2008 financial crisis, such reliance could weaken the stabilizing function of deposit insurance. It could also amplify destabilizing cross-border spillovers insofar as that wholesale funding is from abroad.

it would become easier for individuals as well as banks to shift their balances to the central bank, as just noted. And if interest was paid on those central bank balances, individuals would have an incentive to do so in response to changes in the policy interest rate. Commercial banks would more quickly see the impact of the change in the policy rate on their funding costs, increasing the speed of pass-through from the policy rate to other interest rates (Meaning, Dyson, Barker and Clayton 2018). If a given change in the policy rate elicited a larger shift away from commercial bank retail deposits, the size of the induced change in lending rates might be accentuated. If banks respond to the greater flightiness of demand deposits by increasing their reliance on time deposits and other forms of long-term funding, however, these effects could be eliminated or reversed.

Introduction of a central bank digital currency could also eliminate the zero lower bound on interest rates, since nothing would prevent the central bank from paying negative interest on the balances of retail customers (just as some central banks have paid negative interest rates on reserves). This would represent an increase in the transparency of policy in periods when interest rates are around zero, since at present the central bank is forced to resort to quantitative easing and credit easing, operations that are relatively opaque (Bordo and Levin 2017). This would, however, require the abolition of cash, which individuals can hold to avoid negative rates.[35]

The maintenance of universal digital accounts at the central bank would also be a way of facilitating the use of "helicopter money." The central bank, in lieu of quantitative easing, could simply drop additional currency into everyone's digital account. This assumes, of course, that account holding is universal. It assumes a distribution rule (does everyone get the same absolute amount? Does everyone get an amount proportional to their existing holdings?). One suspects that, even with a central bank digital currency, helicopter money remains in the realm of social science fiction.

[35] Alternatively, the central bank could impose a time-varying paper currency deposit fee on commercial banks at its cash window (Agarwal and Kimball 2015). But this would represent a loss in the policy transparency and simplicity otherwise gained.

Overall, it would appear that the implications for the conduct of monetary policy are consequential but not revolutionary.

4. Conclusion

History is not a linear process. There is no straight line from commodity money to fiat money and from there to crypto, nor from metallic currency to paper currency and from there to digital. Still, some broad trends are evident in the historical record. There has been a tendency over time for political jurisdictions and inhabitants of common economic spaces to converge on a single currency. Political leaders like it this way, since their monopoly of seigniorage is a source of power and a valuable lifeline when sovereignty is threatened. Economic agents like it, since the existence of a uniform currency that is information insensitive (that is free of counterparty and liquidity risk) facilitates transactions and economic activity generally. Followers of Hayek (1976) might prefer otherwise, but history is against them.

To every rule there are exceptions. Early modern Europe was, to some extent, an exception, where different coined monies circulated side by side, trading at different prices vis-à-vis one another owing to clipping, debasement and related practices. The United States from the 1830s to the 1860s was an exception, where competing currency notes circulated side by side, at varying discounts, owing to hostility to the idea of a powerful federal government empowered to regulate the currency supply. Episodes of high inflation are another exception, where agents have an incentive to substitute foreign currencies for the unstable domestic unit. But the broad tendency, it is fair to say, has been in the direction of one currency for each political jurisdiction and common economic space, where in practice those political and economic spheres coincide.[36]

The question is whether digital currencies will now reverse this trend, given the apparent ease with which they can be created. At the moment such digital units are proliferating. But the information sensitivity of those

[36] The Euro Area is of course an interesting exception where the political and economic spheres do not coincide, but it is subject to its own problems (that are properly the subject of another paper).

units, as evident in the fact that they trade at varying prices against one another and the established numeraire, suggests that they fail to provide the core functions of money. So-called stable coins are intended to bridge this gap by providing a reliable store of value, means of payment and unit of account, but whether they can be scaled up at reasonable cost (when fully collateralized) or maintain their stability (when not) is doubtful.

The one unit that can clearly meet these dual challenges of scale and stability is central bank digital currency. But there would be both costs and benefits of such a currency. The case is not a slam dunk.

References

Admati, Anat and Martin Hellwig (2013), "Does Debt Discipline Bankers? An Academic Myth about Bank Indebtedness," unpublished manuscript, Stanford University and Max Planck Institute.

Agarwal, Ruchir and Miles Kimball (2015), "Breaking through the Zero Lower Bound," IMF Working Paper no.15/224 (October).

Al-Naji, Nader, Josh Chen and Lawrence Diao (2018), "Basis: A Price-Stable Cryptocurrency with an Algorithmic Central Bank," http://www.basis.io.

Alesina, Alberto and Robert Barro (2001), "Dollarization," *American Economic Review* 91, pp. 381–385.

Bech, Morten and Rodney Garratt (2018), "Central Bank Cryptocurrencies," *BIS Quarterly Review* (September), pp. 55–71.

Bjerg, Ole (2017), "Designing New Money — The Policy Trilemma of Central Bank Digital Currency," Copenhagen Business School Working Paper (June).

Berentsen, Aleksander and Fabian Schär (2018), "The Case for Central Bank Electronic Money and the Non-case for Central Bank Crypto-Currencies" *Federal Reserve Bank of St Louis Review* (2nd Quarter), pp. 97–106.

Bordo, Michael and Andrew Levin (2017), "Central Bank Digital Currency and the Future of Monetary Policy," NBER Working Paper no. 23711 (August).

Boughton, James and Elmus Wicker (1979), "The Behavior of the Currency-Deposit Ratio during the Great Depression," *Journal of Money, Credit and Banking* 11, pp. 405–418.

Broz, Lawrence (1997), *The International Origins of the Federal Reserve System*, Ithaca, NY: Cornell University Press.

Cipolla, Carlo (1963), "Currency Depreciation in Medieval Europe," *Economic History Review* 15, pp. 413–422.

Claeys, Gregory, Maria Demertzis and Konstantinos Efastathiou (2018), "Cryptocurrencies and Monetary Policy," Policy Contribution no. 10, Brussels: Bruegel (June).

Coats, Warren (2018), "Central Banking in the Digital Age" (1 May), https://wcoats.blog/.

Dang, Tri Vi, Gary Gorton and Bengt Holmstrom (2015), "The Information Sensitivity of a Security," unpublished manuscript, Columbia University, Yale University and MIT (March).

Eichengreen, Barry, Asmaa El-Ganain, Rui Pedro Esteves and Kris James Mitchener (2018), "Public Debt Through the Ages," paper presented to the IMF Conference on Sovereign Debt (September).

Glasner, David (1989), *Free Banking and Monetary Reform*, Cambridge: Cambridge University Press.

Gorton, Gary (2009), "Clearinghouses and the Origin of Central Banking in the United States," *Journal of Economic History* 45, pp. 277–283.

Griffin, John and Amin Shams (2018), "Is Bitcoin Really Untethered?" unpublished manuscript, University of Texas at Austin (June).

Grym, Aleksi, Paivi Heikkinen, Karlo Kauto and Kari Takala (2016), "Central Bank Digital Currency," *Bank of Finland Economic Review* 5, pp. 1–10.

Hammond, Bray (1957), *Banks and Politics in America from the Revolution to the Civil War*, Princeton: Princeton University Press.

Hayek, Friedrich (1976), *The Denationalization of Money*, London: Institute of Economic Affairs.

Hoffman, Philip (2013), *Why Did Europe Conquer the World?* Princeton: Princeton University Press.

Jacobson, Margaret, Eric Leeper and Bruce Preston (2017), "Recovery of 1933," unpublished manuscript, Indiana University and University of Melbourne (February).

Kemmerer, Edwin (1911), *Seasonal Variations in Demands for Currency and Capital*, Washington, D.C.: National Monetary Commission.

Meaning, Jack, Ben Dyson, James Barker and Emily Clayton (2018), "Broadening Narrow Money: Monetary Policy with a Central Bank Digital Currency," Staff Working Paper no. 724, London: Bank of England (May).

Munro, John, ed. (2012), *Money in the Pre-Industrial World: Bullion, Debasements and Coin Substitutes*, London: Routledge.

National Bank of Denmark (2016), "Central Bank Digital Currency in Denmark," Working Paper no. 28 (15 December).

Pauw, Chrisjan (2018), "Stable Coins Analysis: Is there a Viable Solution for the Future?" *Cointelegraph* (14 May).

Peirce, Hester (2016), "Derivatives Clearinghouses: Clearing the Way to Failure," *Cleveland State Law Review* 64, pp. 589–659.

Quinn, Stephen (1997), "Goldsmith-Banking: Mutual Acceptance and Interbank Clearing in Restoration London," *Explorations in Economic History* 34, pp. 411–432.

Riddell, Tom (1989), "Inflationary Impact of the Vietnam War," *The Future of the Past* 1, pp. 42–60.

Rockoff, Hugh (1975), *The Free Banking Era: A Reconsideration*, New York: Arno Press.

Roe, Mark (2013), "Clearinghouse Overconfidence," *California Law Review* 101, pp. 1641–1703.

Rogoff, Kenneth (2016), *The Curse of Cash*, Princeton: Princeton University Press.

Roland Berger (2016), "Think Act — The Rise of Cryptofinance in Central Banking," Munich: Roland Berger.

Rolnick, Arthur and Warren Weber (1983), "New Evidence on the Free Banking Era," *American Economic Review* 83, pp. 1080–1091.

Saga (2018), "Monetary Policy," Saga (May).

Selgin, George (2008), "Milton Friedman and the Case against Currency Monopoly," *Cato Journal* 28, pp. 287–301.

Tobin, James (1963), "Commercial Banks as Creators of 'Money,'" Cowles Foundation Discussion Paper no. 159 (July).

Tolle, Marilyn (2016): "Central Bank Digital Currency: The End of Monetary Policy as we Know It?" *Bank Underground* (25 July).

Wadsworth, Amber (2018), "The Pros and Cons of Issuing a Central Bank Digital Currency," *Reserve Bank of New Zealand Bulletin* 81, pp. 3–21

Walker, John and Harold Vatter (1982), "The Princess and the Pea, or the Alleged Vietnam War Origins of the Current Inflation," *Journal of Economic Issues* 16, pp. 597–599.

Yadav, Yesha (2013), "The Problematic Case for Clearinghouses in Complex Markets," *Georgetown Law Journal* 101, pp. 387–444.

Yang, Yanqing and Xintong Hou (2018), "Interview with David Wen: Developing Countries are Likely to Outrace Developed Countries in Digital Fiat Currency," *YiCai Global* (1 March).

Commodity, Fiat and Crypto: What does history tell us?

Barry Eichengreen
November 2018

My talk is in three parts

- First, I provide an historical perspective on the evolution of currency.
- Second, that history leads me to an analysis of stable coins.
- And, third, that analysis of stable coins leads me to a discussion of the cases for and against central bank digital currency.
    - I like to think that there is a logic for the three parts, but you be the judge...

History

- We currently see a proliferation of private crypto moneys.
- Yet this decentralization of currency emission rests uneasily with historical experience.
- In fact, history shows a tendency for currency and coin issuance to be increasingly *concentrated* in the hands of the central or federal government.
- There are two ways of rationalizing this tendency.
  - First, there is a national defense rationale: the central government needs control of currency creation (and of seigniorage) in order to mobilize exceptional resources in emergencies.
  - Second, there are efficiency advantages of a uniform currency, which is something that only a central authority can reliably provide.

Once upon a time, many polities meant many currencies (and, in practice, coins)

- Early modern polities were fragmented.
- Prior to the Peace of Westphalia (in 1648), for example, the European Continent was fragmented into more than 500 polities.
- It was hard for rulers to govern and control large swathes of land.
- But it was also hard for small states to control their borders.
- Multiple currencies (and coins) therefore circulated across borders.
- In Medieval France, for example, each feudal lord operated his own mint.
- Coins varied in purity (fineness) and traded against one another at variable rates.

After 1648, with the emergence of the modern state system...

- ...Rulers were able to control larger swathes of land with help of modern military technology.
- Philip Hoffman, *Why Did Europe Conquer the World?* (Princeton, 2013) refers to this as "gunpowder technology."
- Standing armies became more important but also more expensive.
- These centralized states controlled the mint (or granted it a royal monopoly), partly in order to be able to raise extraordinary resources in emergencies.

To be sure, that central control was rarely complete

- It was complete neither politically nor monetarily. In the case of money:
    - Scottish banks issued notes alongside the Bank of England (still do).
    - Prior to 1897, Swedish commercial banks were allowed to issue notes alongside the Riksbank.
    - In the US, where there was abiding hostility toward overweening federal power, including over money, a wide variety of moneys circulated.

US case

- After independence, foreign moneys (such as famous Spanish pieces of eight) were the dominant form of circulation.
- State-chartered banks were then permitted to issue their own bank notes.
- These provided only a reasonably uniform circulation when there existed a Bank of the United States to enforce discipline, but not otherwise.
- And after 1846 there no longer existed a Bank of the United States.
- After 1836, free bank notes circulated at varying discounts, giving rise to much contemporary dissatisfaction and inefficiency (although exactly how much is disputed).

US case (continued)

- The Civil War then catalyzed the shift to a National Banking System, which made for a more uniform circulation.
  - It placed a prohibitive tax on note issuance by state banks and required national banks to hold treasury bonds as backing to ensure convertibility.
  - This was essentially an example of the national defense imperative for creating a single currency.
- The Crisis of 1907 then prompted Federal Reserve Act.
  - The crisis pointed up the inefficiencies of this system (requiring the emission of clearing house certificates, in effect multiple private moneys that circulated at discounts and premia against one another).
  - It finally made note issuance a government monopoly.
  - This, in contrast, was essentially an example of the economic efficiency (uniformity) argument for creating a single currency.

So how do I read this history?

- History shows a tendency for currency and coin issuance to increasingly be concentrated in the hands of the central or federal government.
- There's a national defense argument for this.
- There's also an economic efficiency argument.
- Insofar as modern financial systems give governments alternative means, other than debasing the coinage or printing currency, to finance expensive wars, I would argue that the latter is the rationale that increasingly dominated over time and that dominates today.
- Thus, the argument for government monopoly of money issuance, either de facto or de jure, thus must rest on the economic efficiency of a currency that is both uniform (because there is only one issuer) and stable (because it is issued in economically appropriate amounts, for example by an independent central bank with a politically-assigned mandate to pursue price stability).

- A uniform currency minimizes transaction costs. It substitutes for information, in the sense that it is not necessary to have information about the creditworthiness of each and every issuer, there being only one.
- Information being costly to produce, the information insensitivity of government money minimizes these costs (Dang, Gorton and Holmstrom 2015, Berentsen and Schär 2018).
- Thus, the digital payment services provided by Visa and Mastercard are attractive because they are information insensitive. The credit card companies provide the end user with protection from default, and a dollar credit on one's Visa account is convertible into dollars one-to-one.
- It follows that the costs of producing and obtaining information about changes in the actual and prospective value of privately-issued digital currencies is an obstacle to their wider utilization.

Plain-vanilla cryptocoins are highly information sensitive

- Their value fluctuates day to day. Holders therefore require information about not just their current price but also their prospective future prices.
  - Limiting their store-of-value and unit of account functions.
  - Which in limits their means-of-payment function (willingness of agents to accept them in payment).
    - There may also be other technological limits on the means-of-payment function, but I leave these aside.

From this flows the argument for stable coins, which are information insensitive

- You don't need information about their issuer and contingent characteristics in order to accept them, assuming of course that they are really stable.
- Four types of stable coins can be distinguished, with different implications for the future of money and the future of digital money in particular.
  - Fiat fully collateralized
  - Crypto collateralized.
  - Partially collateralized
  - Uncollateralized

Fiat fully collateralized

- Tether is an example of a US dollar-linked fiat fully collateralized stable coin.
- But this type of stable coin is expensive to operate. The issuer must immobilize substantial amounts of collateral in low-yielding liquid form. This gives reasons for doubting that the model is scalable, since large amounts of additional capital would be required.
- Think of it like this. Assuming that the costs are borne by the end user, there is no difference between holding a certain number of dollars in one's commercial bank account and using that account to pay bills and receive wire transfers from one's customers, on the one hand, and using Tether for transactions, on the other — aside from the fact that a conventional bank account may permit one to engage in a larger volume of transactions at lower cost, given the current state of blockchain technology.
  - The crypto alternative is attractive only to those seeking to avoid scrutiny.
- In addition, the search for profitability may encourage issuers to cut corners.

Crypto collateralized

- In this case another cryptocurrency is held as collateral to back the stable coin. This variant frees the issuer from having to deal with, inter alia, Taiwanese banks.
- The problem with this model is that the value of the collateral will fluctuate, since the collateral is not a stable coin. Since the value of the collateral can fall, crypto collateralized stable coins, to be credible, must be generously overcapitalized, making them even more expensive to operate than fiat collateralized stable coins on average.
    - Dai, the leading crypto collateralized stable coin, has a purported collateralization ratio of 300 per cent.
- And, overcapitalization notwithstanding, because nothing prevents the value of the collateral from falling below the par value of the coin issuance, over-collateralization notwithstanding, these coins are vulnerable to bank-run-like problems.

Partially collateralized

- Saga is an example.
- The platform sells and buys Saga tokens in return for Etherium (another cryptocurrency) and invests the proceeds in the fiat currencies making up the SDR basket. Initially the protocol holds 100 per cent reserves in these currencies, essentially replicating what Tether does (or purports to do).
- Over time, however, Saga's reserve ratio will be reduced.
- But just how much is not specified in the Saga white paper, which states only that the reserve ratio will decline "as inherent value becomes less volatile."
- Herein lies the problem. As the white paper notes, "...inherent value is derived from a combination of factors: market confidence, usefulness as means of exchange, sentiment, and future prospects."
- Confidence, as any central banker experienced in operating a currency peg can tell you, is fragile. It is in the eye of the beholder.

- And questions about confidence can become self-fulfilling when the reserve ratio is only fractional. If some holders of Saga tokens develop doubts about the convertibility of their tokens into fixed numbers of SDRs, they will seek to cash out. Other holders, not wishing to be at the end of the queue, will scramble to do likewise before the reserve cupboard is bare. The platform's fractional reserves could be exhausted by the resulting run.

Central banks faced with this situation generally respond in two ways

- First, they devalue the currency, which reduces their ratio of liabilities to reserves. In the present context, this would not be consistent with the stable-coin rationale; it would not be good for confidence and market share.
  - One devaluation would likely create expectations of another.
- Second, they impose capital controls, effectively limiting the access of investors to their reserves. But limiting the convertibility of the crypto token into fiat currency in this way would again be inconsistent with the rationale for creating a stable coin and therefore for with future prospects.

Uncollateralized

- Most interesting, but also most ridiculous.
- Here *smart* contracts are used to manage the supply of the digital coin with the goal of maintaining its value against, inter alia, the dollar.
    - Monetary policy by algorithm....
- The platform issues both digital coins and digital bonds, and sells bonds for coin (coin for bonds) when the price of the latter dips (rises) in terms of dollars.
- Bonds are less liquid than coin, come in larger denominations, and are less useful for transactions, but investors have an incentive to hold them because bondholders are promised interest payments ("dividends") in the form of digital coin when additional quantities of the latter are issued (that is, when the price of the token threatens to exceed $1).
- Dividends are funded out of the commission (seigniorage) taken by the platform when selling additional coin.

- The viability of such schemes obviously depends on success at growing the platform, for without additional stable coin holders/users, there will be no additional issuance with which to pay bondholders.
    - Can you say Ponzi scheme?
- And even if the platform is growing, doubts about its future growth may undermine stability now.
- Doubts about whether the platform will be able to generate sufficient seigniorage in the future to pay the bondholders what they are promised may cause investors to reduce their bids for new bonds, making it even more expensive for the platform to take excess coin out of circulation (increasing the value of claims on dividends relative to remaining circulating coin), which will only heighten preexisting doubts — with good reason.
- It is not hard to imagine a self-reinforcing spiral where investors are unwilling to purchase additional bonds at any price and the platform is therefore unable to prevent the price of the stable coin from collapsing.
- Again, the problem will be familiar to anyone conversant in the literature on speculative attacks on pegged exchange rates.

It follows that the only reliable way of creating a stable-value digital currency is for the central bank to issue it

- 90+ central banks are exploring the possibility.
- Individuals could maintain electronic accounts at the central bank.
- Alternatively, the central bank's digital unit could circulate in a distributed fashion (held in mobile wallets or on electronic smart cards).
- Could be usable only for wholesale payments by businesses, or it could be used more widely.

Downsides

- Rich target for hackers and terrorists.
    - If CB's digital network goes down, the vast majority of cash transactions may be halted.
- Increases the danger of runs on conventional banks.

- Some observers (National Bank of Denmark 2016) have suggested that this risk could be mitigated by limiting the volume of such transfers or limiting the overall size of central bank digital accounts. But this would give rise to the situation where central bank money traded at a premium relative to accounts held at commercial banks, reintroducing all the complications of a non-uniform currency.
  - Shades of 1830s-style free banking....

So I conclude

- Strong economic justification for a uniform circulation.
- The only entity capable of credibly providing a uniform national circulation is the national government.
  - Because stable coin schemes are unlikely to succeed.
- That leaves us with the alternative of central bank digital currencies.
  - On which the jury remains out.

- Thank you.

CHAPTER 4

Chapter 4

Back to the Future with Cryptocurrencies: Comments on "From Commodity to Fiat and Now to Crypto: What Does History Tell Us?" by Barry Eichengreen

Randall Morck

I largely agree with Eichengreen's historical parallels and conclusions, and so can only suggest extensions and amplifications. His discussion of emerging Western nation states monopolizing money creation to capture seigniorage, and more detailed description of US monetary history is excellent. The tension between competing versus monopolistic money creation is actually far older. At the beginning of written history, ancient Egyptians used a competing moneys — metals by weight, oils and grains by volume (Janssen 1975). Are cryptocurrencies resurrecting a world of multiple competing moneys?

A money must serve as a medium of exchange, unit of account and store of value. Eichengreen explains cryptocurrencies' high costs in all three roles. Just as lugging urns of olive oil about gave way to metals by weight, which gave way to coins, costlier cryptocurrencies will be culled by economic selection. Olive oil leaks, spills, spoils, or loses value in a glut from an olive press up the Nile; metal needs reweighing and re-assaying for each transaction; coins are heavy and can be debased; so central bank fiat currencies ultimately won the cost contest (Davies 2010). Eichengreen sees little chance that fiat money will likewise give way to cryptocurrencies. Central banks' seigniorage is secure.

First generation cryptocurrencies, such as bitcoin, are poor mediums of exchange (you must check their fluctuating values every few seconds to reprice olive oil in bitcoin), units of account (successive bitcoin transaction entries in a ledger cannot really be added because the value of the bitcoin changes so fast), and stores of value (big swings relative to the costs of consumer goods make bitcoin a risky investment). "Stable" cryptocurrencies, such as Tether or Etherium, are backed by central bank moneys or government-backed securities. The overcollateralization needed to stabilize their prices is costly; insufficient collateralization invites even costlier asset runs.

Blockchain allegedly provides an anonymity that trumps such issues. But even diehard libertarians are cost-sensitive. Blockchain costs rise sharply with their scale, and all are currently miniscule compared to credit cards. If cryptocurrencies are used on large scales, they will encounter opposition from new quarters. Bitcoin mining already uses enough electricity to power Austria, much of it from coal in China (Krause and Tolaymat 2018). A bitcoin global payments system would make eco-activists are costly foes.

Who would use high-cost cryptocurrencies? Old-fashioned police work (Foley et al. 2019) provides answers. Police raids on dark website servers readily upend cryptocurrency anonymity. Illegal transactions linked to names, shipments of illegal goods and connected accounts reveal up to 70 per cent of bitcoin holdings and up to 60per cent of bitcoin transactions to be illegal.

Eichengreen sees central bank digital currencies, effectively letting individuals have digital demand deposit accounts at central banks, as likelier. These could instantly settle all individual and business transactions, eliminating the roughly 3 per cent overhead in credit cards or check clearing. The Bank of Canada has successfully tested such a system for buying and selling goods, stocks, and foreign exchange. Blockchain anonymity is futile if the central bank knows you anyway; all that is needed is vast computer power and massively redundant storage.

A central bank digital currency (CBDC) would let central banks run "helicopter" monetary policy. Currently, central banks stimulate the economy by creating money to buy treasury securities to increase their prices to lower debt yields to depress bank interest rates to encourage borrowing to stimulate business expansion, consumption and employment. This Rube Goldberg mechanism can be like pushing on a string, perhaps because treasury security sellers are typically wealthy, have low marginal propensities to consume, and use the newly created money to buy other securities. If everyone had CBDC accounts, a recession-fighting central bank, like the Pharaoh meting out grain amid seven years of drought, could drop new money, as if by helicopter, into the accounts of low-income people, more apt to spend it on consumption goods. In a pandemic, or any emergency, new money could instantly materialize in the CBDC accounts of those who need it.

Eichengreen correctly points out that an attack on the central bank could shut down an economy run this way. Massively redundant hardened geographically separated backup computers, each with an isolated dedicated power source might mitigate this. But I see more daunting challenges. Commercial banks, credit card companies, securities brokers, stock exchanges, and providers of all manner of back-office settlement services would lobby intensely to prevent such efficiency, or at least for tollbooths in it they could man (Duffie 2019). Big Finance is a formidable foe (Johnson and Kwak. 2010).

References

Davies, Glyn. 2010. *History of Money*. University of Wales Press.

Duffie, Darrell. 2019. "Digital Currencies and Fast Payment Systems: Disruption is Coming." Unpublished manuscript, Stanford University.

Foley, Sean, Jonathan R. Karlsen & Tālis J. Putniņš. 2019. Sex, drugs, and bitcoin: How much illegal activity is financed through cryptocurrencies? *Review of Financial Studies* 32(5), 1798–1853.

Janssen, Jozef. 1975. *Commodity Prices from the Ramessid Period: An economic study of the village of necropolis workmen at Thebes*. Brill.

Johnson, Simon, and James Kwak. 2010. *13 bankers: The Wall Street takeover and the next financial meltdown*. Vintage.

Krause, Max & Thabet Tolaymat. 2018. Quantification of energy and carbon costs for mining cryptocurrencies. *Nature Sustainability* 1, 711–718

Commodity Money to Fiat Money and Now to Crypto: What Does History Tell Us?

Discussion by Randall Morck
University of Alberta
ABFER, NBER, ECGI

Commodity, Fiat and Crypto: What does history tell us? By B. Eichengreen

- Evolutionary economics explains why state monopolizes money creation
  - National defense (debasement as aggression) & efficiency (rationally reliable uniformity)
  - Peace of Westphalia (1648) + irreg. US monetary history + stability ➔ maybe CBDC viable
  - Fragility (CBDC becomes prime hacking target, solar flares, etc.)

Bad money drives out good.
- Sir Thomas Gresham

The best way to destroy the capitalist system is to debauch the currency
- V. I. Lenin

The central bank must be trusted not to debase the currency, but the history of fiat currencies is full of breaches of that trust.
- Satoshi Nakamoto

The Social Welfare Value of Money

Unit of account
- Uniformity
  - Widespread acceptance
  - Divisibility

Medium of exchange
- Uniformity
- Purity & portability
  - Low cost verification of purity, ...
  - Portability, high value/weight v/v common transactions, ...

Store of value
- Uniformity
- Purity & portability
- Stability over time
  - Central banks v miners

The Social Welfare Value of Moneys

Egypt used multiple commodity monies from 3100 BC to start of modern era (ca 333 BC)

- **Absolutely no coins until 4th century BC**
  - Foreign (e.g. Lydian) coins from 5th C BC valued as lumps of metal
- **Standard units of grain used for small every-day transactions (hktt, ḫr, ...)**

  1 [hieroglyphs] = 1 hkt (barrel) = 4.8 liters

  also the double & quadruple heket

  1 [hieroglyphs] = 1 ḫr (sack) = 20 [hieroglyphs]

1 standard [hieroglyphs]

- **Standard weights of metals for larger transactions, in dbn, qdt, or š'ty**

  1 [hieroglyphs] (ring, also [hieroglyphs])= 1 dbn = 13.6 g.

  1 [hieroglyphs] = 1 qdt (?) = $\frac{1}{10}$ [hieroglyphs]

  1 [hieroglyphs] = 1 š'ty (seal) = $\frac{1}{12}$ [hieroglyphs]

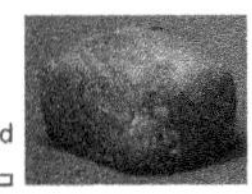

1 standard [hieroglyphs]

- **Standard weights of olive oil, in hnw or hkt**

  1 [hieroglyphs] = 1 hnw (jar)= $\frac{1}{10}$ [hieroglyphs]

Market Transactions Using Multiple Moneys

Issues Running Multiple Units of Account Simultaneously

- **Standard weights and volumes provided in temples/markets & over-seen by official scribes**
- **Surviving mathematics textbooks show scribes learned to convert units in transactions records, contracts, IOUs,**

Examples in Ahmose's (Rhind) Mathematical Papyrus

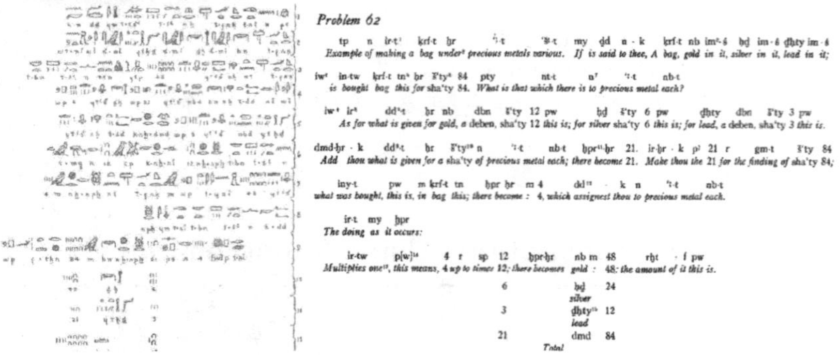

Unit of Account Residuals as a Store of Value as a Medium of Exchange

Ruins of artisans' village at Deir el Medina, Luxor

- **Numerous transactions records on ostraca (pottery fragments)**
- **Copper to silver to gold to grain to olive oil records varied over time**

- Gresham's Law in play: Records cease using a commodity when we have reason to think its price spikes relative to others
- Residuals noted on ostraca appear to record debts
- Did ostraca records make obligations tradeable?
- Ostraca preferred to papyrus for durability? Or survived?

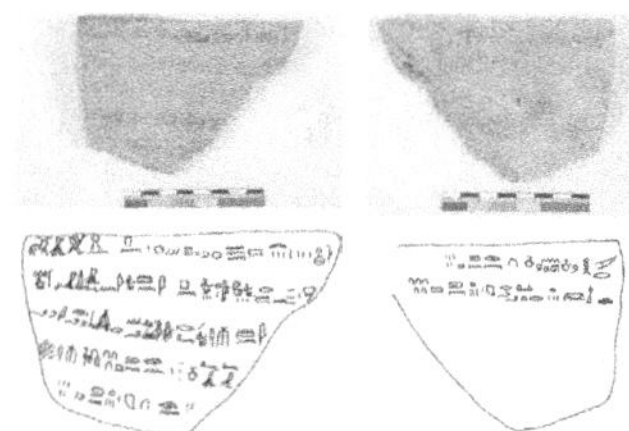

Example: DEM UC ostracon 39606
Year 4, month 3 of summer day 12; on this day purchase of the bull of the crew member Penamun by the security guard Amenmes; amount given in exchange for it:

Meat(-fat) aaat-jar, 1	*making 30 dbn*
Fine woven linen, shirts, 2	*making 5 copper dbn*
Oil, 10 hnw	*making 5 dbn*

Total of value (lit. silver) given for it 50 copper dbn

- Residual = 10 dbn of copper = value of ostracon?

Positive Interest Rates on Private-sector Loans

Literary allusions indicate people could invest wealth to earn interest

The Instruction of Any, 21st–22nd dynasty, in M. Lichtheim Ancient Egyptian Literature Vol. 2, p. 138f

Wealth accrueth to him who guardeth it;
Let thy hand not scatter it to strangers,
lest it turneth to loss for thee.
If wealth be placed where it beareth
interest, it returneth redoubled;
Make a storehouse for thine wealth,
thy people shall find it on thy way.
What is given small returneth
made great.

Extremely high (e.g. 100%) interest in 22nd Dynasty (period of institutional decay) note ➔

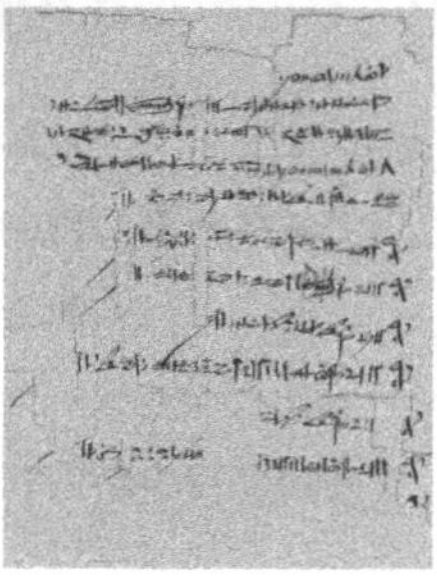

Möller, Georg. 1921. Ein ägyptischer Schuldschein der 22. Dynastie. Sitzungsberichte der preussischen

Akademie der Wissenschaften, Verlag der Akademie der Wissenschaften, Berlin 1921, 298ff.

Petekhons, son of Djedekhonsefankh, speaketh to the prophet of Amen, supervisor of Pharaoh's Treasury, Ankhefenchons, son of Naatefnakht: Thou hast entrusted [me] with 5 dbn of silver from the Treasury of Harsaphes. I shall return them to thee, them being 10, in the year 14, Pakhons, day 11, without having to exchange a word with thee.

– promissory note dated Pakhons 11th, Year 13

Some court records (~ 2600 BC) record no interest in repayment judgments & disputes about commodity exchange rates and item valuations

Gentet, Didier & Jérôme Maucourant. 1991. La question de la monnaie en Egypte ancienne. Revue du Mauss 13, 155–64

Plaintiff: "I acquired this house against payment from scribe Chenti. I paid ten š'ty for it, namely fabric (worth) three š'ty; a bed (worth) four š'ty; material (worth) three š'ty".

Defendant: "Thy payments (of ten š'ty) were made completely by 'conversion' through items representing these values"

– court record from approx. 2600 BC

State Grain Bank System

Grain as money

- Most people were farmers & had to pay their taxes in grain
  - Scribes developed geometry to calculate sizes of irregular fields
  - Grain tax due based on field size

(Some Egyptologists think) people

- Deposited grain in state grain banks after taxes deducted
- Used grain bank deposit receipts as a means of payment

The central grain bank imposed a negative interest rate

- Negative 10% per year in some records
  - Official reason = vermin & rot + storage fee
  - Encouraged consumption rather than saving?

Scribes measuring fields, calculating taxes, organizing grain shipments

Ruins of State Grain Bank silos, Luxor

Government finances operated mainly in grain units

- Farmers' taxes payable in grain
- Negative interest from grain banks
- Intertemporal arbitrage: State grain bank accumulates grain taxes during good crop years & sells grain during bad crop years
- Also production from state copper mines in the Sinai

Monetary stimulus

- Mete out state grain to individuals in 7 years of famine
- Can focus money drop on the needy

How Digital Currencies Compare to Historical Antecedents?

	Grain	Metals	S$	Digital Currency	CB Digital Currency
		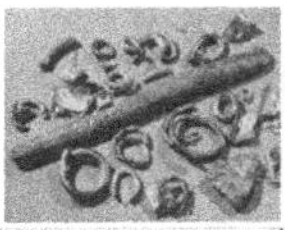		MOS	MAS
Unit of Account	❑ Officially decreed value ❑ Divisible ❑ Quality homogenized by state grain banks	❑ Officially decreed value ❑ Divisible ❑ Purity of metal, but can use metal verified by scribes	❑ Officially decreed value ❑ Divisible ❑ Difficult to counterfeit	❑ Not accepted anywhere ❑ Indivisible ❑ Proliferating near-perfect substitutes	❑ Would probably largely replicate the entries under the S$ ❑ Value contingent on prudence of MOS & political stability of Singapore, advent of quantum computing, ... ❑ Odysseus-like block chain technology allow a central bank to credibly tie itself to the mast? ❑ Or a mechanism for more nuanced discretionary monetary policy?
Medium of Exchange	❑ Universally accepted (including by the state as payment for taxes) ❑ Bulky to carry around, but papyrus depository receipts are portable	❑ Universally accepted ❑ Portable ❑ Gresham's law flips different commodities in & out of use until official exchange rates adjust	❑ Universally accepted (including by the state as payment for taxes) ❑ Portable	❑ Block chain alters scope for fraud ❑ Portability TBA ❑ Not useful for buying anything or paying taxes	
Store of Value	❑ A dry climate ❑ Value (marginal utility) varies inversely with crop yields ❑ Negative interest rates associated with rot & rats	❑ All but gold oxidize ❑ Values fluctuate inversely with mining sector activity ❑ Readily stolen	❑ Value contingent on prudence of MOS & political stability of Singapore ❑ Hackable bank accounts?	❑ Coin supply expands with players' ability to predict the stock market, sports scores, ... ❑ Value contingent on ethics of insiders, advent of quantum computing, ...	

Positive Externalities of a Central Bank Digital Currency

"When the famine had spread over all the land, Joseph opened the storehouses and sold (רֹבְשִׁיַו, 3rd per. sing. imperf., lit. he *returned*) to the Egyptians; for the famine was severe in the land of Egypt. And every nation came to Joseph in Egypt to buy grain, because the famine was severe over all the earth."

Genesis 41 56-7

- Could a modern central bank with a Central Bank Digital Currency replicate such a stimulus?

State Grain Bank at Tel-Edfu

- Newer construction (17th Dynasty, 1630–1520 B.C.) consist of at least 7 round silos of diameters 5.5–6.5 m.
- Earlier stratum is columned hall (early 13th Dynasty, 1773–1650 B.C.) of the sort where official scribes did accounting, opened & sealed containers & dictated or read letters. Ostraca (inscribed pottery shards) in this stratum list commodities.

University of Chicago excavation site

Negative Externalities of a Private Sector Digital Currency

Bitcoin Energy Consumption as % of National Total Energy Use

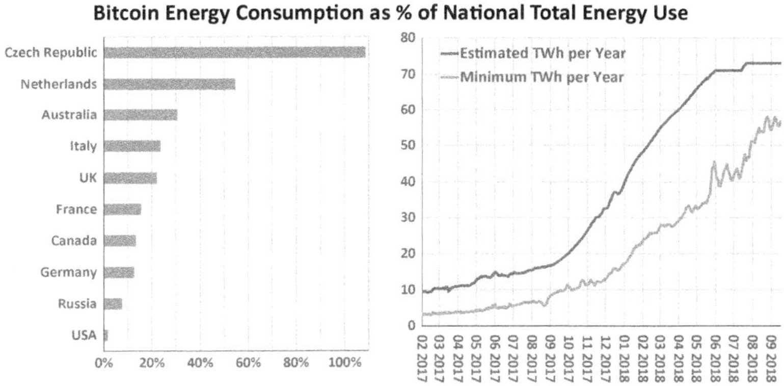

Source: https://digiconomist.net/bitcoin-energy-consumption

Bitcoin Energy Consumption Compared to National Economies

Source: https://powercompare.co.uk/bitcoin

Expensive Barbarous Relics

Max J. Krause, Max & Thabet Tolaymat. 2018. Quantification of energy and carbon costs for mining cryptocurrencies. *Nature Sustainability* 1, 711–718

- **Mining cryptocurrencies requires more energy than mining metals**

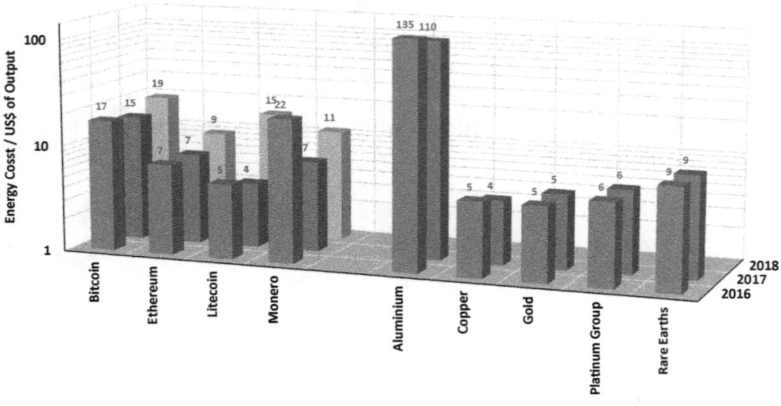

Negative Externalities of a Private Sector Digital Currency

Bitcoin Energy Consumption Becoming Major Contributor to Global Warming

Camilo Mora, Randi Rollins, Katie Taladay, Michael Kantar, Mason Chock, Mio Shimada & Erik Franklin. 2018. Bitcoin emissions alone could push global warming above 2°C. *Nature Climate Change* 8, 931–33.

- **Projected Bitcoin usage, should it follow the rate of adoption of other broadly adopted technologies, could alone produce enough CO2 emissions to push warming above 2 °C within less than three decades**

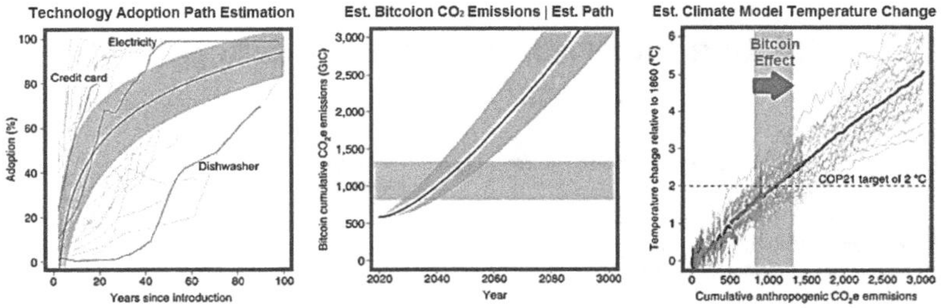

Source: https://digiconomist.net/**bitcoin**-energy-consumption

Positive Externalities of a Central Bank Digital Currency

Inequality issues associated with standard monetary policy

Money expansion via open market operations, quantitative easing, …

- Central bank buys fixed income securities, raising asset prices — direct effect
- Higher prices lower yields, putting downward pressure on interest rates
- Cost of capital to banks falls → more bank lending at lower rates
- Cost of capital to firms & households falls → more investment & consumption — pushing on a string

Owners of financial assets (the rich) become richer

Monetary expansion via CB digital currency creation

- Potential could emulate pharaoh's grain bank distribution of stimulus
- All firms & households have digital currency accounts with central bank
- Central bank simply adds new money to firms' and/or households' accounts
- Better than helicopter money because central bank can do precision money drops on e.g. low-income households with highest marginal propensities to consume?

Transmission to the real economy = chains of events that may or may not actually happen

Precision targeted helicopter money?

Positive Externalities of a Central Bank Digital Currency

Each citizen has a direct account with the treasury or central bank for

- Transfer payment (credits)
  - Micro monetary stimulus; micro fiscal stimulus too
- Tax payment (debits)
- Taxable income payments (credits)
- Bill payments (debits)
- National health care indirect billing & payments

Left v right disagreement on the sign of the externality

- The pharaoh cannot create grain out of nothing. Greenspan can.
- Does block chain technology make Greenspan more like a pharaoh?

"The art of taxation is to pluck the goose to get the most feathers with least hissing."
Jean Baptiste Colbert

Libertarian central bankers?
Alan Greenspan & Ayn Rand

Who To Trust More, Central Banker or Internet Genius?

Thank You

CHAPTER 5

Chapter 5

Digital Money: Private versus Public*

Markus Brunnermeier and Dirk Niepelt

Princeton University; Study Center Gerzensee and University of Bern

The financial system is undergoing fundamental change. Fintech and bigtech firms push the technological frontier, redefine business models and force banks to adapt. In parallel, new forms of money and alternative payment systems emerge. Alipay, Apple Pay, Bitcoin and new types of digital central bank money compete with traditional bank deposits. What are the macroeconomic consequences of these new means of payment? We address five key concerns that are frequently put forward:

(1) Aren't digital currencies just a hype, now that crypto "currencies" like Bitcoin have proved too volatile and expensive to serve as reliable stores of value or mediums of exchange? This confuses things. Central Bank Digital Currency (CBDC) is like cash, only digital; Alipay, Apple Pay, WeChat Pay etc. is like deposits, only handier; and cryptocurrencies are not in any way linked to typical currencies, but they live on the blockchain.

(2) Doesn't CBDC or "Reserves for All" choke investment by cutting into bank deposits? No, because new central bank liabilities (namely CBDC) would fund new investments, and this would not in any way imply socialism or a stronger role of government in investment decisions.

---

*This chapter also appears at the Vox-E-book 2019.

(3) Wouldn't CBDC cut into the profits that banks generate by creating deposits? Less money creation by banks would certainly affect their profits. But if this were deemed undesirable (by the public, not by shareholders and management) then banks could be compensated.
(4) Wouldn't "Reserves for All" render bank runs more likely, undermining financial stability? We argue that, in fact, the opposite seems more plausible.
(5) Aren't deposit insurance, CBDC, "Vollgeld"/sovereign money, or the Chicago plan all alike? There are close parallels indeed between the different monetary regimes. In a sense, money is changing and yet, it stays the same.

Let us be more explicit.

Crypto is private digital money, but different

Apple Pay, Alipay, M-Pesa and other monies issued by fintech and bigtech firms typically constitute claims to central bank money, or claims to central bank money, or ... In this respect, they parallel traditional bank deposits, which also represent commitments to deliver central bank money. Most cryptocurrencies are different. They do not promise euros, dollars, or Swiss francs (unless their issuers actually invest in fiat currencies and render the crypto stuff redeemable). In fact, the prices of cryptocurrencies fluctuate wildly relative to the prices of moneys issued by central banks. This makes cryptocurrencies much less useful as means of payment but maybe more useful for hedging purposes (or as easy-to-hide stores of value). From a macroeconomic point of view, cryptocurrencies pose similar challenges to policy makers as dollarization: The national currency loses its singularity and as a consequence, the central bank part of its influence over domestic monetary conditions.

While cryptocurrencies are quite different from the money issued by banks they are even more different from central bank issued money. What would happen, then, if central banks were to issue digital money for the general public, "Reserves for All," as suggested for example by Tobin (1985, 1987)?

"Reserves for all" would neither choke investment nor herald socialism

True, if people would swap some of their bank deposits into CBDC then banks would lose a source of funding. But the central bank would gain funds, and these would have to be invested somewhere. The central bank could start funding real investment — an experiment in "socialism," and likely a bad one because private banks arguably are better equipped to screen loan applications and monitor projects (and better insulated against political pressure). Alternatively, and preferably, the central bank could pass the funds through to commercial banks, effectively leaving the environment for banks completely unchanged. The important point to note is that a substitution of moneys (CBDC for deposits) only requires new sources of bank funding, not new ownership and control over real assets.

Figure 1 illustrates the effects of the pass-through operation on the balance sheets of banks, the central bank, and households.

Banks can be compensated

When issuing deposits in exchange for loans or other assets banks typically borrow cheaply and lend dearly. (Today, there are some

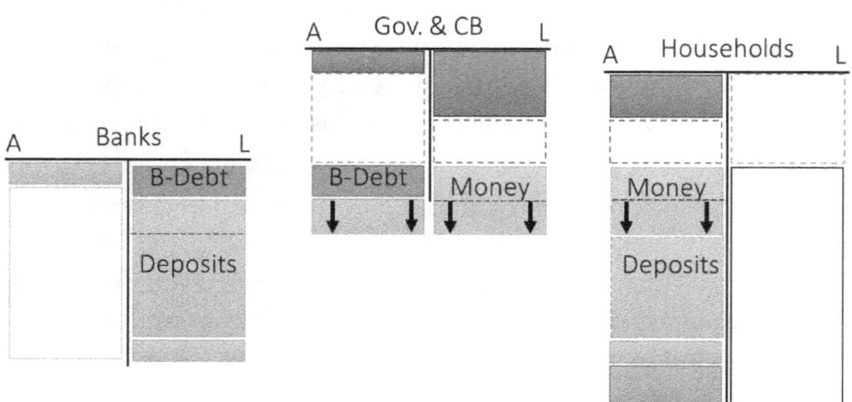

Figure 1: The arrows in the green rectangles indicate that households hold fewer deposits but more central bank issued money, e.g. in the form of CBDC. The central bank passes the funds through to banks by holding more deposits, as depicted by the arrows in the red rectangle on the asset side of the central bank's balance sheet.

exceptions to this rule as some central banks charge negative interest on the reserves banks hold with them, while deposits mostly pay non-negative interest.) Deposit holders go along with this because bank money is useful not only as a store of value but also as a means of payment — money has liquidity value. By creating this value out of "thin air" (subject to limitations), banks generate seigniorage profits. Less bank money creation would eat into those profits.

Some may consider that unfortunate, because they like bank shareholders or are worried about banks' capital base. Others might like it. In any case, the distributive implications of replacing commercial bank by central bank issued money are manageable: banks could easily be compensated if this were so desired.

"Reserves for all" may not increase the risk of bank runs

A frequently made argument against the introduction of CBDC points to the danger of increased run risk. According to this argument, CBDC would not foster "traditional" bank runs where non-banks try to withdraw deposits and convert them into cash. Instead, it would give rise to a novel form with volatile deposit withdrawals in response to swings in sentiment and shifts into safe-haven CBDC since such swaps would be very easy to conduct and nearly costless.

It is far from obvious, however, whether the introduction of CBDC would make bank runs "more likely." First, when the central bank issues CBDC and passes funds through to private banks then the central bank becomes a large, possibly the largest, depositor. But a large depositor that pursues an optimal policy internalizes the run externalities and therefore might refrain from running itself. As a consequence, the incentives for the remaining small depositors to run also fall. Hence, CBDC combined with pass-through funding can make runs less rather than more likely.

Second, with CBDC, the central bank gains an informational advantage because it immediately learns when a run is about to start from fund inflows. The central bank therefore can engage more quickly as a lender of last resort; it can more easily prevent costly fire-sales; and it can better prevent a liquidity problem to morph into a solvency crisis.

If the remaining depositors are aware of this ability to intervene earlier, and more effectively, then they may become less wary themselves which again reduces the risk of a deposit run.[1]

A related question is whether the central bank would lose control over its balance sheet once CBDC is introduced. Indeed, a central bank that passes through funds from non-banks to banks lengthens its balance sheet, and if the volume of funds varies over time, so does the length of the balance sheet. There is no reason, however, to be concerned with the length of the central bank's balance sheet per se (especially if some items on the asset and liability side net out) except for the implications on credit risk exposure. This exposure can be minimized with the appropriate collateral policy.

If today, deposits are perfectly liquid and risk-free because of unconditional deposit insurance backed by government guarantees and a lender of last resort, then CBDC combined with pass-through funding would simply make implicit government guarantees explicit. If deposits are risky, in contrast, then a newly introduced CBDC would have to be accompanied by transfers or taxes in order to exactly replicate outcomes under the contemporaneous regime. In either case, the net wealth and liquidity positions of agents would remain unchanged even if their gross positions reflected in balance sheets might change.

Chicago plan, narrow banks and sovereign money ("Vollgeld")

The Chicago Plan from the 1930s (Knight *et al.* 1933, Fisher 1935, 1936) which argues in favor of narrow banks simply amounts to an introduction of CBDC that fully replaces deposits. As described above, one way to end fractional reserve banking without changing equilibrium outcomes would be for the central bank to supply deposits — at the same price and conditions as depositors currently do — to banks. This is not what the proponents of the sovereign money ("Vollgeld")

[1] The central bank may also set an unattractive (possibly negative) interest rate on CBDC accounts to avoid CBDC becoming more attractive than cash as a safe-haven asset. Of course, the central bank has to be careful that changes in the CBDC interest rate do not serve as a coordination device for households to start a run.

proposal envision. According to their proposal, banks should no longer issue deposits but fund themselves from different sources instead. Banks would lose a source of profits — seigniorage rents from liquidity creation — and change their policies, with potential implications for macroeconomic outcomes. Of course, it is not clear how the abolition of money creation by banks could ever be enforced in the first place.

Money is changing and yet, it stays the same — an equivalence benchmark

In a recent paper (Brunnermeier and Niepelt 2019), we make this discussion precise. We show formally that as long as CBDC can serve as a (not necessarily efficient) means of payment for some transactions currently conducted with deposits, a swap of the former for the latter does not have macroeconomic consequences as long as certain conditions are satisfied. Our equivalence result should be construed as a benchmark result that helps to organize one's thinking about complex economic relationships, in the spirit of Modigliani and Miller (1958), Barro (1974), and many other equivalence results in economics. There may exist only few circumstances under which the sufficient conditions for equivalence literally apply; nevertheless, they give a clear sense of possible sources of non-equivalence in real-world settings.

Maybe the most restrictive condition for the irrelevance of a swap relates to politics (Niepelt 2018). Irrelevance would require, for example, that political decision makers are willing to compensate bank owners for the losses they suffer due to reduced seigniorage profits. We doubt that voters would accept this. In fact, one important motivation for the "Vollgeld" (sovereign money) initiative recently rejected by Swiss voters was to shift rents from banks to taxpayers.

Whether a *non*-neutral monetary reform would be towards the better or the worse is a question that our equivalence result cannot address. Answering this would require an explicit characterization of equilibrium in model economies, as well as serious quantitative and welfare analyses. For policy discussions about monetary reform, our paper therefore does not propose a set of definite answers, but an analytical framework and a robust road map.

References

Barro, R. J. (1974), "Are government bonds net wealth?", *Journal of Political Economy* 82(6), 1095–1117.

Brunnermeier, M. and D. Niepelt (2019), "On the equivalence of private and public money", mimeo, January.

Knight, F. (with seven other Chicago economists) (1933), "Memorandum on banking reform", Franklin D. Roosevelt Presidential Library, President's Personal File 431.

Fisher, I. (1935), 100% *Money*, Adelphi, New York.

Fisher, I. (1936), "100% money and the public debt", *Economic Forum* (April–June), 406–420.

Modigliani, F. and M. Miller (1958), "The cost of capital, corporation finance and the theory of investment", *American Economic Review* 48(3), 261–297.

Niepelt, D. (2018), "Reserves for All? Central Bank Digital Currency, Deposits, and their (Non)-Equivalence", CEPR Discussion Paper 13065, July.

Tobin, J. (1985), "Financial innovation and deregulation in perspective", *Bank of Japan Monetary and Economic Studies* 3(2), 19–29.

Tobin, J. (1987), *The case for preserving regulatory distinctions*, in "Restructuring the Financial System, Proceedings of the Economic Policy Symposium, Jackson Hole," Federal Reserve Bank of Kansas City, Chapter 9, pp. 167–183.

Digital Money Workshop 2018
Markus K. Brunnermeier
Princeton University

NUS, MAS, Singapore FinTech Festival
Singapore, 2018-11-15

The powerpoint presentation material draws from my co-authored papers, "Blockchain Economics" with Joseph Abadi, and "On the Equivalence between Private & Public Money" with Dirk Niepelt.

Digital Economy — Rethinking Money

- Role of cash and other forms of outside money
  - Cash as protector of privacy in an open society
- What new forms of money might emerge?
- Should central banks endorse/fight
  - digital money?
  - cryptocurrencies?
  - Blockchain technology?
- Competition among currencies (and other means of payments, store of value, carrier of info) in a world with declining transaction costs
- Tokenization

Overview

- 3 roles of money & 3 components of asset's value
- Money creation creates rents & resource cost free
- Private vs. public money *with Dirk Niepelt*
  - Who is allowed to issue "money"?
  - Should government compete with private money or disallow it?
    - CDBC vs. Vollgeld/sovereign money
  - Equivalence Theorem
- What's special about digital money?
- What's special about crypto money? *with Joseph Abadi*
  - Blockchain trilemma
  - Fork competition vs. Hayekian currency competition
  - Enforcement: Ownership vs. Possession crypto currencies are special blockchains

Roles of Money

- When is money "essential" a la Hahn?
  - Changes in allocation $\Rightarrow$ MRS/SDF

1. Record-keeping device (information role)
   - Balance of tokens as a crude summary of history
   - Centralized (CBDC) vs. decentralized (cash, DLT)
2. Medium of exchange
   - double-coincidence of wants
   - max $U(x)$ subject to
     - Budget constraint   B = 0
     - Liquidity constraint $L \leq 0$
       - Cash in advance, MIU, shopping time, New monetarism

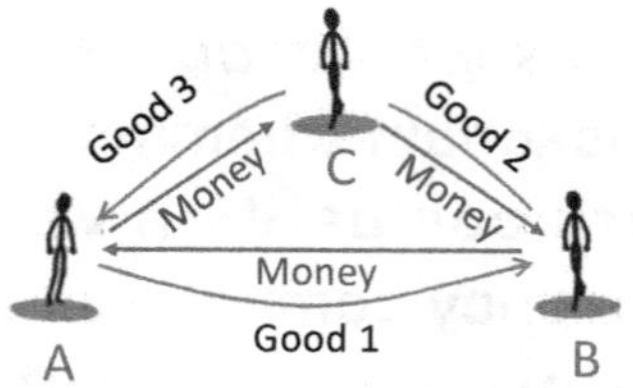

3. Store of value
   - bubble — money changes the asset span

     e.g. Samuelson OLG, Bewley, "I Theory of Money"

3 Components of an Asset's Value

- $p_t = v_t + l_t + b_t$

1. Fundamental value

$$l_t = E_t\left[\sum_{s=t+1}^{T} \beta^s \frac{\partial u / \partial c_s}{\partial u / \partial c_t} CF_s\right]$$

2. Liquidity value

$$l_t = E_t\left[\sum_{s=t+1}^{T} \beta^s \alpha_{s-1} \frac{\partial u / \partial c_s}{\partial u / \partial c_t} CF_s\right]$$

where $\frac{\alpha_t}{\alpha_{t+1}} := \frac{\lambda_t}{\partial u / \partial c_t} L'(\text{velocity})$

- Improves medium of exchange, (relaxes L-constraint)

3. Bubble value

$$b_t = \lim_{T\to\infty} E_t\left[\underbrace{\beta^T}_{<1} \underbrace{\prod_{s=t}^{T-1}(1+\alpha_s)}_{>1} \frac{\partial u / \partial c_T}{\partial u / \partial c_t} b_T\right]$$

- Completes market/OLG

Rents from Money Creation

- Extreme form: issue bubbly liquid asset
  - No (social) resource costs Friedman '69
- More general: hold illiquid asset with high v (cash flow) issue liquid asset with low v

A	L
High v	High l, b
Low l, b	Low v

- Rents:
  - "free lunch"
  - Curse excessive supply, ICOs ⇒ inflation
  - Who has the right to "collect" these rents? Competitiveness

Public/Private Money Competition

- Restrict private money — Chicago plan, Vollgeld
- Compete with private money — CBDC

- Competition among private monies
- Centralized ledgers — Alipay with WeChat Pay
- Decentralized ledger — Blockchain Trilemma, Fork

Classifying Money

Money	Public	Private
Outside	Cash CBDC	Cryptocurrencies
Inside (debt obligation)		Bank deposits Credit cards, e-money (Alipay), ...

- **Gov.-Regulating money supply Limit private money creation or compete with it**
  - **CDBC vs. Chicago Plan/Vollgeld**

Equivalence btw Public and Private Money

- Brunnermeier & Niepelt (2018) "Modigliani-Miller/Ricardian Equivalence type theorem"
- Example: Crowd out public money (CBDC) crowds out private money (deposits)
  s.t. L, L' stay constant insured
  - Resource problem: No, since no social costs (Friedman '69)
  - Wealth problem: Redistributes rents
- Wealth redistribution issue does not arise when
  1. Banks very competitive, so that they had to pass on all rents to borrowers/savers
  2. Banks' ownership structure = tax paying structure (Barro '74)
- Swap banks claims for reduction of implicit tax liability claims
- Any representative agent economy

Equivalence: CBDC vs. Deposits

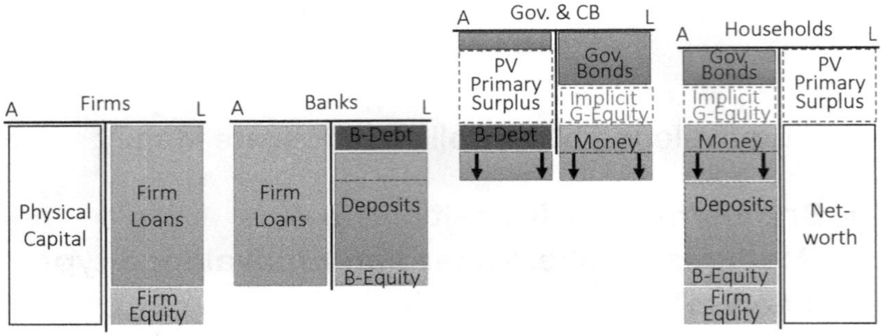

- **Key insight: Central bank "passes through" funding**
- **If banks are non-competitive, CB's supply function has to be such that banks set the same deposit rates**

More Examples

- **CBDC vs. deposits with bank runs**
  - **Transfers needed**
- **Chicago Plan — the end of fractional reserve banking (Fisher, 1935, 1936)**
  - **Equivalence: Central bank buys up all deposits at (possibly distorted) market price**
- **"Vollgeld"/ "sovereign money" (prohibition)**
  - **"Vollgeld" redistributes rents from banks to central bank**
  - **Equivalence only if HH exposures to bank profits = taxes (Ricardian equivalence)**

What's Special about "Digital Money"?

1. Money as record keeping device (token)

- Information role of money
  ⇒ record keeper(s) receives info rents
  - Example: Ant Financial's credit scoring
- Convenience to use ⇒ higher velocity
  - Equivalence can be maintained.
- Easy to exchange
  ⇒ network externalities decline
  ⇒ separates store of value from medium exchange
  ⇒ Lower rents for issues

What's Special about Crypto Currencies?

- Abadi & Brunnermeier (2018) "Blockchain Economics"
- Decentralized record keeping
  - PoW blockchain vs. permissioned blockchain
- Fork competition
  - Info portability + record-keeper competition
  - Instability (split in subgroups)
- Correctness
  - Monopolist's incentives are dynamic PoW-Blockchain incentives are static
  - Rollback

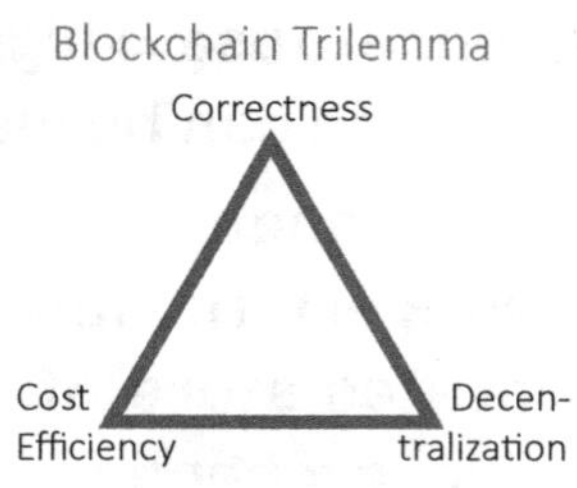

- Enforcement: Ownership vs. Possession

Economically Relevant Differences btw. Centralized Ledger and Blockchain

1. Free entry (for record-keepers)
   - But requires identity management. Hence, PoW
2. Ability to roll back blockchain
3. Portability of Information (for proposers)

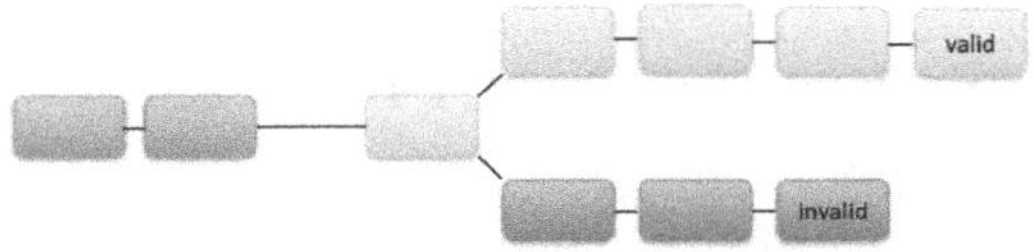

Rollback

- With centralized ledger
  - Future rents/franchise value incentives centralized record keeper to correctly report transactions dynamic incentive scheme
  - No rollback

$\Rightarrow$ Punishment is costly
  - High franchise value needed in order for punishment to be credible
    - For TBTF institution (like Wells-Fargo) must be even higher
- With blockchain
  - Free entry $\Rightarrow$ no future rents/franchise value static incentive scheme
  - Rollback record keepers will compete to write on old chain

$\Rightarrow$ Punishment is not costly
  - No franchise value needed!

2 Forms of Competition

- Competition via entry and forking ("platform competition")

		Ability to FORK	
		yes	no
Ability to ENTER	free entry	Blockchain	
	restricted	Permissioned Blockchain	Monopolistic intermediary

- "Fork competition": 2 necessary ingredients
  - Competition among record-keepers
  - Replication of info

Fork competition

- With centralized ledger, information is not portable
  ⇒ Competition is reduced
  - Example: Alibaba's credit scoring, Amazon's seller rating, Facebook friends
- With Blockchain, information is portable
  ⇒ Competition is fierce (contestable market for platforms)
  - Example: Software developers have incentive to develop new technologies to fork off existing chains Bitcoin Cash, Bitcoin Gold, ...

Fork ≠ Hayekian Currency Competition

- Two types of currency competition:
  - Hayekian: sell old and buy new (price adjusts) -require active decision to participate (ignore new currency and save on info collection cost)
  - Fork: duplicate history + "helicopter drop" of new currency based on current stakes -endowment effect if it is given to you (even if one only sells new currency, pay info collection cost)
- Fork currency competition is fiercer than Hayekian

Enforcement: Cryptocurrency is Special

- So far ignored enforcement distinction btw ownership & possession
  - Ownership is traded in the secondary market
  - Possession is conferred by the previous possessor and enforced by some entity
    - Example: Land registry requires enforcer who "kicks out the squatters"
- Enforcement of land registry, stock registry ... necessary ... central authority needs to be incentivized
  - When to bundle enforcer & record keeper?
- Currency/platform info is special: "Money is a bubble" -no fundamental value/no dividend

... To Sum Up

- Money creation creates rents & resource cost free
- Private vs. public money with Dirk Niepelt
  - Who is allowed to issued "money"?
  - Should government compete with private money or disallow it?
    - CDBC vs. Vollgeld
  - Equivalence
    - Liquidity creation is resource cost free
    - Rent distribution
      - Perfect competitive — passed on to borrowers/savers
      - Ownership structure
- What's special about digital money? with Joseph Abadi
- What's special about crypto money?
  - Blockchain trilemma
  - Fork competition
    - Fork currency competition vs. Hayekian competition
  - Ownership vs. Possession: crypto currencies are special blockchains

CHAPTER 6

Demand and Supply: Discussion of Brunnermeier "Coexistence of Private Digital and Central Bank Currencies"

ABFER-MAS-NUS Business School

Danny Quah
Lee Kuan Yew School of Public Policy

2018 November

NUS

Lee Kuan Yew School of Public Policy

Discussant's outline

1. Brunnermeier's comprehensive account. The deep economics of money, both classical and forward-looking.
2. Demand and supply
   a. Disruption. Digital. AI (Deep learning)
   b. Global order
3. Conclusions

The Demand Side

$$\text{Max } U \text{ (Dynamic)}$$
$$\text{s.t. } B = 0 \text{ (Budget)}$$
$$L \leq 0 \text{ (Liquidity)}$$

$\Rightarrow$ Demand curve

$$E_t\left[MU_{t+1} \times R_{t+1}\right] + \frac{\partial L\lambda}{\partial a\mu} = 1$$

With

$$E_t[MU_{t+1} \times R_{t+1}] = \text{cov}(MU_{t+1}, R_{t+1}) + E_t[MU_{t+1}]E_t[R_{t+1}]$$

$\Rightarrow$ Price $p_t = v_t + l_t + b_t$, functions of $\{MU\}$, $\{R\}$, $\{L\}$

The Supply Side

1. Inelastic?

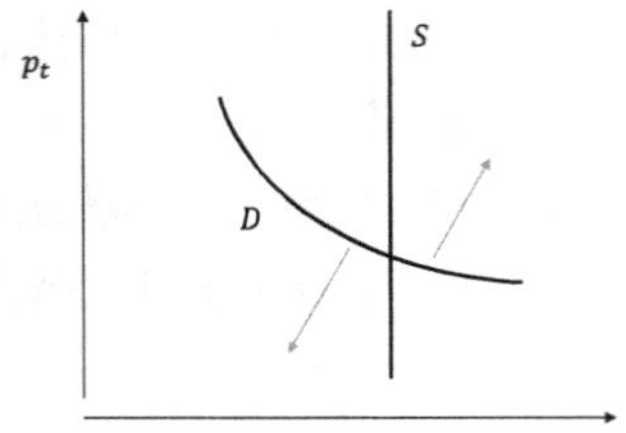

The Supply Side (2) — Competition?

1. Controls (governments vs libertarian fringe?)
2. Blockchain trust. Mining constraints on supply
3. Rogoff government capacity; Eichengreen's uniform national circulation; Yermack's states in emerging markets
    - Not all states alike. Shifting global distribution of power
    - World's reserve currency

The Supply Side (3) — Competition?

3. Intermediate intermediaries
    - Not private providers vs states but private providers vs a fractional reserve banking system
    - Money multiplier; money supply mechanism

The Supply Side (4) — Bundling?

Information management, not just medium of exchange or store of value

- Can digital currency providers whether central banks or private suppliers offer (as a consequence, intended or unintended, in equilibrium):
  - Security and privacy; anonymity?
  - Financial inclusivity (the poor, rural; India)?
  - Bundling and integration with smartphone apps; personal information aggregation dashboard?
  - Lowered transaction costs and AI-driven improved matching of buyers and sellers?
  - Building trust in societies where Delivery vs Payment challenges remain, where rule of law is tenuous?
- Not competition but private-public partnerships on digital currency provision to alleviate concerns

Conclusions

1. Brunnermeier's comprehensive account. The deep economics of money
2. Demand and supply
   a. Different hierarchies and multiple levels
3. Where do we think the disruption to be most powerful, if at all; where do we model that disruption?

Demand and Supply: Discussion of Brunnermeier "Coexistence of Private Digital and Central Bank Currencies"

ABFER-MAS-NUS Business School

Danny Quah
Lee Kuan Yew School of Public Policy

2018 November

NUS

Lee Kuan Yew School of Public Policy

CHAPTER 7

Chapter 7

Lessons for Cryptocurrencies from Foreign Exchange Markets

Charles Engel

University of Wisconsin — Madison
NBER and CEPR
cengel@ssc.wisc.edu

This essay brings insights from the academic literature on foreign exchange rate determination to the analysis of cryptocurrency markets. We present a simple framework to summarize the factors that determine exchange rates. To the extent that cryptocurrencies are like national currencies issued by central banks, their pricing can be analyzed using these models of exchange rates.

As a preliminary, it is helpful to recall the traditional delineation of the three roles of *money*: it is a medium of exchange, a store of value, and a unit of account. The medium of exchange function refers to the usefulness of money for making transactions. Rather than the cumbersome search and matching problem that would arise if trade were by barter, money eases the process by allowing people to sell their goods and services for money, and to buy goods and services from other agents using money. Money is also an asset, which makes it a store of value. Often, money earns very little or no pecuniary return. Forms of money include, for example, currency, demand deposits, and other checkable deposits. All of these pay a lower return than, for instance, short-term paper, but that difference reflects the implicit return to money arising from its utility in performing transactions. Finally, prices of goods and services are quoted in terms of money. Indeed, the convenience of money is connected to the stability of prices. When the prices quoted in terms of money are stable and predictable, people are more willing to hold money for transactions even though money provides little or no direct pecuniary return.

Currency is one form of money and has somewhat different properties than other forms of money such as checking deposits. For transactions that involve small amounts, it is very convenient, but is quite cumbersome relative to other types of money for larger transactions. An important property is that transactions using currency are nearly completely anonymous. It is impossible to trace the buyer or seller of a product or service when the business is conducted with cash.

Money, in turn, is one form of *liquid assets*. Nickolas (2018) defines liquid assets as: "cash on hand or an asset that can be readily converted to cash. An asset that can readily be converted into cash is similar to cash itself because the asset can be sold with little impact on its value." There is a close relationship between liquidity and safety, when safety is defined as in Gorton (2017): "A safe asset is an asset that is (almost always) valued at face value without expensive and prolonged analysis. By design, there is no benefit to producing (private) information about its value, and this is common knowledge." From these definitions, we can conclude that safe assets are liquid, and liquid assets are safe.

Section 1 presents a framework for foreign exchange rate determination. The next section considers the similarities and differences of cryptocurrencies and national currencies, and applies lessons from the model of foreign exchange rates to the pricing of these digital currencies. The third and concluding section discusses implications for policy.

1. Basics of Foreign Exchange Rate Determination

A foreign exchange rate is the price of one money in terms of another — the price of euros in units of US dollars, for example. Like other assets, money is a store of value and it offers a return. Its return comes from its usefulness in making transactions. That is, money is very liquid.

Pecuniary returns and liquidity yield

An asset might pay a tangible monetary return, such as an interest rate, but it also may have an intangible return arising from its liquidity. For example, money has a return even if it does not pay interest because it eases the burden of making transactions. We can designate the monetary return on an asset (designated with a subscript j) at time t as $i_{j,t}$. We label the non-pecuniary return $v_{j,t}$.

To keep to a simple example, suppose money (cash or demand deposits) pays no interest, so that its return arises purely from its usefulness in completing transactions. The return on money is $v_{m,t}$.

A safe, short-term government bond pays interest, but it may also pay a non-pecuniary return. For example, in the United States (US), government bonds are a good asset to use as collateral for overnight interbank borrowing. The market for government bonds is very deep, and there is no private information about their value, so government bonds are liquid. The return on government bonds, then, has a pecuniary and a non-pecuniary component: $i_{g,t} + v_{g,t}$. The non-pecuniary component of the government bond return is often called its "convenience yield."

Money and government bonds have very similar risk characteristics. Both are subject to losing value through inflation. But there is no uncertainty about the nominal return on money or government bonds.[1] Given these similarities, markets will equate the return on the two assets:

$$v_{m,t} = i_{g,t} + v_{g,t}. \tag{1}$$

In words, the return on money that arises from its facilitation of transactions must equal the sum of the monetary and liquidity returns on government bonds. As the interest rate on bonds increases, the liquidity return on money must increase to satisfy the equality in (1). Using the general principle from economics of diminishing returns, as economic agents hold more money, its marginal value for transactions purposes decreases. When interest rates are high, households and businesses economize on cash balances and only hold them for transactions for which it is most valuable to have a liquid asset on hand. For example, when interest rates are very low, households might decide that it saves effort to keep the monthly rent money in their checking account. When

[1] We ignore here the possibility of default on short-term government bonds, though it is easy to extend the analysis to that case by including a premium in the return for default risk.

interest rates are high, the opportunity cost of holding money in their current account is too high, so they may plan to keep the money in an interest-bearing account and then only turn their funds into money on the day that rent is due.

As noted previously, not all money is identical. Currency has different properties than demand deposits — it is more anonymous, but more cumbersome. We can speak of a non-pecuniary return on cash, as distinguished from the liquidity return on demand deposits, $v_{d,t}$. Households and firms adjust their cash balances and checking balances so at the margin those returns are equal, $v_{c,t} = v_{d,t}$, and that equality allows us to refer to the return on money $v_{m,t}(= v_{c,t} = v_{d,t})$.

Returns on foreign currency instruments

How do we compare the returns on the government bills of one country to those from another country? Let us designate one country as the "home" and the other as the "foreign" (and we use a superscript * for returns from the foreign country). The return on a foreign short-term government bond includes its interest rate and its convenience yield: $i^*_{g,t} + v^*_{g,t}$. But those returns are in units of foreign currency. To compare the returns on the foreign government bond to those on the home government bond, we need to convert the foreign currency returns into home currency. Just like shares of stock pay a dividend and a capital gain, the foreign government bond pays its return in foreign currency, $i^*_{g,t} + v^*_{g,t}$, and a capital gain given by the percentage increase in the value of the foreign currency in terms of home currency: $\frac{S_{t+1}-S_t}{S_t}$. Here, S_t is the home currency price of foreign currency. For example, if the US is the home country and France is the foreign country, S_t is the dollar price of euros. If the euro appreciates, so the exchange rate rises between time t and $t + 1$, then $\frac{S_{t+1}-S_t}{S_t}$ is positive and the French government bond has a "capital gain" in terms of US dollars. The return on the French bond, in dollar terms, is $i^*_{g,t} + v^*_{g,t} + \frac{S_{t+1}-S_t}{S_t}$.

Including the currency return introduces two complications into the comparison of returns on home bonds to foreign bonds. First, at the time the investment is made, the future exchange rate is not known. Investors must form expectations of the future exchange rate, S^e_{t+1}, so the expected currency return is $\frac{S_{t+1}^e - S_t}{S_t}$. The *expected* return on the foreign government bond in home currency terms is given by $i_{g,t}^* + v_{g,t}^* + \frac{S_{t+1}^e - S_t}{S_t}$.

Foreign exchange risk premium

The second complication is that given there is uncertainty about the exchange rate, investors face uncertainty about returns. The home investor is uncertain about the return on a foreign government bond because converting foreign currency returns into home currency is subject to the unknown level of the future exchange rate. The uncertainty about the return on the foreign bond might lead the home investor to require a higher expected rate of return on that bond if he is to hold it. But, conversely, the foreign investor might insist on a higher expected return on the home bond in order to compensate for foreign exchange risk. It should be clear that these two conditions cannot both be satisfied — it is not possible for each of the home and foreign investor to earn a higher expected return on the other's bonds.

There is a large theoretical literature that has promulgated various theories of the "risk premium" for foreign exchange, and the models can be quite complicated. It is impossible to give a thorough summary here. But it is important to note is that, just because the return on an asset is uncertain, it does not mean that investors necessarily require a higher expected rate of return to be induced to hold the asset. For example, one could think of fire insurance as being an asset with an uncertain return. Most of the time, its payoffs are negative, because the holder of the policy pays the annual premium but does not make any claims on the insurance company. Only when there is a fire does the "investor" receive a positive payout on the asset. Most fire insurance policyholders never receive any compensation. Surely the expected return on fire insurance is negative. But people are still willing to hold that asset, even though its return is uncertain, and its average payoff is negative. That is because of the timing of the compensation — the fire insurance pays out exactly when the policyholder receives a large negative shock to his wealth. An asset that has properties of insurance — it tends to pay out more during bad times — may have a lower expected return than a riskless asset.

So it is with foreign exchange risk. Investors around the world might be willing to accept lower average returns on US government bonds (or Japanese or Swiss bonds) because those bonds maintain their value during global recessions. That is, the currencies of these countries tend to appreciate during a global downturn, and therefore have properties like fire insurance. While their expected return may be lower than returns on government bonds from other countries, investors are still willing to hold them for their insurance properties.

A complete theory of foreign exchange risk premiums would include the time-varying aversion to risk across countries, the effects of being net borrowers or net lenders to the rest of the world, and the relationship between exchange rate risk and inflation risk.

We can say that the equilibrium condition in global financial markets implies that the return on the home bond must equal the expected return on the foreign bond, adjusted for the expected capital gain, and corrected for the compensation for foreign exchange risk:

$$i_{g,t} + v_{g,t} + rp_t = i^*_{g,t} + v^*_{g,t} + \frac{S^e_{t+1} - S_t}{S_t} \tag{2}$$

Here, rp_t is the foreign exchange risk premium. If rp_t is positive ($rp_t > 0$), then the foreign bond pays a return that is higher than the home bond: $i^*_{g,t} + v^*_{g,t} + \frac{S^e_{t+1} - S_t}{S_t} > i_{g,t} + v_{g,t}$. In this case, the expected return on the foreign bond compensates investors for foreign exchange risk. The home bond pays a lower expected return than the foreign bond, but investors are willing to hold that bond because it provides insurance against foreign exchange risk. It could be the other way around, so that $rp_t < 0$, and it is the home bond that pays a higher expected return because of how the market prices foreign exchange risk.

Basic model of exchange-rate determination

Eq. (2) can be rearranged with a little bit of algebra to give us our basic model of foreign exchange rate determination:

$$S_t = \frac{S^e_{t+1}}{\left(i_{g,t} - i^*_{g,t}\right) + \left(v_{g,t} - v^*_{g,t}\right) + rp_t + 1}. \tag{3}$$

Consider the determinants of exchange rates in Eq. (3). Interest rates play a role. When the home interest rate increases relative to the foreign interest rate, so $i_{g,t} - i^*_{g,t}$ increases, the exchange rate falls. The exchange rate, recall, is the home currency price of foreign currency, so a decrease in S_t is an appreciation of the home currency. For example, when US interest rates rise relative to European interest rates, the dollar appreciates relative to the euro (holding all else constant). That matches the that an increase in home interest rates increases the marginal return on home money, because $v_{m,t} = i_{g,t} + v_{g,t}$, which leads to an appreciation of the home currency.

The relative convenience yields play the same role as the relative interest rates, because the convenience yield is just another source of return on the bonds. When $v_{g,t} - v^*_{g,t}$ rises, the home currency appreciates.

If there is an increase in the riskiness of the foreign bond — that is, if the compensation to investors for foreign exchange risk on the foreign bond increases — the home currency appreciates. When rp_t rises, investors want to switch away from foreign bonds to home bonds. If interest rates do not change, the home currency must appreciate. Holding expectations of the future exchange rate level constant, an appreciation of the home currency today will imply an expectation of a depreciation between time t and $t + 1$. That is, algebraically, if S_t falls, and S^e_{t+1} is held constant, than $\frac{S^e_{t+1} - S_t}{S_t}$ must rise. In order to compensate investors for the increased riskiness of the foreign bond, it must be expected to yield a capital gain in terms of home currency.

Finally, the next period's expected exchange rate affects today's exchange rate. If the foreign currency is expected to have a higher level tomorrow, investors want to buy it today. A higher S^e_{t+1} makes S_t higher. But what determines expectations of next period's exchange rate? One possible answer is that investors are forward looking. They understand that in period $t + 1$, the model given by Eq. (3) will determine the exchange rate:

$$S_{t+1} = \frac{S^e_{t+2}}{\left(i_{g,t+1} - i^*_{g,t+1}\right) + \left(v_{g,t+1} - v^*_{g,t+1}\right) + rp_{t+1} + 1}$$

Then their expectations of the future exchange rate are determined by their expectations of the determinants of the exchange rate that the model posits:

$$S_{t+1}^{e} = \frac{S_{t+2}^{e}}{\left(i_{g,t+1}^{e} - i_{g,t+1}^{*e}\right) + \left(v_{g,t+1}^{e} - v_{g,t+1}^{*e}\right) + rp_{t+1}^{e} + 1}. \tag{4}$$

The superscript *e* represents the market's expectations. We can use this model of the expected exchange rate, S_{t+1}^{e}, and substitute into our exchange rate model, (3), to derive:

$$S_t = \left(\frac{1}{\left(i_{g,t} - i_{g,t}^{*}\right) + \left(v_{g,t} - v_{g,t}^{*}\right) + rp_t + 1}\right) \times \left(\frac{1}{\left(i_{g,t+1}^{e} - i_{g,t+1}^{*e}\right) + \left(v_{g,t+1}^{e} - v_{g,t+1}^{*e}\right) + rp_{t+1}^{e} + 1}\right) \times S_{t+2}^{e}. \tag{5}$$

We can see from (5) that the current exchange rate is affected not only by current interest rates, convenience yields and the risk premium, but also expectations of those variables in the future.

Long-run expectations

Eq. (5) does not fully decide the role of expectations, because it leaves undetermined the expectation of the exchange rate in period $t + 2$. Let's use the letter f_t to denote the "fundamental" determinants of the exchange rate at time t. That is,

$$f_t \equiv \frac{1}{\left(i_{g,t} - i_{g,t}^{*}\right) + \left(v_{g,t} - v_{g,t}^{*}\right) + rp_t + 1}. \tag{6}$$

Then we can write Eq. (5) as:

$$S_t = f_t \times f_{t+1}^{e} \times S_{t+2}^{e}.$$

We can repeatedly substitute for expectations as we did in deriving Eq. (4), to arrive at:

$$S_t = f_t \times f^e_{t+1} \times \cdots f^e_{t+n} \times S^e_{t+n+1} \tag{7}$$

If period $n + 1$ is far enough into the future, then S^e_{t+n+1} can be interpreted as the market's expectation of the long-run exchange rate.

What determines exchange rates in the long run? Note that for some commodities, such as oil, gold, copper, wheat, etc., the *law of one price* holds. That is, the price of the commodity in the home country, P^c_t, equals the price of the commodity in the foreign country when expressed in home currency units, $P^c_t = S_t P^{c*}_t$. In the long run, the price of commodities relative to the overall consumer price index will be determined by fundamentals of supply and demand in each country. That is, $\frac{P^c_{t+n+1}}{P_{t+n+1}}$ and $\frac{P^{c*}_{t+n+1}}{P^*_{t+n+1}}$ are nailed down by factors that affect the supply and demand for the commodity relative to the overall consumption basket. P_{t+n+1} is the consumer price level in the home country and P^*_{t+n+1} the foreign consumer price level. Then in the long-run, if $\frac{P^c_{t+n+1}}{P_{t+n+1}} = \frac{P^{c*}_{t+n+1}}{P^*_{t+n+1}}$, we have $P_{t+n+1} = S_{t+n+1} P^*_{t+n+1}$, a relationship known as long-run *purchasing power parity.* It follows that if this relationship is expected to hold in the long-run, the model of the exchange rate in (7) can be finally rewritten as:

$$S_t = f_t \times f^e_{t+1} \times \cdots f^e_{t+n} \times \left(\frac{P^e_{t+n+1}}{P^{*e}_{t+n+1}} \right). \tag{8}$$

The equation says that the exchange rate is determined by the current economic fundamentals (the interest rates, the liquidity returns, and the risk premium), expectations of future fundamentals, and the long run expectations of nominal prices.

One simple generalization of this model recognizes that purchasing power parity may not hold exactly in the long run. It may be that in the long run (in period $n + 1$), prices in the home country and foreign country are not equal, but instead differ by a factor k: $kP_{t+n+1} = S_{t+n+1} P^*_{t+n+1}$. In this equation, if $k > 1$, prices are higher in the foreign country than the home country in the long run (when both are expressed in units of the home currency). For example, high income countries or urbanized countries might have higher consumer prices than low-income or rural countries.

Economic models allow us to estimate this factor, but a simple way to measure it is using historical data. According to the equation, $k = \frac{S_{t+n+1}P^*_{t+n+1}}{P_{t+n+1}}$, and we can estimate k by looking at the average value of $\frac{S_t P^*_t}{P_t}$ over a long period of time such as the past thirty or forty years. We can modify the above model, then, using $S^e_{t+n+1} = \frac{kP^e_{t+n+1}}{P^{*e}_{t+n+1}}$.

Monetary policy can influence the exchange rate through perhaps four channels. First, if the home country tightens policy by increasing the current interest rate or is expected to increase the interest rate in the near future, the exchange rate will fall — a home appreciation. Second, monetary policy that consistently keeps inflation in check will lead to lower expected nominal prices in the long run, which will imply a stronger currency. Monetary policy could also affect the convenience yield and the foreign exchange risk premium. If policy can stabilize inflation and maintain the value of the currency, more investors will want to hold the country's government bonds. When the market is deep for an asset, it becomes more liquid, and then the third channel of influence of monetary policy is at work through its effect on the convenience yield. Fourth, if monetary policy is successful in preserving the value of the currency during global recessions, the currency will have lower foreign exchange risk, and therefore strengthen. A "safe haven" currency such as the US dollar, Swiss franc or Japanese yen is one that has a high convenience yield and a low, or negative, foreign exchange risk premium.

"Bubbles" in the exchange rate

The model of exchange rates summarized by Eq. (8) is built on economic fundamentals. Expectations are "rational", in the sense that the model assumes that participants in the foreign exchange market form their expectations in a way that is consistent with the model. This formulation does not permit a role for "bubbles." The foundation of the model, given in (3), allows for the possibility that the exchange rate is driven by expectations of future exchange rates. The additional assumption that the long-run expectations are tied down by purchasing power parity rules out a bubble in the exchange rate. From (3), we see that the current exchange rate, S_t, moves one-for-one with expectations of the period $t + 1$ exchange rate, S^e_{t+1}. In turn, Eq. (4) shows us that S^e_{t+1} moves in tandem with S^e_{t+2}. If the market believes the exchange rate will be higher in some future period, it will translate into a higher exchange rate today. If markets' long-run expectations are not tied down, the possibility arises that the exchange rate is entirely driven by expectations, untethered from any economic fundamentals. The price of foreign currency could increase simply because the market expects it to increase.

However, it seems likely that there is a miscalculation by markets if the exchange rate is driven by expectations that are not ever tied to long-run economic conditions. If the exchange rate drifts very far from its long-run purchasing power parity value, economic forces would tend to push it back in line with the PPP value. If foreign prices were much lower than home prices, so $P_t > S_t P^*_t$, businesses and households would find it cheaper to buy goods in the foreign country. If this difference persisted, there would be increasing pressure to buy the foreign currency, pushing up S_t toward its purchasing power parity value. If the exchange rate reverts to the long-run purchasing power parity level, any bubble in the exchange rate must eventually burst. Forward looking agents should recognize this, and if they do, the bubble will never start. That does not mean that bubbles are impossible in foreign exchange markets — but if they exist, it suggests some lack of foresight by the market.

Fixed exchange rates

Finally, it may be worthwhile to consider how an exchange rate could be fixed (to the dollar or another currency) in the context of the model given in Eqs. (6) and (8). Suppose that the monetary policy authority of the foreign country would like to keep its exchange rate fixed (for example, at a rate of one-to-one) to the home currency. There may be forces that would work to change the exchange rate that are not directly controlled by the policy maker — changes in the current or expected future liquidity value of short-term government bonds, or there could be influences that arise because markets are not entirely convinced that the exchange rate will be fixed indefinitely. In that case, events might alter the market's expectations of future interest rates, or future risk premiums, or the long-run price level. For example, if the exchange rate were credibly fixed, then the risk premium, rp_t would be zero since there is no foreign exchange risk under a permanent foreign exchange peg. But if markets believe the peg will not last forever, then markets might expect an increase in the risk premium in some future period, $t + k$, so rp^e_{t+k} would increase. If the monetary authority can control the short-term interest rate, it can always use that instrument to offset any of these changes in demand for its currency and stabilize the exchange rate. Clearly, monetary policy must be entirely devoted to the goal of fixing the exchange rate, to the exclusion of other objectives if the exchange rate peg is to be successful.

For example, suppose that because of some lack of credibility, markets expect higher inflation in the foreign country, leading to a higher expected long-run price level, P^{*e}_{t+n+1}. In the absence of any action by the monetary authority, the foreign currency would depreciate, so would fall. In Eq. (3), the current exchange rate falls because of a decrease in the expected exchange rate, S^e_{t+1}. The foreign policymaker can stabilize the exchange rate by increasing $i^*_{g,t}$ — the decrease in demand for the currency caused by the change in expectations can be offset by making the currency more attractive with a higher interest rate.

It is helpful to consider how the currency could be fixed if the interest rate fell to the zero or to the effective lower bound. Perhaps the monetary policymaker could influence the demand for its currency by effectively communicating about future monetary policy, thus impacting the market's expectations of future interest rates. However, this channel seems difficult to control. Another case would arise with a currency board. Suppose the currency board in the foreign country held one unit of home currency for every unit of foreign currency that it issued. How would the currency board react to changes in $v^*_{g,t}, v^{*e}_{g,t+k}, rp^{*e}_{t+k}$ or P^{*e}_{t+n+1} that led to an incipient depreciation of the foreign currency? It could buy its own currency using its reserves of the home currency. That ought to stabilize the value of the currency, perhaps by increasing its liquidity return, by lowering any expectation of a future foreign exchange risk premium, or, at the very least, by lowering the expected future nominal price level in the foreign country relative to the home country.

Is it possible for the currency board to always effectively stabilize the exchange rate? Yes and no. Yes, in that it can always sell one unit of home currency for one unit of foreign currency, so any agent that holds the foreign currency can always be assured that the currency is backed by the home currency. But the currency board cannot prevent runs that cause it to entirely deplete its holdings of reserves of the home currency. If markets become convinced that the currency peg will not last, they will no longer be complacent about the long-run value of the currency, represented by its expectations of the nominal price level in Eq. (8). That equation tells us that if P^{*e}_{t+n+1} rises enough, then the expected future exchange rate would fall, and the market value of the foreign currency may drop so much that the currency board expends all its reserves defending the currency. If that happens, the original holders of the foreign currency are repaid with one unit of home currency, but the country must create a new currency. More likely, at some point prior to all of its reserves disappearing, the country would abandon the currency board, as Argentina did in 2002. Then the market's expectation of a depreciation would be self-fulfilling. Only a hard-to-define "confidence" in the currency board — like the confidence that markets apparently have in Hong Kong's currency board — can indefinitely stave off a self-fulfilling currency crisis.

In section 2, we use the model of foreign exchange rates to assess the pricing of a cryptocurrency. We draw parallels between the fundamentals of national currencies such as the dollar or yen, and the fundamentals of virtual currencies such as Bitcoin or Ethereum.

2. Cryptocurrency Exchange Rates

If we treat cryptocurrencies like national currencies, then their price (in terms of US dollars or some other national currency) should be determined by the interest or dividend they pay (if any), their liquidity value, their foreign exchange risk premium, and their expected long-run value. We consider each of these factors in turn. It is useful to keep in mind conventional currency (hundred-dollar bills, for example) and gold as analogs to which we can compare cybercurrencies. A third comparison is to a liquid account, such as a checking account, held at a bank or other financial institution.

To keep the analysis simplified, we will examine the typical case in which the cryptocurrency does not pay any interest or dividend. The payoff to the investor comes from the liquidity return, the risk premium and/or the capital gain.

Cryptocurrencies as medium of exchange

Cryptocurrencies can be used to make transactions, but in most cases, at least currently, it is easier and less costly to use traditional money to make payments. For transactions of small amounts, physical currency is quite convenient. For larger amounts, debits to electronic accounts (such as checking accounts in the US, or WeChat in China) work well. In many countries (especially the US), a credit card is a very efficient means of payment. In comparison, payment with cryptocurrencies is not even possible for most transactions and most digital currencies. Even when it can be done, it is slower and more cumbersome than more traditional means of payment.

More importantly, goods and services are not priced in cybercurrencies. Instead, prices are quoted in traditional national currencies, so using digital cash for payments requires conversion into the traditional currency. That is, paying for something with Bitcoin that is priced in US dollars is akin to paying with euros. As noted above, a currency that is used as a unit of account is most useful as a medium of exchange. A traditional currency is a good medium of exchange when we can be certain that prices in units of the currency are pretty stable. Prices are not nearly as stable if we are using euros to pay for goods priced in dollars than if we are using dollars, because the euro per dollar exchange rate is much more volatile than dollar prices of goods. The digital currency price of dollars is far more unstable than the euro price, and so those digital moneys are much less useful as a medium of exchange.

Some proponents of gold as an alternative investment, and as an alternative to holding money, make the point that gold maintains its real value even in the face of high and volatile inflation. But that argument seems antiquated. Figure 1 plots US consumer price inflation, 1871–2018.

Figure 1 shows that US inflation has been tamed and very stable since the mid-1980s. For a period of nearly 40 years, inflation has been low and predictable. The real value of US dollars has not been eroded greatly by inflation, so it seems like dollars are a good vehicle for transactions to buy goods, services and assets priced in dollars. Figure 2 plots inflation

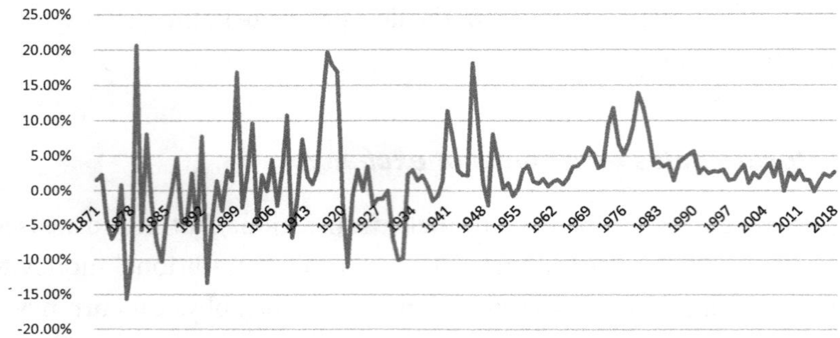

Figure 1 Consumer price inflation in the US, 1871–2018

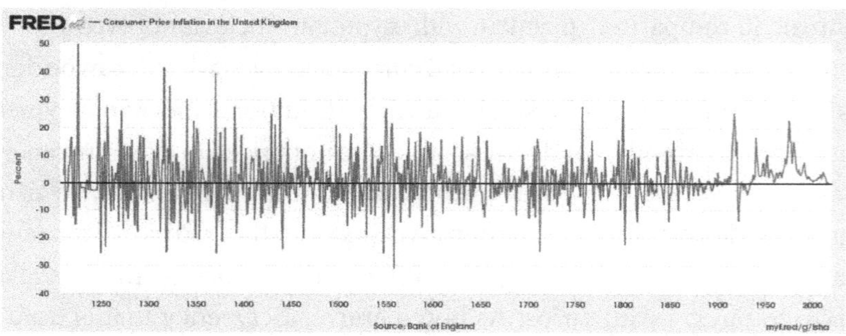

Figure 2 Consumer price inflation in the UK since 1200

in the United Kingdom (UK) since the year 1200. Again, it shows that in recent history, the pound sterling has a very stable value in real purchasing power terms.

In short, the case for using cybercurrencies on the grounds that they provide more stable purchasing power than traditional currencies is weak. It appears that independent central banks that target inflation do a good job of preserving the purchasing power of the currency.

Security and anonymity

One potential desirable feature of cryptocurrencies compared to checking accounts is that the digital currency is not held at a bank or other financial institution. They share the property of physical currency that the holder is not subject to the risk of bank failure. But while that is an advantage in principle, in practice it does not seem to work that way. In the first place, even when banks fail, deposits have been secure. Up to a limit, deposits are insured in many countries. Moreover, depositors generally are more senior to other creditors under bank default. On the other hand, there are cases of cryptocurrencies collapsing, or cryptocurrency exchanges failing, and even elaborate theft schemes that have inflicted damage on holders of cybercurrencies.

The main attractiveness of cryptocurrencies appears to be anonymity. They are like souped-up hundred-dollar bills. It is hard to trace transactions made with digital cash, and digital money is much more convenient for very large transactions than physical currency. In the context of the exchange rate model laid out in Eq. (3) and subsequent equations, the "convenience yield" of cryptocurrencies does not arise from their liquidity or safety, but from their anonymity.

The instability of cybercurrency prices arises in part because of the difficulty of assessing this fundamental value. Who wants anonymity? How much are these agents willing to pay for cybercash that pays no interest, has a volatile price, is clumsy for transactions, and whose long-run value is uncertain (a point addressed below)?

There are, of course, many legal and legitimate reasons for agents in the economy to desire anonymity, secrecy and privacy in their transactions. Households may not want to reveal private information to other households or businesses, and businesses may desire anonymity to protect trade secrets. Strong laws that protect privacy in the traditional financial sector may not be enough. There is a perception that cryptocurrencies provide greater *de facto* protection.

However, it is also the case that there are many illegal activities that are facilitated using cybercurrencies. These include evasion of capital flow management policies, the financing of illegal trade in arms, drugs, terrorist activity, and, money laundering to hide earnings from criminal activities.

Economists are split on the desirability of capital controls as a tool of prudential management. There is not any dispute about the importance of curbing money laundering and terrorist financing. But in the context here, the question is not whether these activities are good or bad, but how they impact the pricing of cryptocurrencies. There is clearly a demand for anonymous means of payment to facilitate illegal activity. A recent blog on the International Monetary Fund (IMF) website offers some anecdotal insight.[2] For decades, until 2016, the one-dollar bill had the greatest volume in circulation of all currency notes printed by the US. However, now it has been overtaken by the hundred-dollar bill. To be clear, this is not a statement about the value of the bills in circulation — the actual number of $100 bills in circulation is greater than the number of $1 bills. Most households in the US use currency to make smaller transactions. It is unusual to use $100 bills for everyday expenses. According to the blog, there are over 13 billion hundred-dollar bills in circulation globally — $130 billion's worth — and it is likely that much of that finances illegal activities. For comparison purposes, this amount is roughly half of the total market capitalization of all cryptocurrencies as of August, 2019.[3] The demand for these $100 bills is evidence of a sizable worldwide demand for secret means of payment to finance illicit transactions. That demand extends also to cryptocurrencies. A recent study estimates that 46 per cent of Bitcoin transactions involved unlawful business.[4]

The difficulty in valuing cryptocurrencies

If in fact much of the demand for cryptocurrencies arises from funding of illegal activities (including evasion of capital controls), there are great difficulties in evaluating their economic value. In the model of equations (6) and (7), the valuation of the currency depends on the convenience yield offered by the digital cash, $v_{g,t}$, but given the uncertainty about who is buying the cryptocurrency and for what reason, this valuation is nearly impossible. Moreover, because the pricing depends not only on the current services offered but also expected future services, markets must form some expectations about how regulations and enforcement will impinge on the value of the digital currency. If governments crack down on the use of cybercurrencies, the value of the currency is affected

---

[2] "US$100 Bill on the Rise" https://blogs.imf.org/2019/07/25/us100-bill-on-the-rise/ July 25, 2019.

[3] See coinmarketcap.com

[4] Foley, Sean; Jonathan R. Karlsen; and, Talis J. Putnins. 2019. "Sex, Drugs and Bitcoin: How Much Illegal Activity is Financed through Cryptocurrencies?" *The Review of Financial Studies* 32, 1798–1853.

directly because demand arising from criminal activities would decline, and indirectly because such regulations may reduce the anonymity of cybercurrency transactions, which is valued even by users that desire privacy for legal business.

The long-run fundamental value of the cryptocurrency is also hard to measure. With conventional currencies, as described above, investors can take advantage of measures of deviations from purchasing power parity to assess the long-run direction of changes in the exchange rate. When the exchange rate is greater than its purchasing power parity level (adjusted for some constant k to account for permanent differences in the cost of living between locations), we can forecast that the exchange rate will fall. That is, if $S_t > S^e_{t+n+1} = \frac{kP^e_{t+n+1}}{P^{*e}_{t+n+1}}$, then the foreign currency is overvalued in the short run, and we can forecast an eventual decline in the exchange rate. But this avenue for assessing the long run value of the currency is not available for cryptocurrencies because, for the most part, goods and services are not priced in cryptocurrencies. That is, usually even when a purchaser can buy goods, services or assets with Bitcoin (for example), the price is set in dollars or euros or some other conventional currency. There is no consumer price index in Bitcoin, and so there is no way to measure the misalignment of the current Bitcoin price relative to its purchasing power parity level.

A common fallacy is that limiting the supply of the currency — a fixed amount in the case of Bitcoin, for example — stabilizes the long-run value of the currency (in terms of dollars, perhaps.) This is not true because the value depends not only on the supply, but also the demand for the currency. It is the components of demand that are uncertain and difficult to measure. Here is a trivial analogy: I can offer a currency called a "charles" which is entirely anonymous. There is only one unit of this currency — its supply is fixed. It is anonymous because payment is made directly with the charles, just as if it were a one-hundred-dollar bill. I personally will create the one unit. (Let's also assume that my artwork is so good that it cannot be counterfeited.) What would somebody be willing to pay me for this cryptocurrency? The supply is fixed, but it can only have value to the extent that people find it a useful store of value or medium of exchange. A less trivial analogy is to monetary policy as it has been practiced in the past thirty years, especially in advanced economies.

There was a time when economists believed that demand for money was very stable, and so a good policy rule was one that set a path for the growth rate of the money stock. Those policies faltered precisely because the demand for money was not stable. More accurately, the demand for whatever measure of money that policy was targeting — M1, M2, or some other measure — was not stable. When policymakers began instead to adopt policies that targeted outcomes, particularly inflation targeting, then the purchasing power of the currencies stabilized. In essence, to stabilize nominal prices, policymakers implicitly alter the supply of money in response to fluctuations in demand for money.

Cryptocurrencies and bubbles

Some economists maintain that cryptocurrencies are purely a bubble that offer no fundamental return. If a currency is a pure bubble, investors value it only because they expect the price to rise. In this view, the bubble is bound to burst at some point because the price cannot rise forever relative to other assets — some sort of balance sheet constraint, or a change in expectations, will lead to the demise of the currency. That is not the view taken here. We have argued that the cybercurrency's fundamental value arises from its relative anonymity for transactions (and possibly its protection from bank failure). However, we have also contended that it is nearly impossible to assess the fundamental value of the currency. Under these circumstances, it is easy for asset price bubbles to arise. Consider Eq. (7). The exchange rate today may change, even when current and expected future fundamental determinants are held constant, if the long-run expected exchange rate changes. That is the essence of a bubble, because movements in the current value of the currency are caused only by changes in the expected future value. However, because it is difficult to measure the fundamentals and the market's expectations of future fundamentals (that is, it is hard to measure $f_t, f^e_{t+1}, f^e_{t+2}, \ldots$), an investor would not be able to tell whether the exchange rate fluctuation is being caused purely by an expectation-driven bubble, or by changes in expectations about future fundamental determinants. In the case of conventional currencies, a bubble will not last long because knowledgeable investors will be able to ascertain when the currency is far out of line with the value pinned down by economic forces (as in Eq. (8)). Those bubble-bursting, fundamentals-trading investors must have a smaller role in pricing cryptocurrencies given the ambiguity about fundamental values. The pricing of these cyber assets then is amorphous both because it is hard to assess the value of fundamentals and because it is easy for bubbles to at least temporarily drive the price.

Another possible fundamental value to a cryptocurrency is as a hedge against global risks. Gold is said to have that property. During a crisis, many assets lose value, and even conventional currencies lose value if inflation spikes up during a global downturn. Since gold is a real commodity, gold investors believe that it will maintain its value during such times, and so it serves as a hedge against fluctuations in the value of the investor's portfolio. A difference between gold and cryptocurrencies is that the fundamental long-run price of gold is connected to real demand from its usage in industry and fine art, while the real long-run value of cryptocurrencies is harder to pin down. Cryptocurrency prices have been very volatile over both day-to-day and longer-run horizons and have not proven to be a good portfolio hedge.

To summarize, while exchange rate models are far from perfect in accounting for the level and movement of conventional currency prices, they offer some guidance on measurable economic factors that affect these prices. Short-run movements are more difficult to account for, but long-run values are tethered by purchasing power parity (or some variant of that long-run model.) Cryptocurrencies are nearly impossible to price both because we cannot assess the value of its principle attribute, anonymity, and because there is no clear long-run anchor.

Stable coins and fixed exchange rates

Speaking of tethering, the application of the model in Section 1 to pegged currencies is also helpful in the consideration of "stable currencies". "Stable coins" share many characteristics of traditional currencies that have an exchange rate fixed to another currency. In fact, the most successful (so far) of the stable coins, Tether, is operated much like a currency board. Tether claims to back each of its coins by one US dollar.

There are a few interesting properties of stable coins that relate to traditional currencies and currency boards. Exactly as the discussion above of currency boards highlights, stable coins are subject to runs that are precipitated by a lack of confidence. Even if a coin pegged to the US truly is backed 100 per cent by very liquid dollar assets, there could be a run on the coin if investors have doubts about the future backing of the coin.

Coins that are not backed 100 per cent by liquid, riskless assets are even more vulnerable to a run. In fact, the business model for most stable coins involves holding assets that have some risk but pay an expected return that compensates for that risk. Certainly stable coins are not backed by hundred dollar bills kept in a safe somewhere. When these risky assets lose value, investors in the stable coin may doubt the soundness of the backing, and a run could occur.

What are the advantages of a stable coin? Usually this question is answered comparing stable coins to other digital cash, and the answer is obvious: as long as a run does not occur, the value in terms of dollars (or whatever currency the stable coin is pegged to) is much less volatile. Since ultimately investors value wealth for what it can buy, and the goods and services they buy are priced in dollars or other traditional currencies, then this stability is desirable. A different comparison is to a liquid account denominated in a traditional currency. Why hold Tether (which is pegged to the US dollar) when one can hold a liquid account in US dollars at a bank? As we have noted, one potential advantage of any cybercurrency compared to bank deposits is the immunity from bank failure. The main advantage might be the higher security, anonymity and privacy offered by digital currencies relative to bank accounts. If the digital cash value is credibly fixed to the dollar, then the investor can balance his portfolio of liquid assets between those that are widely accepted, convenient, and subject to consumer regulatory protection with those that offer greater anonymity. Until now, the demand for stable coins is small relative to other liquid assets.

3. Policy Implications and Conclusions

Because cybercurrency holdings are small relative to other forms of liquid assets (in August, 2019, the market capitalization of digital currencies was approximately US$260 billion, which by comparison is less than 2 percent of US Treasury debt held by the public, which measured around US$16.17 trillion[5]), the digital currency market is not a major concern for monetary policy currently. Regulatory issues should be the focus of policymakers at central banks.

Price stability is the primary concern of central bank monetary policymakers. As long as goods and services are priced in traditional national currencies, the existence of the cybercurrency market should not impede the achievement of an inflation target. A concern would be if "currency substitution" occurred. Currency substitution refers to the situation in which a national currency is replaced by a different currency. Consumer prices are set in the new currency, and transactions take place using the new currency. Examples of currency substitution have arisen in countries when prices in the national currency experience high and volatile inflation. Many central banks around the world have adopted inflation targeting practices, and no countries — with the exception of Venezuela — appear to be susceptible to currency substitution. If currency substitution occurs, then the national central bank no longer can control inflation, but this only occurs when the policymaker has lost control in the first place.

Another concern of monetary policymakers is to insure liquidity in the market for loans to households and businesses. A potential looming problem arises from loans denominated in cryptocurrencies. However, this problem is a mere speck currently — the market for such loans is tiny. The problem such loans raise is exactly analogous to foreign-currency loans using traditional currencies. A business whose revenue is in pesos may find it very difficult to repay a dollar-denominated loan if there is an unexpected peso depreciation, just as a household that earns income Polish zloty is taking on risk with a mortgage denominated in euros. Financial stability could be threatened if a large market evolved with unsophisticated agents amassing debt in some cybercurrency. This is a possible macroprudential concern, but it must be far down the list of financial stability concerns at this point.

---

[5] See coinmarketcap.com for the cryptocurrency figures and treasurydirect.gov for the US government debt numbers.

Monetary policymakers are sometimes concerned about exchange-rate stability. Emerging markets in which households and businesses hold a lot of dollar debt may be fragile if the exchange rate is volatile. It is hard to imagine a point at which any monetary policymaker would begin to worry about the stability of its exchange rate with a cryptocurrency. At the present time, it is the creators of these currencies that are working on different ways to insure greater exchange rate stability.

It is likely that if the crypto market grows, regulators will impose greater restrictions and tighter control on the buying and selling of these currencies. One concern is unsophisticated investors that are insufficiently aware of the risks of investing in digital currencies. Perhaps more important is the use of these assets to launder money and conduct illegal operations. However, increased regulation is likely to make these assets less valuable to investors that desire the properties of cryptocurrencies — their anonymity and their independence from the traditional financial system. They will constitute a strong lobby opposed to stricter rules.

There are at least a couple of things that can be done to ease the path toward tighter regulation. The first is education. Regulators should forewarn the public of their concerns about cryptocurrencies, and why they might require stronger controls. Legitimate investors stand to suffer large losses if major regulations are imposed without much warning. Second, governments can step up efforts to increase the safety, security, and privacy of the traditional sector — banks, credit cards, and other financial institutions. Such a step may reduce the demand for alternatives to the traditional financial system.

We have maintained that cryptocurrencies do have a fundamental value, arising principally from their ability to potentially provide greater privacy and anonymity compared to the conventional banking system. But that feature is difficult to value, which makes cryptocurrency exchange rates volatile and subject to bubbles. In addition, that very feature makes these assets desirable for the conduct of illegal activities, which is likely to invite increasing surveillance and regulation. In turn, those controls will work to reduce the value of cryptocurrencies, not only for use in illicit transactions, but for legitimate users as well.

The Implications of Digital Currencies for Monetary Policy and the International Monetary System

Charles Engel
University of Wisconsin — Madison

Cryptocurrencies and Monetary Policy

- Private cryptocurrencies.
  - Might be analogous to currency substitution regimes.
  - But with the special feature that they are like “souped up” $100 bills.
- Central bank cryptocurrencies.
  - Retail central bank cryptocurrencies.
  - Analogous to “reserves for all” or CBDC.

Features of private cryptocurrencies

- Anonymity.
  - Might be analogous to dual-currency regimes.
  - But with the special feature that they are like "souped up" $100 bills.
- "Monetary policy".
  - For example, a fixed supply of Bitcoin (subject to change?).
  - Analogous to gold standard, perhaps.
- Private information.
  - There is largely little private information about these assets.

Features of central bank cryptocurrencies

- Very similar to deposit accounts offered by central banks.
- Deposit accounts versus cryptocurrencies.
  - Anonymity.
- Monetary Policy Rule.
- Private information.
  - There is largely little private information about these assets.
  - There may be asymmetric information about monetary policy.

What I will not discuss

- Blockchain, distributed ledger, etc., etc.
    - May be important, but not my comparative advantage.
- Determination of cryptocurrency exchange rates.
- Many, many other aspects of cryptocurrencies and policy.
    - Financial Regulation.
    - Bank profitability and implications for banking system.
    - Implications for payments system efficiencies and risks.
- I consider "aspects" of monetary policy, but do not offer a comprehensive or systematic analysis.

I will take cryptocurrencies seriously

- Many economists are skeptical and consider cryptocurrencies to be a fad.
- They may be right. But I will consider policy implications conditional on cryptocurrencies becoming viable and successful.
- It seems possible that many of the technical difficulties present in Bitcoin, for example, may be overcome in the future — but maybe not!

Anonymity of private cryptocurrencies

- To some, anonymity is an appealing feature.
- Anonymity, at this point, does not seem total. Some clever law enforcement officials have used tools to break it.
- But it is fair to say that it presents a challenge to regulation.
- My specific focus is that cryptocurrencies make it much easier to evade capital flow management policies.

Is that a bad thing?

- The "traditional" view of economists (and the IMF) was that it is desirable to allow capital to flow freely.
- Capital controls were considered undesirable because:
  - They prevent capital from flowing to its most productive use.
  - They hamper diversification.
  - Capital flow regulations are costly and difficult to enforce.
  - They promote corruption.
- Nonetheless, there has been a revival of interest in this tool.

Why capital flow management?

- Long-run considerations to regulate capital outflows:
  - Stifle "hiding" of ill-gotten gains and tax evasion.
  - Externalities of investment: private returns < social returns.
- "Overborrowing" in the sense of Bianchi (2011).
  - Individual borrowers don't take into account fire-sale externalities.
- Macroprudential policy.
  - Regulation of local financial institutions is insufficient.
  - Regulation of foreign financial institutions is not possible.

Hot capital flows

- Maturity mismatch — foreign lending is short-term, to finance long-term projects.
  - Rollover risk.
  - Why is lending short term? May reflect political risk.
- Currency mismatch.
  - As Maggiori, *et al.* (2018) has shown, foreign debt is almost always in currency of lender.
  - Currency mismatch presents special risks for emerging markets.

Exchange rate management

- Trilemma — not possible to manage exchange rate and domestic policy objectives with perfectly free capital mobility.
- Capital account restrictions make sterilized intervention possible.
- Exchange rate changes, whether driven by irrational bubbles or by rational investors taking into account news and risk aversion, may lead to misalignments.
    - Prices and wages do not move flexibly.

What misalignments?

- Terms of trade.
- Relative price of traded goods to nontraded goods.
- Inefficient pricing to market.
- Trade balance misalignments.
  - For example, persistent deficits may lead to unsustainable foreign debt.

Can cryptocurrencies be regulated?

- It may be very hard to regulate the flow of capital through private cryptocurrencies.
  - Anonymity and bypassing of the financial system.
- China's "ban" on trading and VPNs.
- Perhaps regulation can hamper spending cryptocurrencies.
  - But one could imagine giant Bitcoin malls opening in the Grand Cayman Islands, where people come to spend their cryptocurrencies.

Why do we need cryptocurrencies?

- Anonymity — though the contribution to social welfare is questionable.
  - Marvin Goodfriend and Rand Paul.
- Monetary policy effectiveness.
  - Central banks have done a good job of maintaining a stable purchasing power of their currencies.
  - Gold standard did not.
  - I will return to this question later when considering central bank cryptocurrencies.

US Inflation, 1871–2018

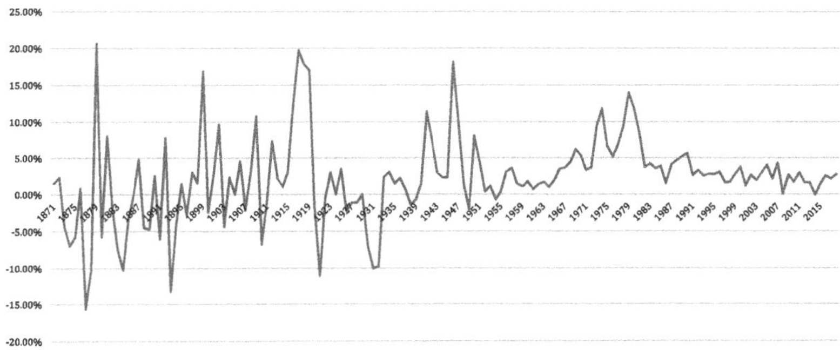

UK Inflation since 1200

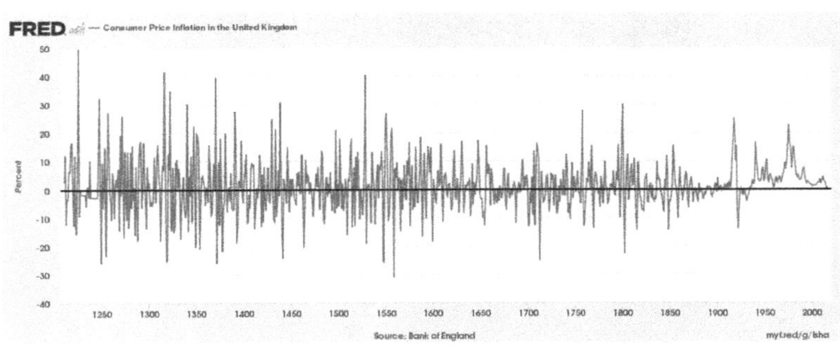

Private information

- Gorton has defined a "safe asset" as an asset about which an investor can be confident that no other investor has private information.
- That describes cryptocurrencies in the ideal.
- It also describes regular currencies (subject to caveat discussed later.)
    - What challenges does the presence of private cryptocurrencies pose for monetary policy?

Currency substitution

- There is an old economics literature on "currency substitution" that is relevant here.
- The key point to note is that currency substitution is possible already, but it is rare.
- Only countries with very high inflation rates have experienced currency substitution.
- Of course, investors can freely diversify investments in different currencies, and may find some hedging gains to diversifying the currency composition of the portfolio.

Currency substitution in practice

- **The key characteristic of countries experiencing currency substitution is that transactions are denominated in two different currencies.**
- **The host country cannot influence the inflation rate of the guest currency.**
- **The effectiveness of countercyclical monetary policy is weakened to the extent that transactions take place in the guest currency.**
- **But this is a cumbersome system, which is why it is rare.**

Practical implications

- Private currencies are unlikely to replace government currencies for well-managed economies.
- Even a significant dual-currency regime is implausible.
  - It is cumbersome to have a dual system of pricing.
  - If prices are set in local currency, then circulation of a private currency does not pose more problems than the presence of 180 government-issued currencies.

Practical implications (continued)

- Can cryptocurrencies find a policy that does a better job maintaining real value of currency than central banks?.
- One possible implication is that monetary policymakers will adopt more discipline in order to prevent currency substitution.
  - However, this is analogous to dollarization in hyperinflation countries. Clearly the threat of loss of seignorage is not always effective.
- The threat from cryptocurrencies may be somewhat greater since it is harder to regulate their use compared to dollars.

100000000000000
RESERVE BANK OF ZIMBABWE
100000000000000
I promise to pay
the bearer on demand
ONE HUNDRED
TRILLION
DOLLARS
for the Reserve Bank of Zimbabwe
100 000 000 000 000
HARARE
AA1701201

100 000 000 000 000
RESERVE BANK OF ZIMBABWE
100 000 000 000 000

Central bank cryptocurrencies

- The concept is very similar to central banks offering deposit accounts — so-called “reserves for all”.
- One possible distinction is that central bank cryptocurrencies could still maintain the anonymity feature.
    - But is this something that central banks want?.
- In contrast to private cryptocurrencies, the value of the central bank variety is controlled by monetary policy makers.

Liquid asset

- Safe asset in the Gorton sense — no private information about the value.
- Default risk is low.
- Maintains real value.
- Easy and safe to use and store.

Central bank deposits versus other assets

- Central bank deposits are easier to spend than Treasury bills.
  - Less default risk if there is monetary policy independence.
- Central bank deposits are easier to store and safer than cash.
- Central bank deposits are less liable to asymmetric information than insured checking deposits.
  - That is because there is a limit on insurance.
  - In turn, the limit exists because of moral hazard issues.
- However, the central bank controls the real value of the central bank deposits.

Analogy to denomination of sovereign debt

- No private investor has private information about monetary policy (usually!).
- But the monetary policy maker cannot commit to maintaining the real value of central bank deposits.
- It might be tempted to abuse its seigniorage privilege.
- Why can some countries borrow in debt denominated in their own currency?
  - A partial answer is commitment to inflation targeting.

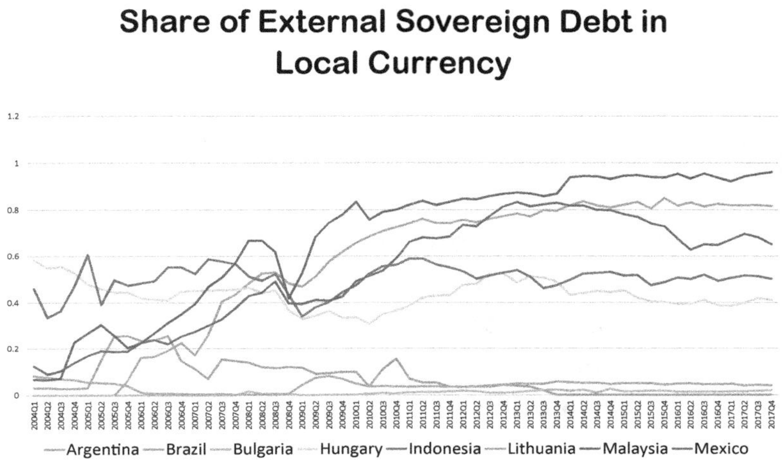
Share of External Sovereign Debt in Local Currency
Argentina
Brazil
Bulgaria
Hungary
Indonesia
Lithuania
Malaysia
Mexico

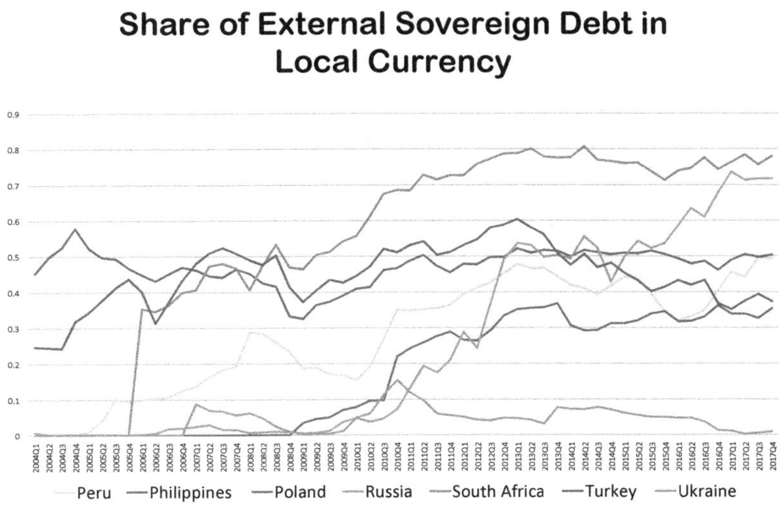
Share of External Sovereign Debt in Local Currency
Peru
Philippines
Poland
Russia
South Africa
Turkey
Ukraine

How is bank profitability affected?

- If monetary policy is credible, I assume central bank deposits are more desirable than commercial bank deposits.
- Does this erode bank profits? Banks would protest, for sure.
- One should not mistake the partial equilibrium view of a single bank for the general equilibrium outcome.
- By the way, CBDCs are much less of a problem for traditional banking models than Fintech and Big Tech.
- Commercial banks may still have a role for maturity transformation.

Equilibrium effects

- Assume on the asset side, central bank holds government bonds and foreign reserves.
- Funding becomes more expensive for commercial banks.
- Will increase cost of funds, so increase lending rates, discourage investment.
- In essence, country adjusts portfolio toward more liquid assets and less capital.
- International capital flows modify this.

Alternative central bank model

- One suggestion in the literature is that the central bank provide funding to commercial banks.
- This strikes me as very much like a system with unlimited deposit insurance.
- In such a scheme, the regulators would need to be very vigilant about moral hazard and adverse selection.

Safe asset supplied by a non-US country?

- The literature has made much of the "exorbitant privilege" of the US.
  - Its government assets are valued as safe, liquid assets and so can pay a lower return.
- Does the market even value government assets from any other country for their liquidity?
- We can test this by asking whether the country's currency value responds to the convenience yield of the government assets.

Exchange rate determination

- In work with Steve Pak Yeung Wu, we consider a modification to "standard" models of exchange rates
- We include traditional determinants: interest rates and an error-correction term.
- But we also consider the so-called "convenience" yield of a country's Treasury assets: the difference between its government bond yields and the interest rate on a "safe" interbank loan.
- The larger the difference (the smaller the relative return on government bonds), the stronger is the currency.

US Dollar relative to 9-country panel

Regression:

$\Delta S_t = \alpha_1 + \beta_1 s_{t-1} + \beta_2 \Delta\, basis_t + \beta_3 \Delta\, (foreign\ yield\text{-}home\ yield)_t + \beta_4 basis_{t-1} + \beta_5 (foreign\ yield\text{-}home\ yield)_{t-1} + \varepsilon_t$

LHS:ΔS_t	USD	USD
S_{t-1}	−0.0223***	−0.0924***
	(0.0061)	(0.0218)
$\Delta basis_t$	4.9372***	11.0358***
	(0.4824)	(1.0995)
$\Delta(foreign\ yield$	−5.3315***	−10.2294***
$—\ home\ yield)_t$	(0.2745)	(0.5382)
Period	1988M1–2018M1	2008M–2018M1

Standard errors in parentheses
*p<0.1, **p<0.05, ***p<0.01

Table for all countries 1988M1–2018M1

LHS:ΔS_t	AUD	CAD	DEM	JPY	NZD	NOK	SEK	CHF	GBP
S_{t-1}	–	–	–	–	–	–	–	–	–
	***	***	***	***	***	***	***	***	***
$\Delta basis_t$	+	+	+	+	+	+	+	+	+
	***	***	***	***	***	***	***	***	***
$\Delta(foreign$	–	–	–	–	+	–	–	–	–
$yield$ —	***	***	***	***	***	***	***	***	***
$home\ yield)_t$									
Period	1988M1–2018M1								

Standard errors in parentheses
*p<0.1, **p<0.05, ***p<0.01

Implications (speculative)

- If countries are able to issue more safe assets, the exorbitant privilege of the US will be diminished.
- The dominance of US Treasuries as safe assets may be tied to the dominance of the US dollar in invoicing and in denomination of loans.
- Greater holdings of safe assets in local currency may encourage more lending in local currency, so exchange rate risks are balanced.
- In turn, less corporate debt in dollars mitigates the need to invoice in dollars to hedge exchange-rate risk for exporters.

Less dollar dominance

- To the extent that trade is denominated in local-currency, the pass-through of exchange rates to inflation is diminished.
- Perhaps a greater issue is the fragility of the financial system when corporate debt is denominated in dollars.
    - Financial accelerator effect from currency depreciation.
- An early mover in the establishment of a CBDC may establish a regional dominance if it attracts not only local but regional investors.
    - Network effects tend to entrench the leadership of early movers.

How much can policymakers prepare?

- The immediate "threat" to monetary policy and the international financial system seems small (except for evasion of capital controls.)
- The challenges for the future depend completely on how the role of cryptocurrencies evolves:
  - Widespread use in transactions?
  - Held as reserves?
  - Supplant weak national currencies?

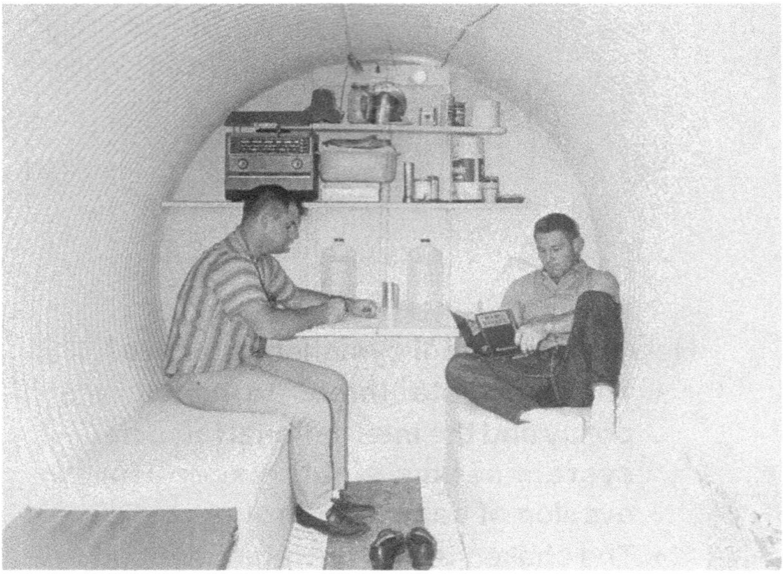

LIBERTY
AMMUNITION
CIVIL
DEFENSE
9mm +P
50gr 2000 fps

CHAPTER 8

Comments on "The Implications of Digital Currencies for Monetary Policy and the International Monetary System"

Andrew K. Rose

Berkeley-Haas, ABFER, CEPR and NBER

(Dean of NUS Business School since Jun 2019)

Much that is good, little that is not

... and some that is irrelevant
(to the topic)

Agree wholeheartedly with the main conclusion:

- No immediate effects on monetary policy and/or international monetary system.
  - Exception: loosening of capital controls.

Disagree (mildly) about long-run

- Uncertainty overstated.

Caveat: hard to have clarity in slides!

What I like most

Digital Currency has *Potential* for Increase in Capital Mobility

- Lowered costs of currency substitution.
- Could have worked harder on implications (e.g., through Mundell's Trilemma).
- More importantly: how important is this effect?
    - Crypto currencies are small compared to current capital flows.
    - Currency substitutes already exist (foreign currencies), as Engel points out.
        - Most foreign currencies inconvertible/small and hence irrelevant ... just like most cryptocurrencies.
        - Introduction of a cryptocurrency similar to entry of a new country with its own currency.
            - How much of an effect have South Sudan, Kosovo, and Montenegro had on capital mobility?.
        - How different are cryptocurrencies?
- Seems reasonable that the choice between fixing and monetary sovereignty will slowly become sharper.
    - But little GDP in countries that fix ... so little relevance.

Worth remembering

- Most Money is *already* digital/ electronic.
  - Most of American M2, half of M1 *de jure,* more in practice ($100 bills are US).
  - Credit cards, reserves, ...
  - Substitution of cash with electronic money ... not a big thing historically.
    - Money has evolved continuously for decades (gold ... notes ... cheques ... credit cards ...)
    - My FX acquisition; direct → traveler's checks → credit cards → ATM card → Apple Pay.
      - Recent transition from "no cash trip" to "no credit card trip".
- But these technologies have not compromised effectiveness of monetary policy!

Size: How big is cryptocurrency?
Small

- *All* (>2000) cryptocurrencies at market value (Oct 11, 2018): $202b.
  - About half in Bitcoin (and 35 variants).
  - 10% in Ethereum (and 24 variants).
- *Very* small compared to relevant benchmarks.
  - <4% of *daily* FX turnover, capital flows (BIS: $5.1t, April 2016).
  - Stock of notes and coins (transactions).
    - <13% of US Federal Reserve currency ($1.6t in circulation, Sept 2018).
    - <2% of Worldwide currency ($8t).

Compared to money (M1)?

Crypto insignificant

- *To repeat: All* (>2000) cryptocurrencies ≈ \$202b.
- US M1 currently \$3.7t (18x).
    - M2 \$14.2t (70x).
    - Crypto currently around size of Danish M1 (26th largest national money supply).
- Denmark interesting for gauging currency substitution effect.
    - July 2012, short interest rates: Euro (.5%); Norway (2.2%); Sweden (1.1%).
    - But Denmark still introduced negative nominal interest rates without problems!
    - So currency substitution effects likely *small.*
- These are stocks. But *even smaller* in flow/transaction terms (crypto transactions primitive).

How money is crypto?

- Need clear taxonomy on different types of digital currencies.
  - Engel: private vs central bank cryptocurrencies.
- Private cryptocurrency *isn't currently money.*
  - Doesn't satisfy any roles:
    1. Medium of exchange.
    2. Unit of account.
    3. Store of value.
- Unlike currencies, even of inflationary developing countries!

Difficult to see how crypto could, *in principle*, evolve into money

- Could private, digital, crypto (enabling peer-to-peer transactions) eventually become *money*?
- Far from it now!
  - Money is a social institution.
  - Historically, currencies are successful with stable value and large user network.
  - Crypto *WAY* short of that now, for *intrinsic reasons.*
    - *Volatility* stems from inelastic supply (also unstable demand).
    - This instability precludes use as either unit of account or store of value.
    - High transactions costs also limit network size, use as medium of exchange.
    - Private crypto has no extrinsic backing or possibility of coercion.
  - So currently a speculative asset (not money) and will remain so.

Which leads to inelastic supply of crypto

- Little direct confrontation of issue posed in title.
  - Part of Bitcoin idea was to limit inflation via formulaic growth.
  - Preclusion of discretionary policy might be inseparable from idea of crypto currencies.
    - Inelastic supply big part of appeal to libertarians.
    - Built into Bitcoin.
      - Potentially modifiable with widespread consensus.
      - Not part of all cryptocurrencies (*many* Bitcoin splinters ... Basis ...).
      - But most cryptos are failures.

Discretionary monetary policy *key* to titular issue!

- Could *decentralized* (private) cryptocurrencies be designed with monetary policies that include feedback or even discretion?
  - Need to if want to substitute for Central Bank roles:
    1. Avoid inflation/deflation ("Cross of Crypto").
    2. Provide counter-cyclic monetary policy.
    3. Act as lender of last resort in crises, support financial stability.
  - A future of algorithmic central banking?

Can we write *complete* rules for monetary policy?
Could we eliminate *all* discretion? (Would we?)

- **If so, can write central bank reaction function into mining rules.**
- **But if we could, why do we still have central bankers?**
- **Knightian uncertainty: we're a long way from this knowledge!**
  - **Hard to believe we will *ever* be there.**

But even ignoring all this ...

- Why should *any* form of **money** matter, even in principle?
  - Indeed, why should the stock of money matter?
  - Central banks use prices/interest rates, not money supplies/growth.
- *Highly* relevant in this context because cash does create effective lower bound on nominal interest rates.
  - So digital currency facilitates negative nominal interest rates, more counter-cyclic monetary policy.
  - Can reduce exchange rate/currency war issues associated with ZLB/ELB (Caballero, Farhi and Gourinchas).
  - More analysis here warranted.

Which leads to Central Bank digital currency

Modern Central Bank could issue e-currency

- **Not (private) cryptocurrency, merely another digital form of money.**
- ***Could* lower costs, increase access to money.**
- **But without offering anonymity of private cryptocurrency.**

Most issues are micro, not macro

- Technical problems in providing fast transactions, prevent hacking.
- Do central banks want money launderers and bad consumers to deposit directly, encouraging illicit behavior?.
- How much does digital money *per se* facilitate settlement, esp. international?.
- Does central bank have an obligation to provide public with access to risk-free central bank money like currency *if latter fails market test*?.

But some are ...
Suppose anyone could deposit directly with central bank

- Small Pro: (even) easier to have negative interest rates.
    - Easier to handle business cycles, avoid de/inflation with time-varying/low real rates.
    - But ... doesn't require central bank deposits for all: just less cash, more commercial bank digital money (Rogoff).
- Big Con: bad for commercial banks.
    - Central Bank Digital Currency: totally safe.
    - So raises risk and spreads for commercial banks, reduces private credit, monitoring.
    - Commercial banks already squawking about negative nominal interest rates.
- Agree with Engel: tradeoff likely to seem bad for society.

But even if central bank Issues digital money

- Central bank still controls central bank deposits.
    - No obvious negative effect on ability to conduct monetary policy.
    - Keeps ability to control monetary policy for cyclic, counter-in/deflationary reasons.
    - Seigniorage retained (small).

Will central banks ever surrender monopoly on money creation?

- **If central bank is NOT monopoly supplier of reserves, it loses its ability to control interest rates and carry out monetary policy.**
  - **If central bank does not control unit of account, its monetary policy becomes irrelevant (think of dollarized economies).**
  - **Seems unlikely for almost any central bank (Venezuela).**
- **Society wouldn't *allow* central banks to lose power.**
  - **Social contract: central bank power and independence to create stable money in return for trust-generating accountability.**
    - **Checks and balances required for durable institutions like money.**

Conclusion

- Seems like private cryptocurrency may *eventually* facilitate some transactions.
  - Will enhance capital mobility *a little.*
    - A *little* more pressure on fixers.
  - Unlikely to change monetary policy.
- An analogy.
  - Transition from paper airline tickets to electronic tickets.

CHAPTER 9

Chapter 9

Cellular Structure for a Digital Fiat Currency

Robleh Ali
MIT Digital Currency Initiative

Abstract

Bitcoin introduced digital money without banks. It showed that functions of the financial system could be reliably executed by decentralized networks and in doing so raised the prospect of a new financial system. Almost a decade later, Bitcoin still works despite frequent predictions of its demise but the overwhelming majority of payments still use fiat currencies and the financial system is unchanged. We propose a cellular structure in which digital fiat currency issuers and transaction validators create functionally separate ledgers, decentralized but capable of cohering into a single system for moving digital money. The primary benefit of the cellular structure is that it lowers barriers to entry for payments by using trustless intermediation between cells in the system. The larger purpose of this structure is to create an open foundation for a decentralized financial system in which competition can thrive but which cannot be captured by private interests.

1. Introduction

This paper addresses how digital fiat currency (DFC) could be provided to the financial system in the future. The goal of doing so is a changed organizational structure for payments with greater competition by reducing barriers to entry for participants in the system.

Existing payment systems usually comprise an operator which is responsible for running the system and members who participate in it. Together, the operator and members provide services to end users. Large payment systems tend to be centralized, the practical effect is that control over payment systems is concentrated making it difficult for new entrants to compete. This problem has manifest itself across different jurisdictions, leading to antitrust cases against payment system operators.[1]

1.1. *Trust and its effect on structure*

The core problem facing any digital payment system is how to prevent double spending. This is done with rules defining how the system should work and enforcement mechanisms to ensure the rules are followed. How rules are constructed and enforced affects the structure of the system. In existing payment systems, rules are extrinsic to the technology meaning that a combination of contractual obligations and regulations are needed to maintain the integrity of the system. The mechanisms for ensuring compliance with these rules are (a) new members need permission to join the system and (b) once inside the system there are penalties if the rules are not followed. Ultimately, these systems require trusted participants to operate, the rules are there to ensure they are worthy of that trust.

Bitcoin demonstrated that it was possible to solve the double spend problem without trusted participants. It achieves this by making the rules and enforcement intrinsic to the protocol and technology. Participants do not need to be trusted because if they don't follow the rules, their transactions will be rejected. The only requirement for joining the system is running the software necessary to conform to the protocol — there are no requirements beyond that. The absence of prerequisites flowing from extrinsic rules reduces the barriers to entry for the system.

[1] See, for example the European Union case against Visa (https://ec.europa.eu/competition/elojade/isef/case_details.cfm?proc_code=1_39398) and the United States (US) Justice Department cases against Visa and American Express (https://www.justice.gov/atr/case-document/brief-united-states-final-version; https://www.justice.gov/opa/pr/us-district-court-rules-american-express-violated-antitrust-laws).

It is true that the barriers to entry for Bitcoin mining have steadily increased over time through rising infrastructure costs. This has led to centralization of the mining network because small scale mining operations are now uneconomic. There is debate about the extent to which this is problematic for Bitcoin but it is the current reality. It does demonstrate that decentralized architecture alone is insufficient to prevent increased barriers to entry. In spite of this, Bitcoin is largely an open system, and it is still possible to participate in the system (for example by running a full node) and build services on top of the platform without anyone's permission.

Generally the more trust is needed for a system to function, the higher barriers to entry will be. The DFC structure we propose is different from Bitcoin because a DFC is not the sole manifestation of the currency and requires backing as a result. When proposing the design for the system we do make use of the general concept of reducing trust in a system leading to lower barriers to entry overall.

2. Cellular Structure

The structure we propose is a system built up from multiple different ledgers recording transactions for the same currency. Each ledger, or cell, in the system would have an issuer — a private entity which holds central bank money equal to the amount of DFC in issue on their cell. Routing payments between cells in the system would be done trustlessly.

2.1. *Backing*

The most significant difference between existing cryptocurrencies and DFC is backing. Cryptocurrencies have no backing and the value of the currency is set by the market whereas in DFC the issuer of the money on any given cell has to maintain 1:1 backing. How this backing works also affects the structure of the system. The goal is to minimise the underlying risks of the backing asset such that the regulatory structure can be kept simple. A characteristic of the existing financial system is its complexity which makes it difficult to manage risks for participants and regulators alike — see Haldane and Madouros (2012)[7]. Complexity makes regulation more costly to comply with and raises barriers to entry.

In our model, each cell in the system is backed by central bank money. This model of issuers holding cash at the central bank to back the DFC is a simplified version of the requirements placed on issuers of private banknotes in the United Kingdom (UK).[2] In the UK system the assets held at the central bank are ringfenced and this allows all the privately issued notes to circulate at par with central bank issued banknotes. It is possible to back a DFC with alternative assets but these introduce either credit or market risk into the system, making it less stable and more complex. We have not addressed these potential models of a DFC system because the risk they introduce would require additional complexity to manage with no obvious benefit.

2.2. *Single cell*

A single DFC cell is comprised of an issuer and validators. In addition to providing the backing, the issuer is responsible for the software and protocol used to make transactions within the cell. The validators record transactions and maintain up to date copies of the ledger.

Figure 1 shows a decentralized model in which the validators are separate entities from the issuer and in which validators use distributed consensus to synchronize their ledgers. It would also be possible to have an internal construction for a cell which was more centralized where the issuer also undertook the validation of transactions and maintenance of the ledger. Our DFC implementation will use a Cryptokernel[3] based blockchain with validators separate from the issuer.

Regardless of the internal structure of an individual DFC cell, the presence of an issuer does create a degree of centralization (as compared to a permissionless cryptocurrency). Having multiple DFC cells ensures

---

[2] For more information, see Bank of England: Scottish and Northern Ireland banknotes. (https://www.bankofengland.co.uk/banknotes/scottish-and-northern-ireland-banknotes)

[3] Cryptokernel is a blockchain tooklit developed by James Lovejoy at the MIT Digital Currency Initiative.

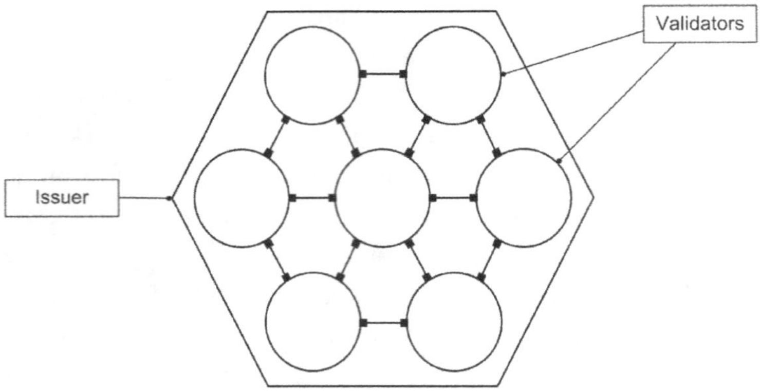

Figure 1: Single DFC cell

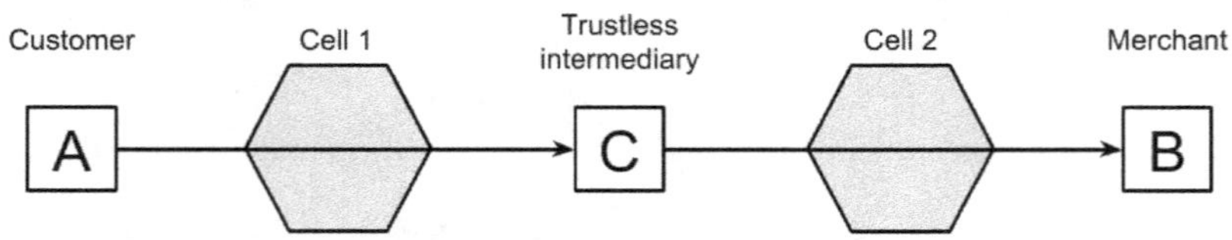

Figure 2: DFC system structure — trustless routing using HTLCs

that the system does not become reliant on a single issuer. All the DFC cells must support Hashed Timelock Contracts to enable trustless intermediation between the cells.

2.3. *One currency — multiple cells*

Having multiple cells allows for trustless routing of payments between them. This allows the system to reduce the barriers to entry for intermediaries as the rules are intrinsic to the technology, in this case Hashed Timelock Contracts (HTLCs).

Figure 2 shows a payment from A to B via C, a trustless intermediary, using HTLCs. This example assumes that there are pre-existing payment channels between both A and C as well as B and C (for a description of how payment channels work see Poon and Dryja (2016)[10]).

In essence, HTLCs work by B creating the hash of a secret "R" (HashR) which is then used by A and C to create HTLCs, one sending money from A to C and one sending from C to B. The money held in the HTLCs can be claimed by revealing R. A and C can compare HashR to verify that receiving R will allow both HTLCs in the path to complete. B triggers the payment from C by revealing R to C. This allows C to trigger the payment from A to C and complete the transaction. Neither A nor B need to trust C because she can only claim the funds from A after she has paid to B. C does not need to trust A because she knows the secret she receives from B will trigger the HTLC with A. This allows intermediation between cells to be trustless. If B never reveals R, then A and C can cancel the payment after a timeout and retrieve their funds, creating a strong incentive for B to reveal R immediately (Figure 3).

Under this structure there are two ways for holding balances. One is for an end user to hold all their funds on a single cell and rely on intermediaries to route money when they need to make payments to other users holding money on different cells in the system. In this model, risk arises from users being exposed to the operational failure of the cell they are using to hold their funds. This risk is similar to the current financial system in which users generally hold their funds at one bank.

An alternative is for users to hold balances across multiple cells. This increases a user's risk of being exposed to failure of a given cell but the consequences are less severe as they would still be able to access their balances on other cells while the faulty cell is recovered.

In both models intermediaries would be required to route payments between different cells. Intermediaries in the cellular structure essentially perform the same function payment systems do today by connecting the

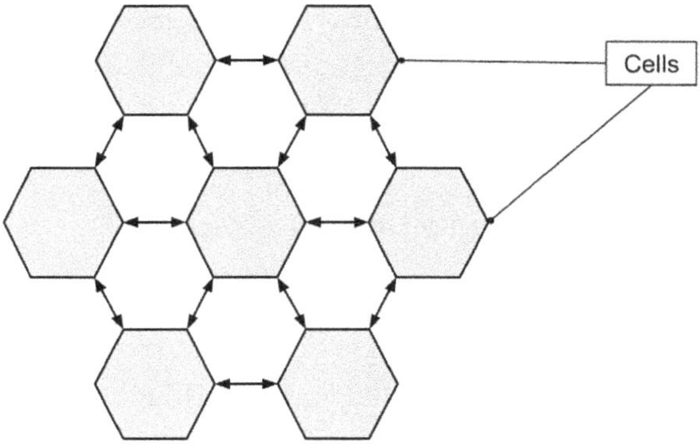

Figure 3: DFC system structure — one currency

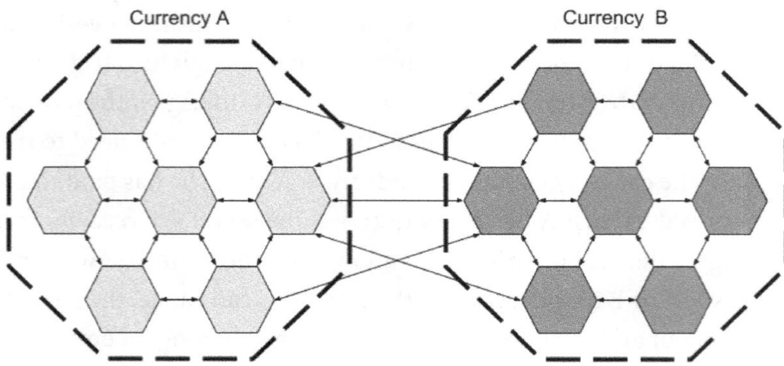

Figure 4: DFC system structure — multiple currencies

ledgers of commercial banks, albeit in a different way. The difference is that intermediaries in a cellular system do not have to manage credit and liquidity risk in the way existing payment systems do, just the payment channels needed to route the money.

2.4. *Multiple currencies*

One advantage of the cellular structure is that the same infrastructure used to route payments between cells of the same currency can also be used to make transactions between different currencies. In addition to routing the payments between different cells, intermediaries would also have to make markets for the currency pairs users wanted to transact (Figure 4). Whether the same intermediaries would do both the market making and transaction settlement is an open question, the functions could be separated but this is not necessary and there may be benefits to allowing the same intermediary to do both.

3. Rationale for DFC with a Cellular Structure

The most commonly asked question when discussing DFC is why bother at all — payment systems to transact these currencies already exist and function adequately. The short answer is to add competition and innovation while improving the stability and resilience of a financial system whose serious flaws were exposed during the 2008 financial crisis. While it is true that the crisis did not emanate from payment systems, fundamentally reforming the financial system has to start with its foundation which is money and payments.

3.1. *Competition*

The cellular structure increases competition in the system by lowering barriers to entry. It achieves this in two ways. One is at the individual cell level, the relative simplicity of the regulatory structure means that the barriers to adding a cell are as low as possible. The other is by making routing between cells trustless, this also minimises barriers to entry for intermediation. The cellular structure accommodates competition from multiple private participants at both the infrastructure and intermediation levels which makes it more difficult for a single entity to capture the platform.

Payment systems are the foundation of the financial system. The goal of creating a DFC is an infrastructure model where new entrants have equal access without the permission of their competitors. This is one way in which the cellular structure supports competition within the DFC system. It also provides competitive pressure to existing payment providers, giving merchants and their customers a viable alternative. This is especially important as cash usage declines for day to day payments.

Equally important is ensuring the future infrastructure is not itself captured by any commercial interest which can then extract rents from use of the system and control who has access. It is absolutely critical that any software employed for transacting in a future financial system is not dependent on any cryptocurrency, current or future.

Many existing cryptocurrencies have inflated values predicated on the notion that many or all future financial transactions will flow across their networks, increasing demand for their tokens. The prospect of the financial system becoming reliant on a single cryptocurrency or small handful of cryptocurrencies would be a disastrous outcome. Putting aside the issue of whether these networks will ever be capable of processing the number of transactions needed to support the entire financial system, the prospect of access to the financial system requiring the use of a token whose ownership is highly concentrated is the antithesis of decentralization, whatever the underlying architecture of the system. Changing the technology but keeping the same organizational structure (or making it even worse) is an exercise in futility.

3.2. *Innovation*

There are two different types of innovation to consider, technological and organizational. Technological innovation enables organizational innovation but doesn't guarantee it. In Chapter 7 of their book, Brynjoflsson and McAfee (2014)[2] give the example of electrification of factories (technological innovation) not leading to any significant productivity for more than thirty years. The change only came after a generation of factory managers had retired and were replaced by a new generation who saw that electric dynamos could be shrunk, allowing machines to be individually powered and factories remodeled around the flow of materials (organizational innovation). David (1990)[3] found that it was these organizational changes that the new technology enabled were primarily responsible for the productivity gains — not the mere introduction of new technology.

There is an analogy to the financial system and the emergence of cryptocurrencies. Digitizing money and other financial assets (technological innovation) happened as soon as computers were deployed in the financial system but there was no accompanying organizational innovation so the system didn't change. The current model of the financial system is for institutions to handle trust related aspects of the system and for software to handle record keeping. The change Bitcoin introduced was to handle both the trust element and record keeping using a combination of software and cryptographic methods. Trust in this context means two things: (a) the integrity of the record keeping; and (b) the conduct of monetary policy.[4]

It was Bitcoin that first demonstrated that creating digital money without banks (organizational innovation) was possible. One goal of creating a DFC with a cellular structure is to lay the foundation for

[4] Monetary policy could in theory be handled automatically, but this would require a more fundamental set of changes to the way money is created in the economy and is beyond the scope of this paper, for a discussion see Friedman (1960)[5].

organizational innovation in the broader financial system. It would be perfectly possible to implement a DFC without any accompanying organizational change but doing this would be akin to factory managers' first use of electricity and the result would likely be the same — no appreciable gain in productivity.

Subsequent innovations in cryptocurrencies such as Hashed Timelock Contracts (HTLCs) and smart contracts[5] have demonstrated how other functions of the financial system (payment versus payment, delivery versus payment, derivatives) could be handled using software rather than institutions. For example, in a future where both DFC and tokenized shares exist, HTLCs eliminate the need for a trusted intermediary as the software ensures simultaneous transfer of the cash and asset — enabling delivery versus payment. The same method can be used to exchange two DFCs trustlessly to facilitate payment versus payment. This has systemic implications as the market for intermediation will become much more competitive as barriers to entry are lower. Any intermediary overcharging for services could be immediately routed around by users. This is a significant difference with the existing system in which the costs of intermediating payments means setting up a new payment system and getting all the existing banks to use it — a very high bar to competition.

Smart contracts allow two parties making a prediction on a future event such as the price of an asset at a specified date with the settlement enforced using software. Smart contracts have to be fully collateralized and are not completely trustless as they require an oracle to determine price of the asset on the execution date. A risk is that the oracle is compromised, one way of mitigating this risk is to use multiple oracles and use some subset of them to settle the transaction but this does not eliminate the risk completely. At present, smart contracts still have limitations which would prevent them from replicating the complete functions of existing derivatives. For example, because smart contracts are prefunded on both sides, derivatives using DLCs only work in a relatively small price window (unless the counterparties are prepared to prefund with increasingly large amounts). There is also no netting which would make using smart

[5] On Bitcoin, for example, see Discreet Log Contracts by Thaddeus Dryja at the MIT Digital Currency Initiative (https://adiabat.github.io/dlc.pdf).

contracts at scale in their current form very capital intensive. Smart contracts are the subject of ongoing research to address these limitations and the technology will continue to develop. They are also an example of an innovation from cryptocurrencies with the potential to alter the organizational structure of the financial system by using software to perform functions previously undertaken by institutions.

3.3. *Financial stability and resilience*

The primary way in which a DFC increases financial stability is by creating a payment system separated from credit risk. This reduces the risk of a macroeconomic shock from the simultaneous failure of the banking system and payments in the economy, reducing one incentive for the state to bailout the banking system.

Partially separating payment and credit in this way would have costs. The advantage of fusing deposit taking and lending is that it allows more efficient liquidity management such that money used for payments doesn't lie inactive on commercial banks' balance sheets, it can simultaneously support productive enterprise, see Kashyap, Rajan and Stein (2002)[8]. The cost of this efficiency is structural fragility which is mitigated but not eliminated by deposit insurance and regulation. These measures introduce government subsidy and barriers to entry to the financial system which alter incentives and create costs of their own. Depositors no longer need to scrutinize the safety of banks because their deposits are government guaranteed. Banks can take greater risks, reduce capital and increase leverage in the knowledge that the losses will ultimately be borne by the taxpayer. In theory, regulation addresses this moral hazard problem but experience shows financial institutions will both push to the limit of what regulation allows and lobby for looser regulation. In addition, risky activity is shifted outside the regulatory perimeter and the financial crisis a decade ago demonstrated how risks in the shadow banking system can spill into the rest of the system — see Gorton and Metrick (2010)[6].

As the DFC in our model is fully backed by central bank money, there is a risk that in a crisis bank depositors could run to the DFC as a perceived lower risk form of money. Broadbent (2016)[1] describes this risk in the context of a central bank issued digital currency and also the potential effects on lending. As a DFC is a private system and deposit insurance would still exist these risks would be lower but the critique is still relevant to a DFC backed with central bank money. The risks could be mitigated by adopting the 'pawnbroker for all seasons' proposal in King (2016)[9] which has the additional benefit of increasing the discipline on commercial banks. Shifting funding of productive enterprise from banks to capital markets would also reduce the systemic reliance on commercial banks — see Véron and Wolff (2016)[11] and Draghi (2014)[4].

The cellular structure increases resilience by ensuring the system can still function and route payments even if one or more of the cells isn't functioning. This structure also allows for multiple issuers, reducing the probability of any individual provider dominating the system.

4. Conclusion

Bitcoin showed that digital money could be separated from banks. It also demonstrated that functions of the financial system could be executed trustlessly by a decentralized network without the current set of institutions. Although Bitcoin has shown remarkable resilience since it first emerged almost a decade ago, it has not evolved into a platform capable of replicating all the functions of the existing financial system either in terms of complexity or scale.

Our work on DFC is aimed at progressing the concept introduced by Bitcoin — that of a decentralized financial system which is easy to access but hard to capture. There are levels to it. The cellular structure we have outlined in this paper shows how a DFC can be constructed in a decentralized way to preserve the possibility of organizational innovation in the levels above. This is important because money is the base level of any financial system and its structure affects how the rest of the financial system built on top develops.

References

1. Ben Broadbent. "Central banks and digital currencies". In: *Speech at the London School of Economics* 2 (2016).
2. Erik Brynjolfsson and Andrew McAfee. *The second machine age: Work, progress, and prosperity in a time of brilliant technologies.* WW Norton & Company, 2014.

3. Paul A David. "The dynamo and the computer: An historical perspective on the modern productivity paradox". In: *The American Economic Review* 80.2 (1990), pp. 355–361.
4. Mario Draghi. "Keynote speech at the Eurofi Financial Forum in Milan". In: *European Central Bank, September,* available at https://www.ecb.europa.eu/press/key/date/2014/html/sp140911_1.en.html (2014).
5. Milton Friedman. *A program for monetary stability*. Vol. 541. Fordham University Press New York, 1960.
6. Gary Gorton and Andrew Metrick. "Regulating the shadow banking system". In: *Brookings papers on economic activity* 2010.2 (2010), pp. 261–297.
7. Andrew Haldane and V Madouros. "The dog and the Frisbee. Bank of England". In: *Speech given at the Federal Reserve Bank of Kansas City's 36th economic policy symposium, "The Changing Policy Landscape", Jackson Hole, Wyoming*. Vol. 31. 2012.
8. Anil K Kashyap, Raghuram Rajan, and Jeremy C Stein. "Banks as liquidity providers: An explanation for the coexistence of lending and deposit taking". In: *The Journal of Finance* 57.1 (2002), pp. 33–73.
9. Mervyn King. *The end of alchemy: Money, banking, and the future of the global economy*. WW Norton & Company, 2016.
10. Joseph Poon and Thaddeus Dryja. "The bitcoin lightning network: Scalable off-chain instant payments". Whitepaper. Draft Version 0.5.9.2. https://lightning.network/lightning-network-paper.pdf.
11. Nicolas Véron and Guntram B Wolff. "Capital Markets Union: A vision for the long term". In: *Journal of Financial Regulation* 2.1 (2016), pp. 130–153.

Cellular Structure for a Digital Fiat Currency

Robleh Ali
MIT Media Lab Digital Currency Initiative

Cellular structure for a digital fiat currency (DFC)

- **Goals.**
- **Cellular structure.**
- **Rationale for cellular structure.**
- **Central bank digital currency.**

Goals of a DFC

Goals

- Financial stability/resilience — Having an alternative infrastructure to make fiat currency payments enhances stability in two ways (a) providing a payment system separated out from the balance sheets of commercial banks and the risks they face, (b) allow a DFC to operate independently of operational failure or cyber attack on the banking system and vice versa.
- Competition — Separate infrastructure, service providers and fee structure for a DFC provides competition to existing payment providers, giving merchants and customers a viable alternative. Greater competition lowers costs of payment system, clearing and settlement.
- Innovation — A DFC can incorporate innovations from the cryptocurrency system and provide a platform for building new financial services which incorporate fiat currencies.

Backing

- Direct issue by central bank (Central bank digital currency or CBDC).
  - Effect on the existing banking system.
  - Wider discussion of credit creation, maturity transformation and how productive enterprise is financed.
- Privately issued (Digital fiat currency or DFC).
  - Cash at central bank (no market or credit risk).
  - Government bonds (minimal to no credit risk, market risk).
  - Other assets such as corporate bonds, loans (credit and market risk).
  - Commercial bank money (credit risk, no market risk).

Cellular structure

DFC single cell

- Issuer.
  - Holds cash at the central bank (systemic stability).
  - Simplified version of UK commercial banknotes system.
  - One ledger, one cell.
  - Decides how the cell functions internally (consensus mechanism, software, validators, fees).
- Validators.
  - Order transactions.
  - Maintain copies of the ledger.

DFC single cell

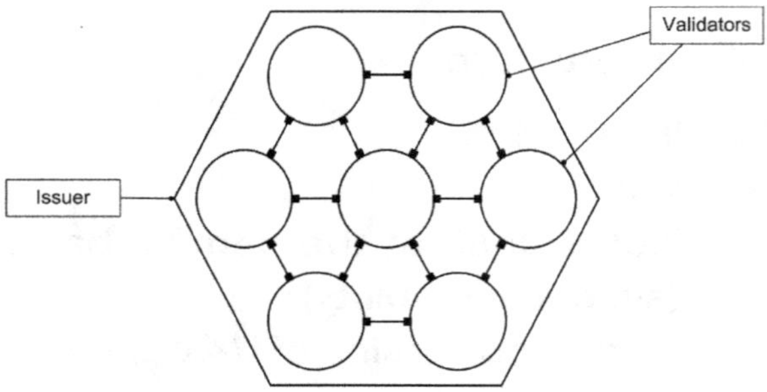

DFC system — single currency

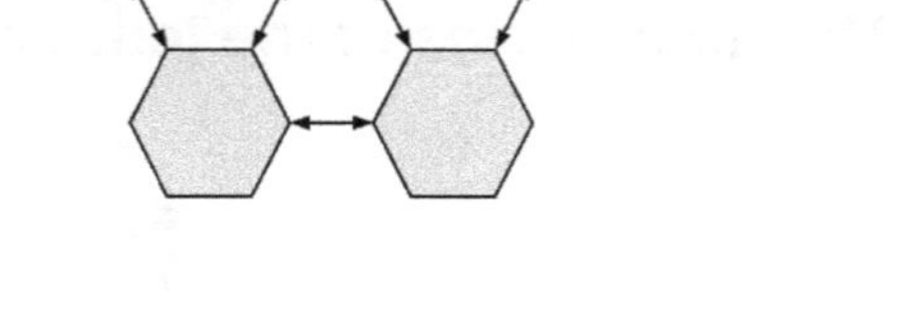

DFC system — single currency

- Holding DFC.
    - With a single issuer.
    - Across multiple issuers.
    - Cost of fragmented liquidity.
- Inter-chain transactions.
    - Routing payments — multi-hop.
    - Trustless intermediaries.
    - Lower barriers to entry for intermediation.
    - More competitive market for liquidity provision.

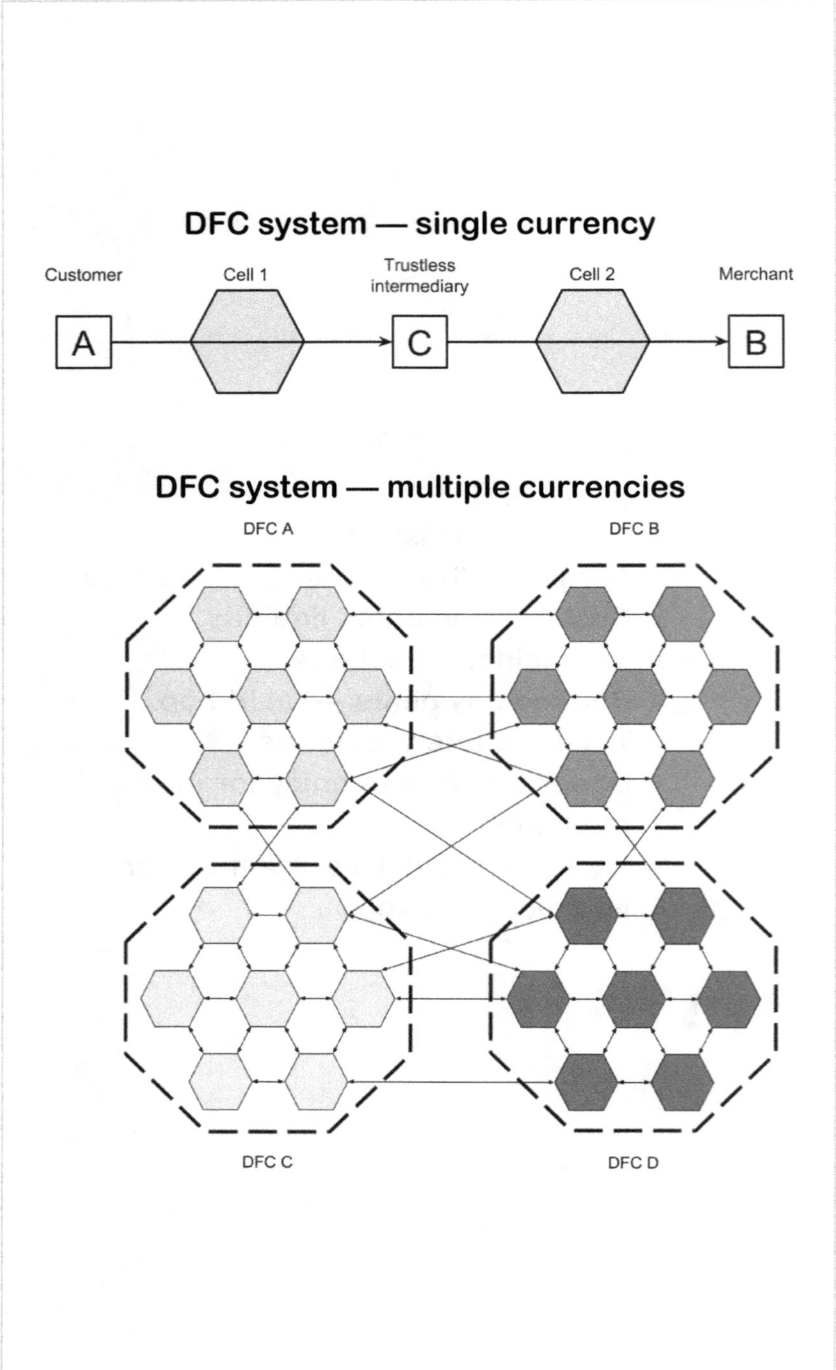
DFC system — single currency
Customer
Cell 1
Trustless
intermediary
Cell 2
Merchant
A
C
B
DFC system — multiple currencies
DFC A
DFC B
DFC C
DFC D

DFC system — multiple currencies

- Intermediaries.
  - Routing payments (payment versus payment).
  - Market making for currency pairs.
- Application to other tokenized assets (delivery versus payment).
  - Shares.
  - Bonds.
  - Commodities.

Rationale for cellular structure

Financial stability/resilience

- Existing system.
  - Efficiency of matching money and credit (Kashyap *et al.*, liquidity paper).
  - Structural fragility from maturity transformation.
  - Deposit insurance, regulation, lobbying, shadow banking.
  - Credit and liquidity risks in payment systems — PFMIs.
- DFC.
  - Parallel system immune from contagion (fully collateralized).
  - Structural elimination of credit risk.
  - System can survive failure of individual cells (resilience).

Competition

- Present competition.
    - Merchant payments.
    - Decline of cash.
- Future competition.
    - Cryptocurrency strategy.
    - Changing the organizational structure.

Innovation

- Technological and organizational change.
  - Parallel with dynamos in factories.
  - Technological change alone did not produce significant productivity gains.
- Bitcoin as organizational change.
  - Payments without banks.
  - Financial system as a set of functions.
  - How to extend this concept to the existing financial system.
    - Cross chain atomic swaps (PvP, DvP).
    - Discreet log contracts (derivatives).

CHAPTER 10

Cellular DFC Design:
Technological Perspectives
Prateek Saxena
Asst. Professor of Computer Science
NUS
National University of Singapore
School of Computing

The Premise: Decentralized Digital Payments

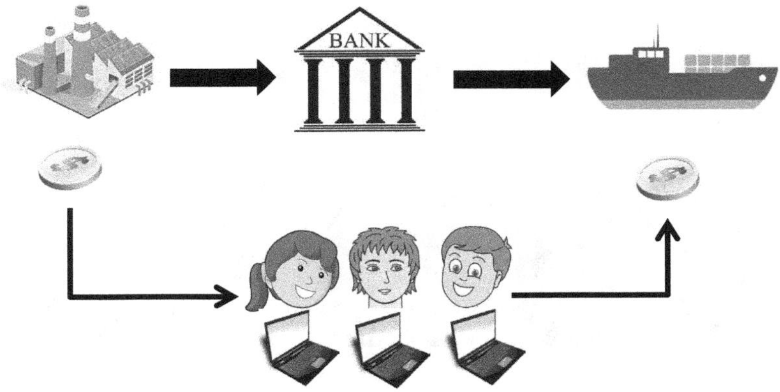

But, Why?

- **Resilience, Auditability and Reconciliation.**
- **"Tokenization": Improves Liquidity, Fractionalization.**
- **Levelling the playing field.**

Better Resilience

Better Resilience: No Single Point of Failure

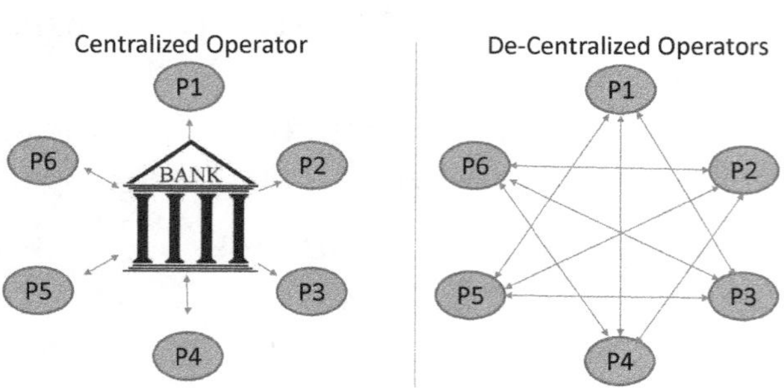

Tokenization

30 Million Dollar Real Estate Tokenized — Oct 2018

Tokenization

- **Fractional Ownership.**
- **Liquidity.**
- **Processing.**

Leveling the Playing Field: Access to Capital/Services

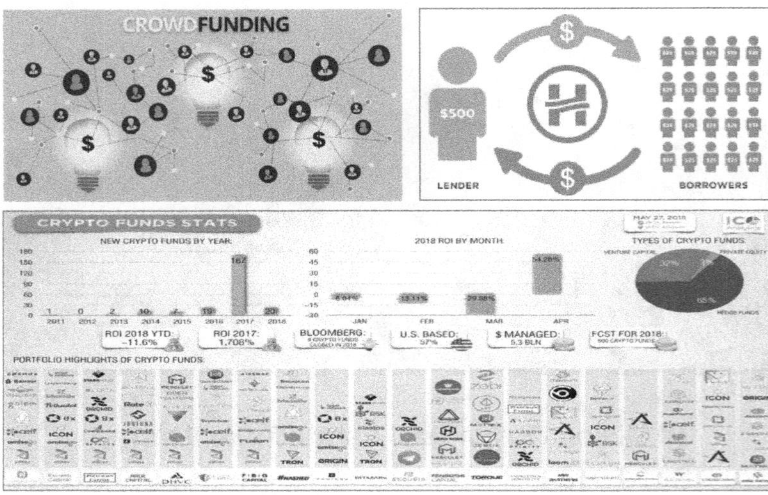

Technological Advances

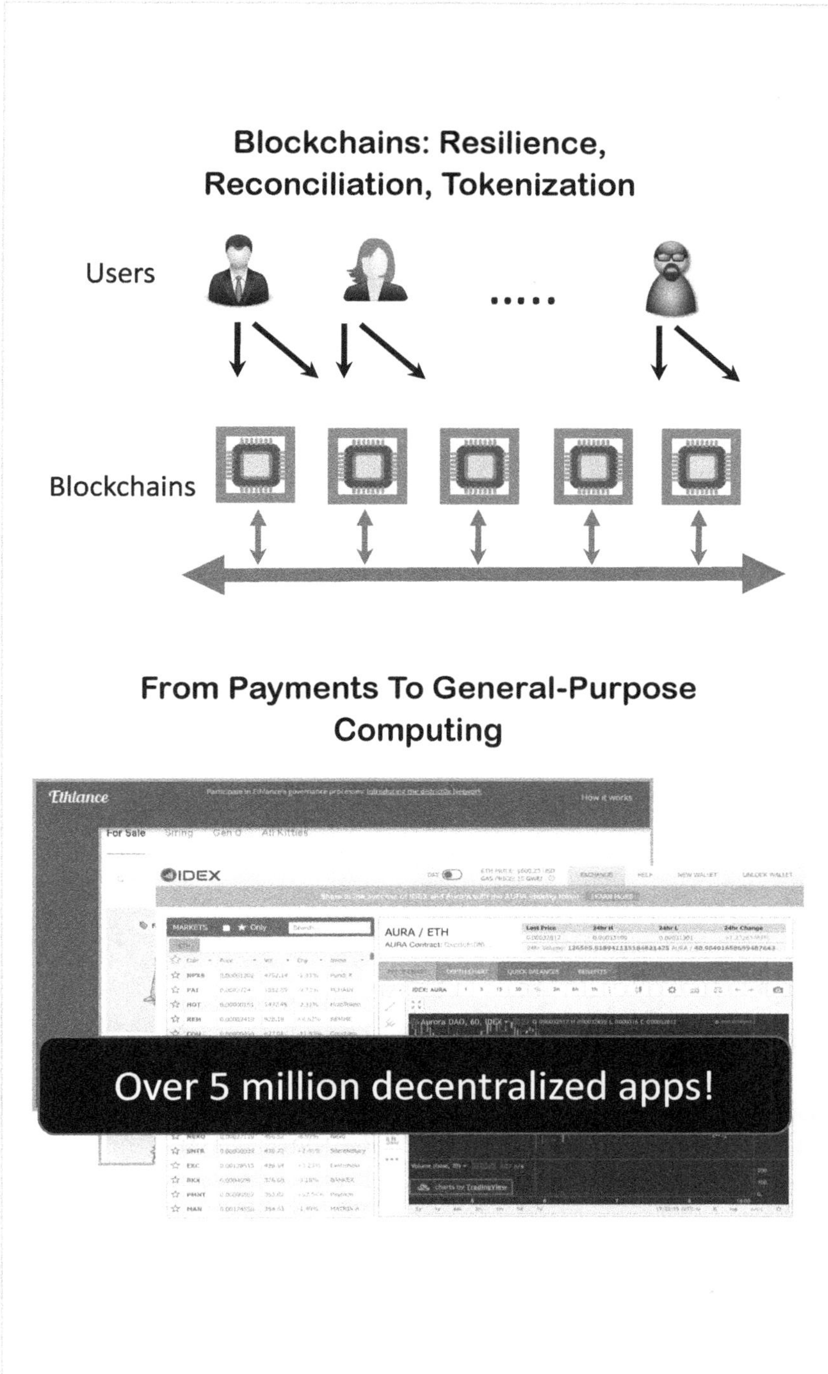
Blockchains: Resilience, Reconciliation, Tokenization
Users
Blockchains
From Payments To General-Purpose Computing
Ethlance
For Sale
IDEX
MARKETS
AURA / ETH
Over 5 million decentralized apps!

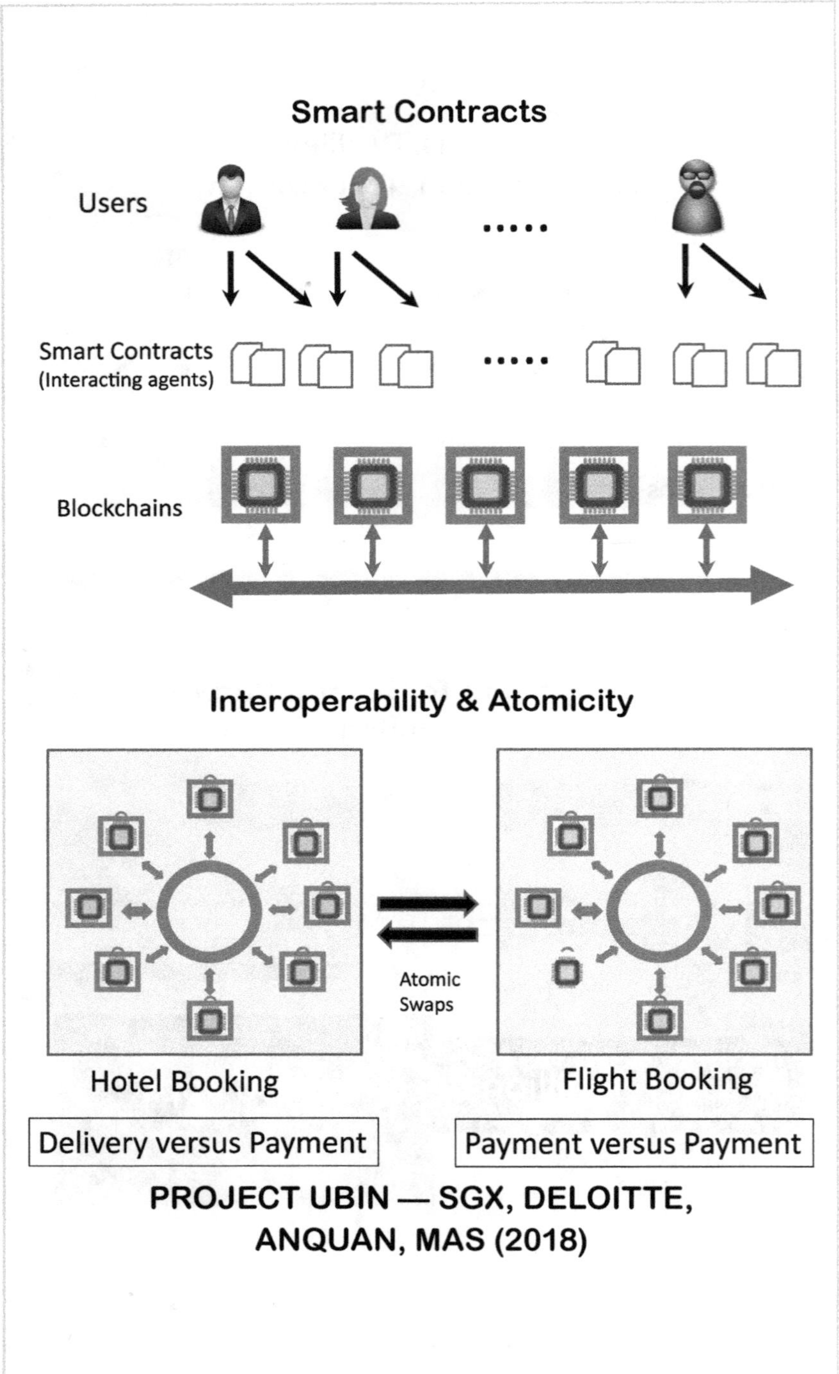
Smart Contracts
Users
.....
Smart Contracts
(Interacting agents)
.....
Blockchains
Interoperability & Atomicity
Atomic
Swaps
Hotel Booking
Flight Booking
Delivery versus Payment
Payment versus Payment
PROJECT UBIN — SGX, DELOITTE,
ANQUAN, MAS (2018)

Scalability & Security

- Scalability (2015).
  - 10 transactions per second.
- Scalability (2018):
  - 10,000 transactions per second (e.g. Zilliqa).
- High Resilience:
  - 20%–50% fail. tolerance.
- Latency at high decentralization:
  - 5–60 seconds.

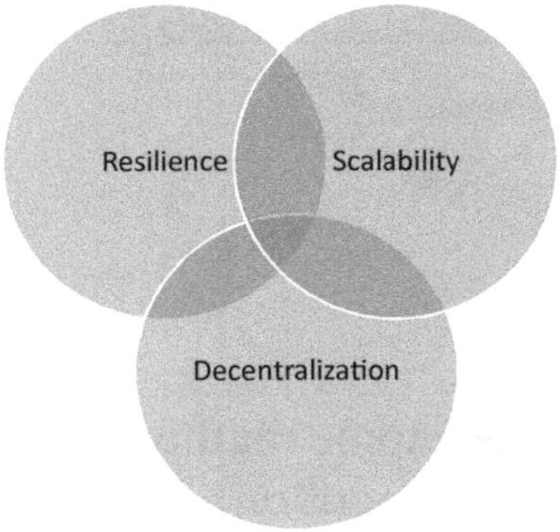

Privacy & Information Controls

- Allow information owners to control:
  - Who share with.
  - What computation can be done.

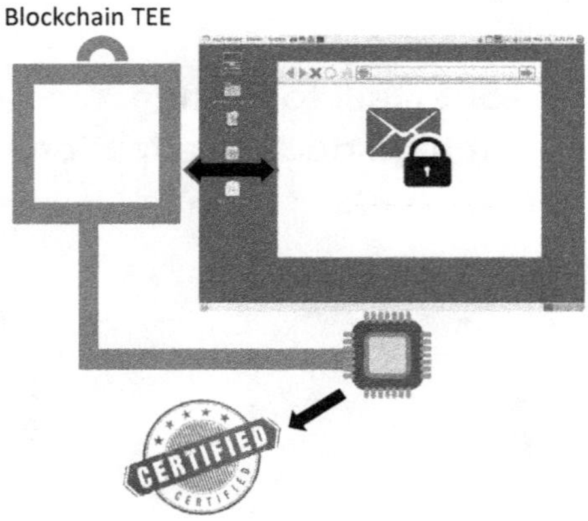

- Solutions:
  - Cryptographic methods.
  - Trusted Execution Environments (TEEs).

Enabling A New Experience

- Resiliency and Auditability of Information sources.
- Real-time Reconciliation.
- Programmable trust and actions.
- Better speech & natural language Interfaces.
- Smarter Analytics.
- Strong information Controls.
- Low barriers to Innovation.

Questions?

CHAPTER 11

Chapter 11

How do Private Digital Currencies Affect Government Policy?

Max Raskin, Fahad Saleh, and David Yermack

March 26, 2020

Throughout history, everything from beaver pelts to cigarettes has been used as money, and as the world has become more digital, so too has its currencies. For the developed world, this has meant fractional reserve banking systems based on fiat currency managed by government-run central banks and intermediated through private banking systems. For emerging markets, however, this has meant a number of different approaches, from sound monetary policy and dollarization to grey markets and monetary instability. Emerging markets have always faced the specter of currency crises, and in recent years, countries like Argentina and Turkey have also experienced such crises. What makes these crises different is that they are the first to have occurred in a world with digital currencies such as bitcoin.

In developed markets, stable currencies like the US dollar have served as a safe haven asset during recent times of economic and financial uncertainty — including the Financial Crisis and the Coronavirus Crisis. In the developing world, however, currencies are more volatile. The creation of private digital currencies raises a number of important questions for monetary theory. We are primarily concerned with the question of how digital currencies impact central bank behavior in an emerging market economy.

The contribution of our work is twofold: first, we lay out a typology of digital assets; and second, we examine the impact of a particular type of currency, the private decentralized currency, on government behavior in corrupt emerging markets. We establish three findings from our economic analysis. First, that private decentralized currencies enhance citizen welfare, second, that they encourage local investment in some economies, and third, that they may be desirable for corrupt sovereign governments to adopt or at least to not prohibit.

The term digital currency can refer to a number of different types of assets, and so it is important to define terms early on. Our typology exists along two axes: private/public and centralized/decentralized. These two axes meaningfully categorize different innovations in a way that facilitates further refinement and research.

With respect to the public/private axis, a digital asset is classified as public or private based on whether it has some relation to a sovereign state. State-sponsored public digital currencies have a government behind them that is able to enforce certain protections and privileges of that currency. Legal tender laws, for instance, mandate that the sovereign's preferred currency shall be legal tender for debts and payments regardless of what two individual parties have contracted *ex ante*. Private digital currencies have none of these protections and operate in accord with pure market forces of supply and demand and with no special recourse to the legal system beyond the protections that are normally afforded civil litigants.

With respect to the centralized/decentralized axis, we define centralization as existing if formal barriers exist that prevent participation in the software writing and validation process of a given digital asset network. What this essentially asks is whether parties, not necessarily connected to the project, have the ability to make or prevent changes to the protocol. The focus on formal barriers is important because in the context of emerging markets with unstable monetary systems, it is relevant to look at the ability to offer competing alternatives.

Private decentralized digital currencies, like Bitcoin, are one of the four possible categorizations based along these axes, and they are the most novel from a monetary theory perspective. The reason for this is that they have properties of non-discretionary monetary policy without the ability for a centralized party to manipulate in accord with certain political ends. In other words, they are exogenous from the sovereign. While private centralized digital currencies also have this exogeneity, they contain both central points of failure and corruptibility. In markets with a corrupt sovereign, an exogenous monetary force is an important point of analysis because it offers a benchmark against which the sovereign's own policy can be judged.

Our formal economic analysis examines how private decentralized digital currencies influence economic policy within corrupt emerging markets. We define a corrupt emerging market as an economy with high volatility and a government that sets policies based on selfish interests rather than considering the welfare of its citizens. We model the interaction of the government and citizenry within that setting. We establish three main findings.

Our first finding is that citizens gain from the presence of the private digital currency. Citizens accrue those gains through two channels. First, private decentralized digital currencies offer diversification which, in turn, generates welfare gains for citizens. Second, the private decentralized digital currency serves as an alternative to local investment so that the private digital currency's presence restrains monetary policy, thereby generating lower inflation.

Our second finding highlights that the presence of the private digital currency encourages local investment. This finding also operates through two economic channels. First, as noted, the private digital currency's presence disciplines monetary policy by creating an alternative to local fiat. The referenced monetary policy discipline, in turn, reduces inflation and results in higher returns from investment which then encourages higher local investment. Second, as discussed, a private digital currency provides diversification for those investing in the local economy. As such, when the government employs appropriately restrained monetary policy, access to a private digital currency not only induces investment in the private digital currency but also expands investment in the local economy.

Our third finding demonstrates that a selfish government may gain from permitting the private digital currency within the local economy. This result arises because the government extracts revenue from citizens through taxation. Permitting the private digital currency generates higher local investment by citizens for previously discussed reasons. That higher local investment generates higher tax revenues for the government, thereby creating an incentive for the government to permit the private digital currency. Importantly, this incentive exists even when the government disregards citizen welfare. This last finding is particularly important, because it implies that the previously discussed citizen welfare gains arise even when governments may crack down on the private digital currency, precisely because the government may prefer not to prohibit the private digital currency.

For the developed world, private digital currencies have not supplanted sovereign currencies like the dollar or euro. There are many reasons for this, but the skepticism over central banking shared by many early bitcoin and crypto adopters is not widespread in these societies. The same cannot be said for emerging markets. These countries have citizens who are less trusting of their central banks' monetary policy and have witnessed numerous crises in recent years that attest to this fact. For such countries, private digital currencies have a definite impact on societal welfare.

How do private digital currencies affect government policy?

Max Raskin
NYU School of Law

Fahad Saleh
McGill University — Desautels

David Yermack
NYU Stern School of Business,
NBER & ECGI

November 16, 2018

We have the first global currency crises since the invention of private digital currency

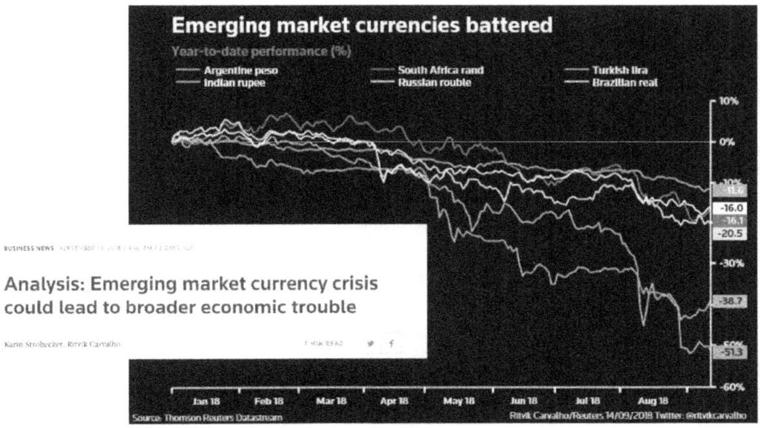

Digital currencies, most prominently Bitcoin, circulate alongside unstable fiat currencies

Main Finding 1:
Digital currencies enhance citizen welfare

- **Risk Reduction.**
  Non-positive correlation with local economic risks provides investors with a diversification opportunity
- **Restrained Monetary Policy.**
  The difficulty of excluding digital currencies from the market reduces gains from seigniorage, thereby inducing lower inflation

Main Finding 2:
Digital currencies encourage local investment

- **Diversification.**
  Digital currencies serve as a hedge asset, thereby facilitating investment in high-risk economies
- **Credible Commitment.**
  Digital currenciess facilitate a credible commitment to disciplined monetary policy, thereby enhancing expected returns from local investment

Main Finding 3:
Digital currencies may be desirable for corrupt sovereigns

- **Local Investment.**
  Increased local investment yields higher tax revenue (holding tax rates constant)
- **Welfare Gains.**
  Governments may extract some of the welfare gains via increased tax rates

Typology

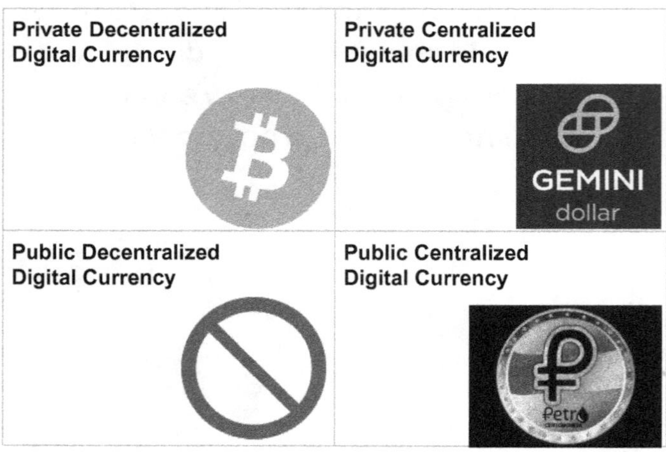

Centralized digital currencies

- Public.
  - Many investigating, few implementing.
    - E.g., Sweden, Ecuador, Venezuela.
  - Narrowing of banking system,
    - Similar to Chicago Plan of 1933.
  - Central bank retains monopoly power.
  - Can alter ledger or rules to defeat private choice.
- Private.
  - Easier to regulate companies than individuals.
  - History of numerous shutdowns.
    - E.g., Liberty Reserve.
  - Stablecoins, such as Tether, interact with traditional banking system.

Decentralized digital currencies

- Often politically motivated.
  - E.g., Nakamoto and Bitcoin.
- Rules-based monetary policy, implemented by decentralized consensus.
- Can only be suppressed by closing extraterritorial nodes.
  - Compare BitTorrent.

THE TIMES

Eat Out from £5

Israel prepares to send tanks and troops into Gaza

Chancellor on brink of second bailout for banks

- Capital control resistant.
  - Bearer instruments, with no recognition needed from legal system.
  - Similar to gold, cigarettes, shells, etc.
  - Requires user to control private key.

Related literature

- **Central banks and digital currency.** Raskin and Yermack (2016), Bordo and Levin (2017), Fung and Halaburda (2017)
- **Digital currency return properties.** Yermack (2015), Dyhrberg (2016a, 2016b), Liu and Tsyvinski (2018), Hinzen (2018)
- **Digital currency economic design.** Routledge and Zetlin-Jones (2018), Saleh (2018)

Model

- Two agents.
  - — Government.
  - — Citizen.
- Three assets.
  - — Local productive capital.
  - — Unproductive capital.
  - — Private digital currency (if permitted).
- Two dates (i.e., agents are short-lived).

Model: Assets

- Local productive capital.
  - Taxable.
  - Proxy for local investment.
- Private digital currency.
  - Untaxable (reflects enforcement difficulty).
  - Non-positively correlated with local economy.
- Unproductive capital.
  - Zero real return.

Model: Government

max E[Tax revenue] + E[Seigniorage])

- $t = 0$.
  - Government decides whether to permit private digital currency.
  - Government sets tax rate for local investment.
- $t = 1$.
  - Government sets inflation rate.
  - Government consumes.

Model: Citizen

$\max(E[R_p] - 0.5\,Var[R_p])$

- $t = 0$.
  - — Citizen invests among available assets.
    - Local productive capital.
    - Unproductive capital.
    - Private digital currency (if permitted).
- $t = 1$.
  - — Payoffs realized.
  - — Citizen pays taxes; faces inflation.
  - — Citizen consumes.

Model: Monetary policy ($t = 1$)

Seigniorage = Money Growth x Real Money Demand

- Higher inflation directly increases seigniorage.
- Higher inflation indirectly lowers seigniorage revenue by lowering real money demand.
- Interior optimal inflation rate (Cagan, 1956).

Model: Monetary policy ($t = 1$)

- Private digital currency strengthens the negative effect of inflation on local fiat money demand by creating an outside option.
- Outside fiat cannot fill identical role, because traditional fiats are easier for governments to restrict.
- Private digital currency enables credible commitment by the sovereign to (more) restrained monetary policy.

Model: Fiscal policy ($t = 0$)

Tax Revenue = Tax Rate x Local Investment Return

- Higher tax rate directly increases tax revenue.
- Higher tax rate indirectly lowers tax revenue by discouraging local investment.
- Private digital currency serves as alternative asset and therefore restrains fiscal policy.

Model: Regulatory policy ($t = 0$)

- Digital currency as a complement to local investment.
  - Permitting digital currency facilitates diversification which encourages local investment.
- Digital currency as a substitute for local investment.
  - Permitting digital currency enables citizens to substitute away from local investment.
- Digital currency is not taxable, so government optimizes based on revenue extracted from local investment.

Results: Citizen welfare

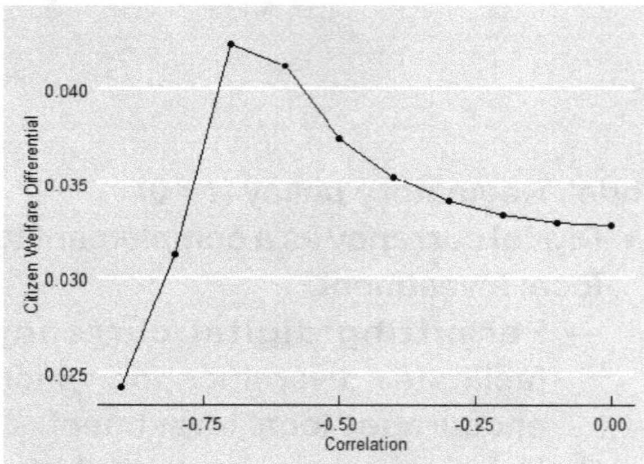

Results: Local investment

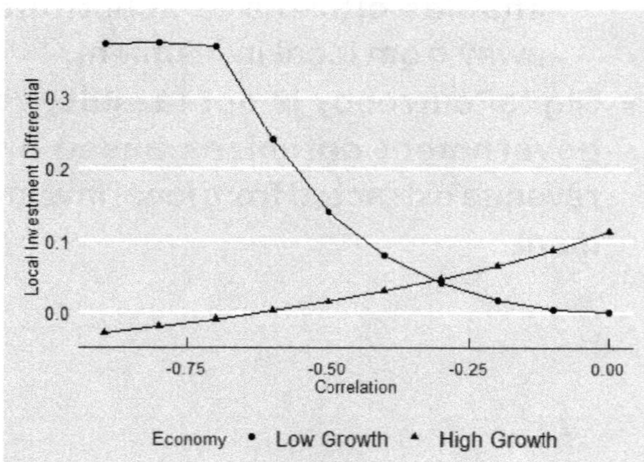

Results: Government welfare

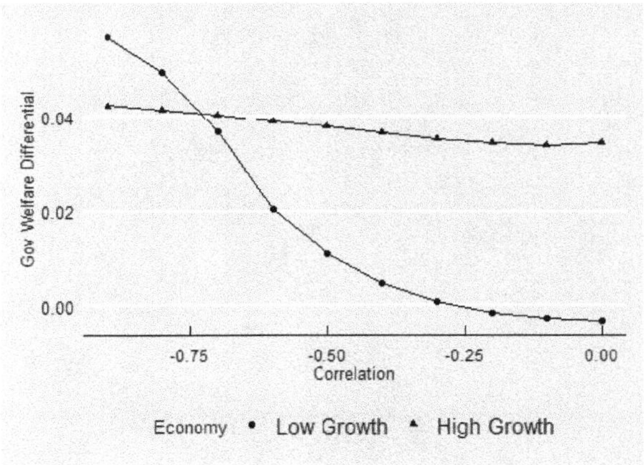

What if private digital currencies were better designed?

- **Higher productivity (Cong, Li and Wang 2018).**
- **Lower volatility (Saleh 2018).**

Results: Government welfare

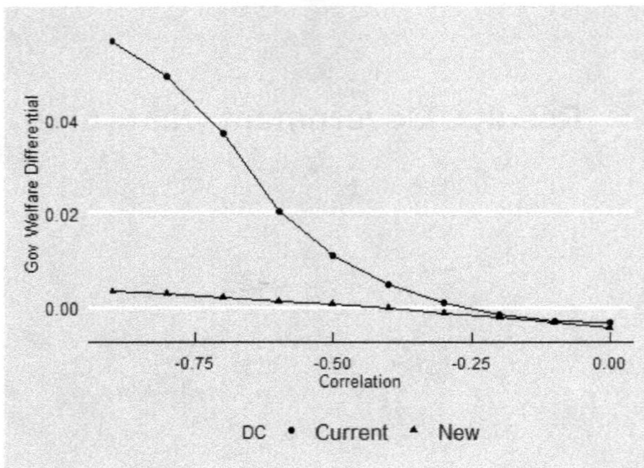

Results: Citizen welfare

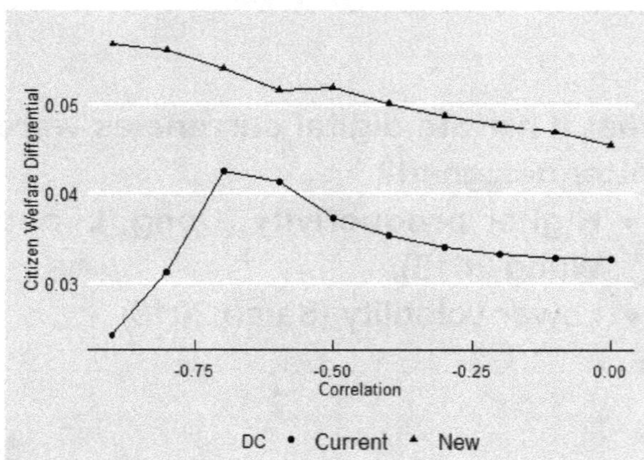

Conclusions

- Private digital currencies may improve welfare in some emerging market economies.
- Selfish governments may wish to permit trading of private digital currencies.
- Our results highlight the need for work on the economic design of private digital currencies.

CHAPTER 12

How do Private Digital Currencies Affect Government Policy?
By Raskin, Saleh, Yermack

Discussion by Gur Huberman
Columbia Business School

Singapore, November 2018

Agenda

- The model's background vision & relevance.
- Digital currency governance & its implications.
  - Single/streamlined control Vs Protocol guided/controlled.
- The model's main findings.

Context

- A corrupt regime.
- Presumably W/O much credibility.

Creates (?)
Welcomes (?)
Tolerates (?)

PRIVATE DIGITAL CURRENCY

Territory, Time Frames

- Single period.
- Territorially, political & monetary regimes identical.

Agenda

- The model's background vision & relevance.
- Digital currency governance & its implications.
    - Single/streamlined control Vs Protocol guided/controlled.
- The model's main findings.

Typology

Private Decentralized Digital Currency	**Private Centralized Digital Currency**
Public Decentralized Digital Currency	**Public Centralized Digital Currency**

Private Digital Currencies

- Control? Regulation?
  - Who controls balances/transfers? Identities? Disputes?
- Territorial relevance? Is it an international currency?
- Temporal relevance?
  - How do you start the digital currency?
  - How do you stop it?
- If used to evade capital controls, is it welfare enhancing?
- The mechanism that confers credibility & value on the digital currency?
- Bitcoin is one model.

If a Trusted Party is Necessary...

- It has some control/discretion.

=>

- Can extract rents.
- Can adapt to changing circumstances.

Economics of the Bitcoin Payment System

Gur Huberman, Columbia Business School
Jacob D. Leshno, Chicago Booth
Ciamac Moallemi, Columbia Business School

Cryptocurrencies

- Decentralized Electronic payment systems.
  - Bitcoin being the first, many other followed and offer different functions.
- Decentralized, two-sided markets.
  - Users receive similar services to PayPal, Fedwire; Miners provide infrastructure.
  - Security and Market design enabled by blockchain protocol.
- Novel economic structure.
  - Owned by no one.
  - Rules fixed by a protocol.
  - Participants are price-takers.

Traditional Payment Systems vs. Bitcoin

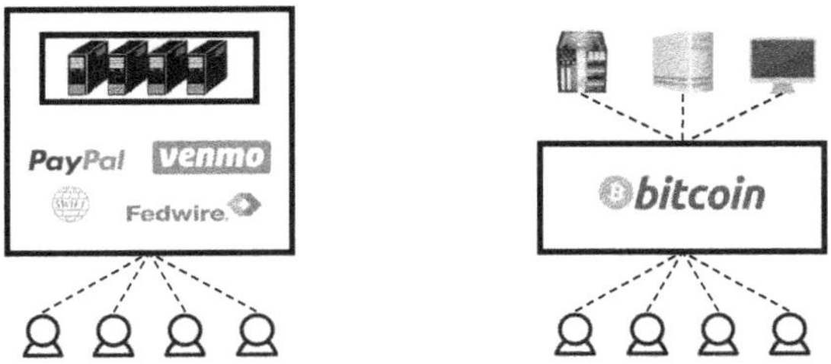

Rules	Set by firm/org	Fixed by protocol
Infrastructure	Procured by firm/org	*Revenue, entry/exit*
Revenue	Fees set by firm/org	*Equilibrium congestion pricing, all agents served*

Protocol Rules, No Policy Discretion

- Even when circumstances change.

Two & a Half Constituencies

- Users — send transactions (TX).
- Miners — provide computing infrastructure.
- TX recipients — confer value on the coin.

Miners are Crucial

- Must be compensated — in native coin.
- Native coin loses value => miners quit => system collapses.
- Should the model incorporate this possibility?

No Trusted Party => Crypto, or Protocol-governed

  - =>
  - Commitment to rules.
  - Rules are hard to change even when circumstances change.

Agenda

  - The model's background vision & relevance.
  - Digital currency governance & its implications.
    - Single/streamlined control Vs Protocol guided/controlled.
  - The model's main findings.

Main Finding 1:
Digital currencies enhance citizen welfare

- Risk Reduction.
  Non-positive correlation with local economic risks provides investors with a diversification opportunity
  - Who is supplying the digital currency & is on the other side of the diversification position?
  - Is the digital currency the issuer's liability?
- Restrained Monetary Policy.
  The difficulty of excluding digital currencies from the market reduces gains from seigniorage, thereby inducing lower inflation
- Difficulty of exclusion?
- E.g., Outlaw wiring money into/from exchanges.

Main Finding 2:
Digital currencies encourage local investment

- **Diversification.**
  Digital currencies serve as a hedge asset, thereby facilitating investment in high-risk economies
- In what sense are currencies an asset? If we make more, are we wealthier?
- **Credible Commitment.**
  Digital currencies facilitate a credible commitment to disciplined monetary policy, thereby enhancing expected returns from local investment
- Can terms of digital currencies adapt as circumstances change?

Main Finding 3:

Digital currencies may be desirable for corrupt sovereigns

Desirable also for non-corrupt sovereigns? Who is corrupt? Who is to say who is corrupt? Where's corruption in the model?

- **Local Investment.**
  Increased local investment yields higher tax revenue (holding tax rates constant)
- **Higher revenue to the corrupt is good?**
- **Welfare Gains.**
  Digital & original money side by side? Foregone network benefits of a single money?

Model: Assets

- Local productive capital.
  - — Taxable.
  - — Proxy for local investment.
- Private digital currency.
  - — Untaxable (reflects enforcement difficulty).
  - — Non-positively correlated with local economy.

Source of (negative) correlation?
Source of value fluctuations?

- Unproductive capital.
  - — Zero real return.

Agenda

- The model's background vision & relevance.
- Digital currency governance & its implications.
  - ○ Single/streamlined control Vs Protocol guided/controlled.
- The model's main findings.

The Stuff Dreams Are Made Of

- A small sliver of the population understands blockchain technology well enough to engage in fierce, esoteric debate over the meaning and relative importance of various ideas and terms.
- At the highest levels, everyone practices a kind of obscurantism, unwitting or otherwise.
- Elsewhere, people fake it.

CHAPTER 13

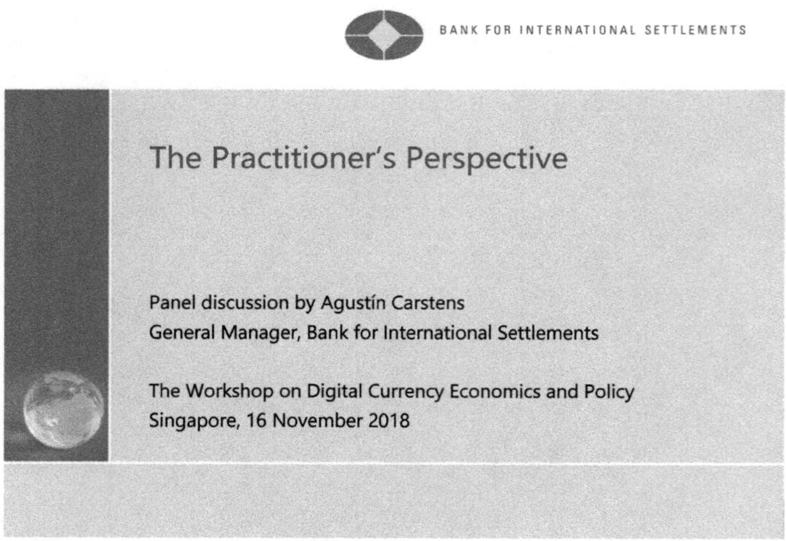
BANK FOR INTERNATIONAL SETTLEMENTS
The Practitioner's Perspective
Panel discussion by Agustín Carstens
General Manager, Bank for International Settlements
The Workshop on Digital Currency Economics and Policy
Singapore, 16 November 2018

The Money Flower: a taxonomy of money

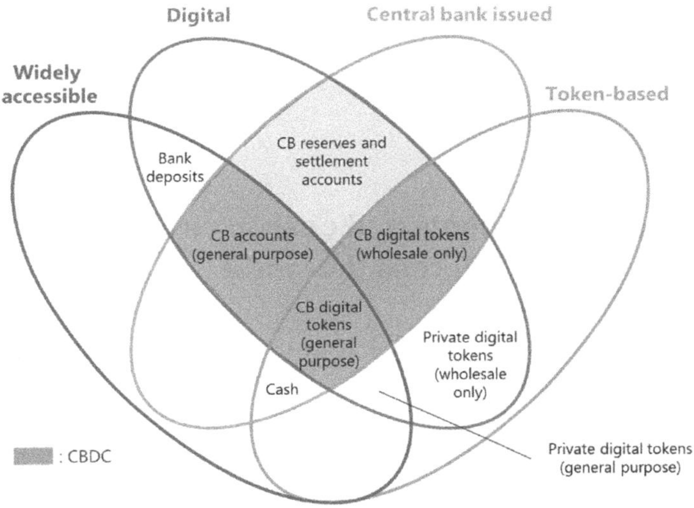

The Venn diagram illustrates the four key properties of money: issuer (central bank or not); form (digital or physical); accessibility (widely or restricted); and technology (account-based or token-based). CB = central bank; CBDC = central bank digital currency (excluding digital central bank money already available to monetary counterparties and some non-monetary counterparties). Private digital tokens (general purpose) include cryptoassets and currencies, such as bitcoin and ethereum. Bank deposits are not widely accessible in all jurisdictions. For examples of how other forms of money may fit in the diagram, please refer to the source.
***Source*: Based on M Bech and R Garratt, "Central bank cryptocurrencies", *BIS Quarterly Review*, September 2017, pp 55–70.**

Card payments and cash in circulation across the world

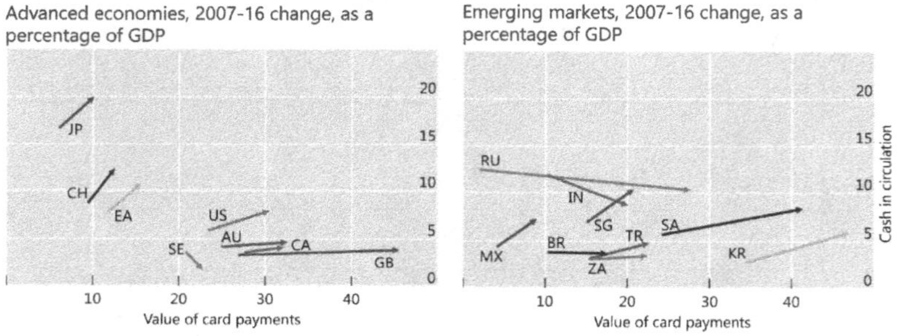

Source: **M Bech, U Faruqui, F Ougaard and C Picillo (2018): "Payments are a-changin' but cash still rules",** ***BIS Quarterly Review,*** **March 2018, pp 67–80.**

Card payments and cash in circulation in Sweden

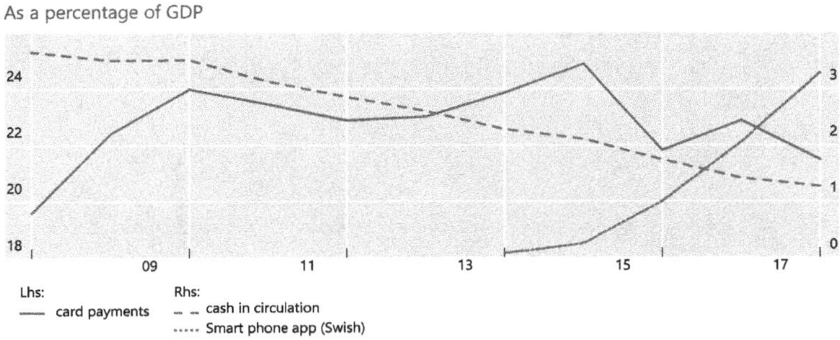

Source: **CPMI Red Book and Swish statistics 2012–2017.**

CBDC work
Share of respondents

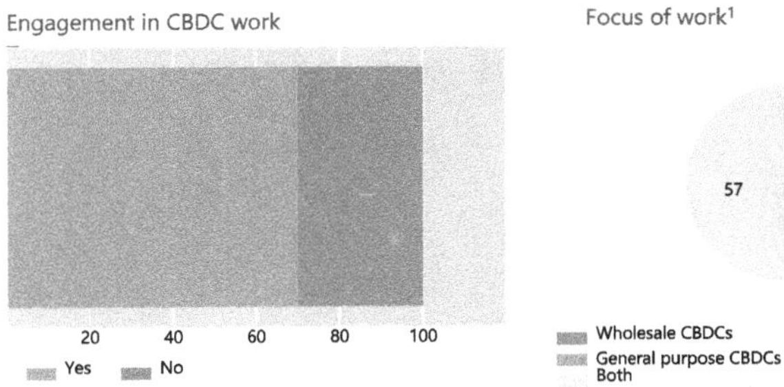

[1] Share of respondents who are conducting work on CBDC

***Sources*: CPMI central bank survey on CBDC and digital tokens.**

Type of CBDC work

Share of respondents who are conducting work on CBDC

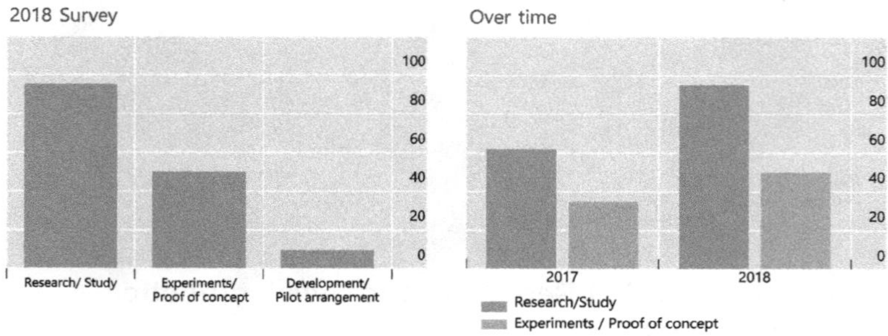

***Sources*: CPMI central bank survey on CBDC and digital tokens.**

Likelihood of issuing a CBDC Share of respondents

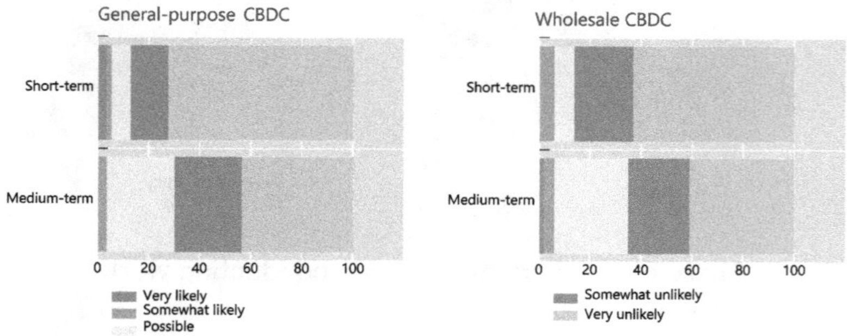

***Sources*: CPMI central bank survey on CBDC and digital tokens.**

CHAPTER 14

Chapter 14

Initial Coin Offerings, Corporate Finance and Financial Regulation

Franklin Allen*

Imperial College London

12 July 2020

Abstract

Initial Coin Offerings (ICOs) have grown substantially in recent years. They involve issuing coins that are recorded on a blockchain. These can be used to purchase the service or good that the firm they finance produces. The coins can be exchanged for currency on cryptocurrency exchanges. Although many ICOs are fraudulent, most studies find positive average and median returns. Theoretical analyses suggest they can have several advantages compared to Initial Public Offerings (IPOs). They are regulated in widely differing ways with the UK, Switzerland and Singapore having regimes that make them easier to undertake than other countries.

Introduction

Initial Coin Offerings (ICOs), where firm promoters issue electronic "coins" recorded on a blockchain that can be used to buy goods and

---

* Presented at the Asian Bureau of Finance and Economic Research workshop on Digital Currency Economics and Policy from 14–16 November 2018. I am grateful to my discussant Beatrice Weder di Mauro, workshop participants, Antonio Fatas, and Risto Karjalainen for helpful comments and discussions.

Table 1: ICOs from 2014–18

Year	Number of ICOs	Amount Raised (millions $)
2014	2	16
2015	3	6
2016	29	90
2017	875	6,227
2018	1,253	7,812

Source: ICODATA.IO: https://www.icodata.io/stats/2018

Table 2: The Geography of ICOs

Country	Number of ICOs	% ICOs
United States	178	19.5
Russia	111	12.1
United Kingdom	80	8.7
Singapore	75	8.2
Switzerland	46	5.0
Canada	29	3.2

Source: Adapted from Table 1 in Huang et al. (2018).

services, are a rapidly growing form of corporate finance. Table 1 shows the amount raised and the number of ICOs that occurred from 2014–2018. It can be seen that they were almost unknown in 2014 and 2015 with there being 2 and 3 ICOs, respectively, and the amounts raised being a few million dollars. 2016 was a transition year with 29 ICOs and $90 million raised. In 2017, ICOs took off with 875 issues and $6.227 billion raised and in 2018 there were 1,253 issues and $7.812 billion.

Although there are ICOs in many countries, some countries have significantly more than others. Table 2 shows the top 6 countries out of 18 with at least 12 for ICOs in 2017 and the first quarter of 2018 (Huang et al, 2018). The United States (US) and Russia are the largest with the United Kingdom (UK), Singapore and Switzerland next. While the first two are large countries, the next three are not, particularly Singapore and Switzerland. It is argued below that regulation plays a significant role in this distribution and the UK, Singapore, and Switzerland are particularly accommodative of this kind of financial technology.

There are a whole range of interesting issues associated with ICOs. We start by considering the typical sequence of events in an ICO. An important role is played by the information that is released in ICOs and how this helps to protect ICO investors. While ICOs have a number of advantages, they also have a number of disadvantages that are discussed.

An example of an ICO called Streamr is considered next to illustrate how these offerings often work. Streamr is a platform that allows data to be bought and sold using coins called DATAcoins that are special to the firm. These were issued in the initial offering to raise money to fund the firm and who owns them as they change hands are recorded on a blockchain. A proportion is held by those launching the firm to provide incentives for them to actually construct the firm so that the coins can be used to buy and sell the data. It is an interesting example because it could evolve into a new organizational form, namely a Decentralized Autonomous Organization (DAO). This kind of organization is essentially a computer program that is held on many computers so that it is decentralized. It can also be fully autonomous with no human intervention. As a result, equity is not needed.

There is a growing literature on the returns to investing in ICOs that is documented. While many are scams, many are not and overall returns appear to be positive. There is also a literature that considers the determinants of success of ICOs and this is discussed.

A number of theoretical models of ICOs have been developed. These usually argue that equity is a superior funding mechanism but we shall suggest this result depends on a number of assumptions of the models.

A key question that has come up in many countries is how ICOs should be regulated. We consider various models that are being used and argue that the UK, Singapore and Switzerland have developed the best form of regulation. However, there is room for improvement if the full benefits of ICOs for the economy are to be obtained. Finally, there are concluding remarks.

Typical Sequence of Events with ICOs

Since in many places ICOs are unregulated, they are done in a number of ways. Here we consider a typical sequence of events.

1. The promoters making the ICO issue a "White Paper" — these take many different forms but usually describe the nature of the

technology being funded and the uses the technology can be put to.
2. Possible investors then have the opportunity to ask the promoters questions about the technology and the business that is being founded.
3. An initial sale of coins is made and the promoters use the funds to implement the project. The promoters keep a proportion of the coins so that they have an incentive to complete the project, in which case the coins will have value.
4. Coins can be used on the platform to buy and sell the service or good the firm produces. These transactions are recorded on a blockchain.
5. The coins can be bought and sold for conventional currencies on cryptocurrency exchanges.

Information Released and Protection of Investors in ICOs compared to IPOs

Cohney, Hoffman, Sklaroff and Wishnick (2019) compare the information released in ICOs and protection of investors through computer code or what are known as "smart contracts" with traditional legal mechanisms in Initial Public Offerings (IPOs). They consider the top fifty ICOs in terms of funds raised in 2017 and collect the white papers and other available information. Their focus is on three issues regarding promises made in the documentation and whether they were coded in the smart contracts.

1. Did the promoters promise to restrict coin supply?
2. Was the vesting of coins to promoters to provide incentives as promised?
3. Did promoters retain the right to modify the code and was this disclosed?

The authors found that the ICO code and ICO disclosures often do not match. The code often fails to deliver key investor protections such as limiting the number of coins and providing the incentives to complete the project as promised. Also, the code often allows the promoters considerable ability to change the terms of engagement in ways that were not disclosed. Overall, the degree of protection is considerably less than in IPOs.

Advantages and Disadvantages of ICOs

Kaal (2018) points to several advantages of ICOs compared to conventional ways of raising capital:

1. ICOs enable borderless online sales with very few costs by enabling promoters to bypass the usual legal and jurisdictional hurdles and directly selling to a worldwide pool of investors
2. They provide excellent liquidity because global cryptocurrency exchanges provide continuous access to trading ICO tokens from the early stages of the business
3. ICOs provide liquidity to investors faster than other forms of capital formation such as venture capital, because investors can avoid the long and complex processes leading up to an IPO or sale and can simply sell their coins on an exchange

The main disadvantage of ICOs is the lack of regulatory oversight and legal recourse to the promoters as discussed by Cohney et al. (2019).

Example of an ICO — Streamr

An example of an ICO is described to illustrate some of the main features. To continue the example used above, Streamr is a platform that is designed to allow agents to buy and sell continuous streams of data for various applications. For instance, an asset manager might want to buy data on stock market prices, macroeconomic variables, and so on to drive its asset allocation model. Sellers of this data will find Streamr a useful platform to connect with such buyers.

Full details of the firm, its vision and in particular its whitepaper can be found at https://token.streamr.com/ (last accessed on 14 July 2020). The ICO raised 30 million Swiss Francs. The coins that were issued are called DATAcoins and there are a fixed number of these. DATAcoins are not mined but can be earned by selling data or can be bought or sold at a cryptocurrency exchange. The following link gives access to a page with details of the current price of DATAcoins and various other information such as the total market capitalization of the company: https://coinmarketcap.com/currencies/streamr-datacoin/ (last accessed on 14 July 2020).

New Organizational Forms: The Decentralized Autonomous Organization (DAO)

Streamr provides an example of a new type of organisational form. In the long run when it is fully completed, it has the potential to run autonomously without any human intervention. The programs that underlie the platform will be housed on many computers in many diverse places. If one or a few fails, then this will not lead to the service Streamr provides being lost. This decentralised structure and the fully automatic nature of the platform means that it is not necessary to have equity and governance structures in the way that traditional firms do. This feature becomes a key characteristic in terms of potential advantages of ICOs. We will return to this issue when we discuss theories of ICOs below. Karjalainen (2020) contains a full discussion of governance paradigms for firms such as Streamr.

Returns on ICOs

One problem with ICOs is that many are fraudulent. It is possible for the promoters to simply take the money raised in the ICO and disappear without creating the firm that allows the coins to be used. One of the important issues with ICOs is whether this possibility of fraud means that the returns are negative or whether the non-fraudulent ICOs earn sufficient positive returns to offset the scams. There are a number of papers that consider the returns on a sample of ICOs. They find widely differing results mainly because the samples used are quite different.

Benedetti and Kostovetsky (2018) create a dataset with 2,390 completed ICOs that were mostly executed between the start of 2017 and the end of April 2018, with a few being earlier. They find that there is a 179% average return from the final ICO price to the first day's opening market price on a cryptocurrency exchange that on average occurred 16 days later. The authors suggest ICOs that don't list within 60 days can be interpreted as fraudulent. If they are assigned a return of –100%, the average return falls to 82%. During the first 30 days of trading, the average buy and hold returns are 48%.

A study by Hu, Parlour and Rajan (2019) uses a dataset consisting of 64 of the largest ICOs by market capitalization based on white papers that were available in August 2017. In their sample, the median return on tokens that were purchased at the average ICO offering price and the end of the first day was 115%. At the end of the first month, the median increase was a further 29%. They create a sample that is 25% larger by adding firms that they do not have ICO prices for but do have price data for secondary trading on cryptocurrency exchanges. With these extra observations, the median returns from the end of the first day until the end of the first month are –16.1%. However, the average return is 46.3% because of some large positive returns in the extended sample.

In a series of empirical studies of ICOs, Momtaz (2019; 2020) finds that the price rises by 8.2% on average on the first day. Despite this average increase, the price falls on the first day of trading in 40% of cases. Momtaz (2019) investigates long term returns. Over the three years the average return is 15% while the median return is 3%.

Fahlenbrach and Frattaroli (2019) consider a hand-collected sample of 306 ICOs that successfully raised money between March 2016 and March 2018. On average the firms have 4,700 ICO investors. The median investor invests $1,200 and usually sells before the product is developed so the liquidity of ICOs seems to be valuable to them. The average return using weightings based on the initial amounts raised over 270 days in their sample is 104.8% but most of this is due to the rise in the price of cryptocurrencies generally. They therefore consider the excess return relative to the Ethereum cryptocurrency. Using equal weights, the excess return relative to Ethereum was –1.5% but with initial value weights it was +37.0%.

The point that Fahlenbrach and Frattaroli (2019) make, that returns on ICOs can be related to the price changes of cryptocurrencies, is borne out by Allen, Fatas and di Mauro (2019). They investigate the correlation between the returns on the 50 largest ICOs and Bitcoin and Ethereum. Correlations are positive but low while Bitcoin and Ethereum were becoming established and their prices were rising. When their prices fell dramatically in late 2017 and early 2018, the correlations increase and reach a very high level.

Overall, despite the many scams and unsuccessful projects that lead to large numbers of firms with negative coin returns, there is substantial evidence in the literature of a positive average return and, to a lesser extent, positive median returns over a multitude of holding periods. Thus, this type of financing does appear to have some social value and may well survive in the long run.

Determinants of Success of ICOs

One of the issues that has received some attention in the literature is what is needed to ensure an ICO is a success. An early paper investigating these issues is Adhami, Giudici, and Martinozzi (2018). They consider 253 ICOs from the beginning of 2014 until August 2017. They find that the probability of an ICO's success in terms of raising funds is increased if the source code the enterprise is based on is available, and if there is a presale of tokens that allows the purchase of the firm's output.

Howell, Niessner, and Yermack (2019) contains a thorough investigation of 1,520 ICOs that are listed on the TokenData website as of April 2018. They focus on 451 offerings where the coins subsequently trade on secondary exchanges for at least 90 days. Among these, firms are more successful in terms of avoiding failure and increasing employment if they issue a white paper that includes a budget, there is a vesting period for the tokens owned by the top management, and when top management have venture capital, entrepreneurial and computer science experience. While Howell et al. find that success is improved by allocating some tokens to an incentive pool, Roosenboom, van der Kolk, and de Jong (2020) find that bonus schemes hurt success. Otherwise, their results are similar, except that the latter also additionally show higher quality ratings by experts and having a pre-ICO GitHub repository are significant factors for success. Finally, Bourveau, De George, Ellahie and Macciocchi (2019) stress the stress the importance of the role of information intermediaries in the success of ICOs.

Theoretical Analysis of ICOs

As the previous sections have outlined, ICOs have been used to fund a significant number of entrepreneurial ventures. They also appear to have positive returns initially. How can these observations be explained? A number of theoretical studies have investigated the circumstances where token-based finance might be superior to traditional Initial Public Offerings (IPOs).

An early contribution is Catalini and Gans (2019). They develop a partial equilibrium model where an entrepreneur is raising funds for an innovative venture through an ICO and compare it with raising funds through a traditional equity offering. The products of the firm are paid for with the coin that is issued. Their main result is that issuing equity is superior to issuing coins because it can monetize the future equity return stream and so raise more money. This result suggests that ICOs will be a fleeting phenomenon that will soon die out. However, they have not done so yet.

Malinova and Park (2018) start by developing a model where a simple token structure is not as good as equity. However, an optimal token contract that combines pre-selling output with the sharing of marginal revenue is equivalent to equity. Finally, they show that with entrepreneurial moral hazard, tokens can finance more ventures than equity. Li and Mann (2018) adopt a different approach to show that tokens can be superior to equity. They focus on firms that develop peer-to-peer platforms. Their main result is to show that selling tokens before the platform is operating can overcome subsequent network effects. They argue their model is consistent with a number of empirically observed patterns associated with ICOs. Asymmetric information and agency problems are the focus of Chod and Lyandres (2019) when comparing equity and tokens. They show that tokens can be a superior form of finance for firms providing information goods or services, for those where entrepreneurial effort is important and those with relatively low payoff volatility. They can also be superior in signalling the quality of the firm to investors.

In addition to the factors stressed by these theories arguing that tokens can be superior, there are many other potential advantages of tokens. In some places, they allow regulation to be avoided. They provide liquidity from the beginning and do not tie up funds until there is an IPO or a firm is sold. There may also be tax advantages if appreciations in currency or tokens are not taxed. There may also be significant corporate governance advantages, as, for example, in the case of Streamr. There the platform is based on many nodes and ultimately may be fully autonomous with no human intervention. In this case, there will be no stream of equity returns and it will be a DAO where no decisions are required. The incentives to finish the platform are provided by the appreciation in the value of the coins that are issued. Understanding the operation of DAOs and how they compare to regular equity funded firms is an important area for future research.

Regulation of ICOs

ICOs raise a whole set of interesting regulation issues. Often ICOs are structured to avoid regulation. For example, in 51% of Zetzsche, Buckley, Arner and Föhr's (2017) sample, investors from certain countries were excluded from participation while 80% had no mention of the regulatory status of the ICO. In the Streamr example mentioned above, the website starts with the following message:

> *By continuing you agree that you are not a citizen of the following countries: The United States of America, Japan, Finland, or any other jurisdiction in which it is not permissible to participate in token crowd contributions.*

There is wide range of ways in which the regulation of ICOs works in different countries.

- In China and South Korea, there is an outright ban.
- In the US, the Securities and Exchange Commission (SEC) in July 2017 released a Report of Investigation that found a blockchain-based token qualified as a security requiring registration under the Securities Act of 1933.

- Many regulatory authorities have issued a warning concerning the risks of investing in ICOs including the US, Singapore, Hong Kong, UK, Australia, Germany, and the European Union's European Securities and Markets Authority (ESMA).

However, there are a few countries where the regulation of ICOs is relatively benign. These include the UK, Switzerland and Singapore. In general, the UK's "Regulatory sandbox" approach is helpful for allowing Fintech innovations. This allows businesses to test innovative products in the market provided they have a clear objective such as reducing costs to consumers and they are conducted on a small scale (see Financial Conduct Authority (2020)). With regard to ICOs, the UK Financial Conduct Authority (FCA) has stated that utility tokens, which are neither transferable securities nor regulated products, fall outside their regulatory product provided they only allow access to a network or product with no other legal rights attached (Linklaters, 2020). In this case, ICOs are effectively unregulated.

Switzerland provides another good example of a regulatory system that encourages ICOs by being more permissive. The Swiss Financial Market Supervisory Authority, FINMA, divides tokens into three types (FINMA, 2018):

- Payment tokens
- Utility tokens
- Asset tokens

The first are synonymous with cryptocurrencies, the second are intended for the purchase of a service or good, and the third are like equities, bonds, or derivatives.

The regulations that are most applicable are those concerned with anti-money laundering and securities regulation. Payment tokens must comply with anti-money laundering requirements and asset tokens with securities regulation. However, utility tokens are not treated as securities, provided they can already be used to purchase a good or services when they are issued. Thus, by issuing utility tokens in their ICOs, companies can avoid regulation of the type that accompanies IPOs.

The main regulator of ICOs in Singapore is the Monetary Authority of Singapore (MAS). ICOs are largely unregulated in Singapore, provided the tokens offered do not qualify as securities under Singapore law as defined by the Securities and Futures Act. The MAS holds ICO investors accountable for conducting their own legal due diligence and for addressing any risks associated with money laundering and terrorism financing (MAS, 2017; Sleek, 2020).

The difficulty with regulation is to design rules that protect investors while at the same time allowing innovation. Outright bans like those in China and South Korea clearly protect investors but prevent innovation. Defining coins as securities, as the US SEC does, achieves a similar outcome. The approach of the UK, Switzerland, Singapore allows innovation but protects investors mainly through warnings about the pitfalls of ICOs. These are designed to deter retail investors with small amounts to invest without preventing sophisticated investors from participating. It works reasonably well in these three countries. However, there does remain a considerable amount of fraud and, where deterrence works, the funds from small retail investors are not used to finance the new ventures. The results of Fahlenbrach and Frattaroli (2019) on ICO investors suggest these funds can be substantial. The question is whether it is possible to do better than the current regulations.

One possible approach is to use rules similar to Rule 144A restrictions on private placements that have been quite successful in the US for the issuance of securities outside the public markets. These ICO rules could ensure that only qualified investors (both in terms of computer science, the law and finance) can participate in ICOs. Another possible approach is self-regulation. Since the market for ICOs is global to a large extent, an industry body could suggest guidelines for the structure of white papers and what they should disclose. These could benefit not only information intermediaries, whose role Bourveau et al. (2019) stress, but also retail investors.

Conclusion

ICOs are becoming an increasingly important way of raising funds for innovative ventures. However, they are still small relative to more traditional ways of funding innovation such as angel investing and venture capitalists. There is evidence they provide positive investor returns on average and they have a number of theoretical advantages that the literature has identified. The UK, Switzerland and Singapore have structured liberal rules that have encouraged this kind of finance in their jurisdictions. However, fraud remains high. Regulation should aim at excluding unknowledgeable investors from ICOs while providing the knowledgeable ones with significant freedom to invest in firms that innovate. If this can be done well, there is potentially substantial scope for increasing innovation and thus growth in the economy.

References

Adhimi, S., G. Giudici and S. Martinozzi (2018). "Why do Businesses go Crypto? An Empirical Analysis of Initial Coin Offerings," *Journal of Economics and Business* 100 (November-December), 64–75.

Allen, F., A. Fatas, B. Weder di Mauro (2019). "Understanding Initial Coin Offerings and its Relatives," working paper, INSEAD.

Beneditti, H. and L. Kostovetsky (2018). "Digital Tulips? Returns to Investors in Initial Coin Offerings," working paper, Boston College, SSRN-id3182169.

Bourveau, T., E. De George, A. Ellahie and D. Macciocchi (2019). "Information Intermediaries in the Crypto-Tokens Market," SSRN-id 3193392.

Catalini, C. and J. Gans (2018). "Initial Coin Offerings and the Value of Crypto Tokens," working paper, MIT, SSRN-id 3137213.

Chod, J. and E. Lyandres (2019). "A Theory of ICOs: Diversification, Agency, and Information Asymmetry," SSRN-id 3159528.

Cohney, S., D. Hoffman, J. Sklaroff and D. Wishnick (2019). "Coin-Operated Capitalism," *Columbia Law Review* 119(3), 591–676.

Fahlenbrach, R. and M. Frattaroli (2019). "ICO Investors" European Corporate Governance Institute Working Paper 618/2019, SSRN-id 341994.

Financial Conduct Authority (2020). *Regulatory sandbox.* https://www.fca.org.uk/firms/innovation/regulatory-sandbox

FIMA (2018). *ICO Guidelines.* https://www.finma.ch/en/news/2018/02/20180216-mm-ico-wegleitung/.

Howell, S., M. Niessner and D. Yermack (2019). "Initial Coin Offerings: Financing Growth with Cryptocurrency Token Sales," *Review of Financial Studies* (forthcoming).

Hu, A., C. Parlour and U. Rajan (2019). "Cryptocurrencies: Stylized Facts on a New Investible Instrument," *Financial Management* 48, 1049–1068.

Huang, W., M. Meoli and S. Vismara (2018). "The Geography of Initial Coin Offerings," working paper, University of Bergamo, SSRN id3206234.

Linklaters (2020). *ICOs and Regulation in the United Kingdom*. https://www.linklaters.com/en/insights/thought-leadership/fintech/a-global-view-of-icos-and-regulation/icos-and-regulation-united-kingdom.

Kaal, W. (2018). "Initial Coin Offerings: The Top 25 Jurisdictions and their Comparative Regulatory Responses," working paper, University of St.Thomas School of Law, SSRN-id3117224.

Karjalainen, R. (2020). "Governance in Decentralized Networks," SSRN-id 3551099.

Li, J. and W. Mann (2018). "Initial Coin Offerings and Platform Building," SSRN-id 3088726.

Malinova, K. and A. Park (2018). "Tokenomics: When Tokens Beat Equity," SSRN-id 3286825.

Momtaz, P. (2020). "Initial Coin Offerings," SSRN-id 3166709.

Momtaz, P. (2019). "The Pricing and Performance of Cryptocurrency," *European Journal of Finance* (forthcoming), SSRN-id 3169682.

MAS (2020). *A Guide to Digital Token Offerings*. https://www.mas.gov.sg/regulation/explainers/a-guide-to-digital-token-offerings.

Roosenboom, P., T. van der Kolk and A. de Jong (2020). "What Determines Success in Initial Coin Offerings?" *Venture Capital* 22:2, 161–183.

Sleek (2020). *ICOs in Singapore* sleek.com/sg/resources/icos-in-singapore/.

Zetzsche, D., R. Buckley, D. Arner and L. Föhr (2017, 2018). "The ICO Gold Rush: It's a Scam, it's a Bubble, it's a Super Challenge for Regulators," University of Luxemburg Law Working Paper 2017-011, SSRN-id 3072298.

Digital Tokens and Financial Regulation

Franklin Allen

Imperial College London

ABFER Conference

National University of Singapore

16 November 2018

1. Introduction
   - Initial Coin Offerings (ICOs) are a rapidly growing form of corporate finance — in 2017 there were 18 a month and total of $3.7 billion raised for the year while up to July 2018 there were 99 a month and $17 billion had been raised (*Economist*, 1 September 2018).
   - There are a whole range of interesting questions associated with ICOs including the fact that they can represent a new form of corporation, e.g., Streamr.
   - Zetzsche *et al.* (2017, 2018) give the following classification and statistics for their hand-collected sample of over 1,000 ICOs out of 3,000 that they estimate have been made so far.

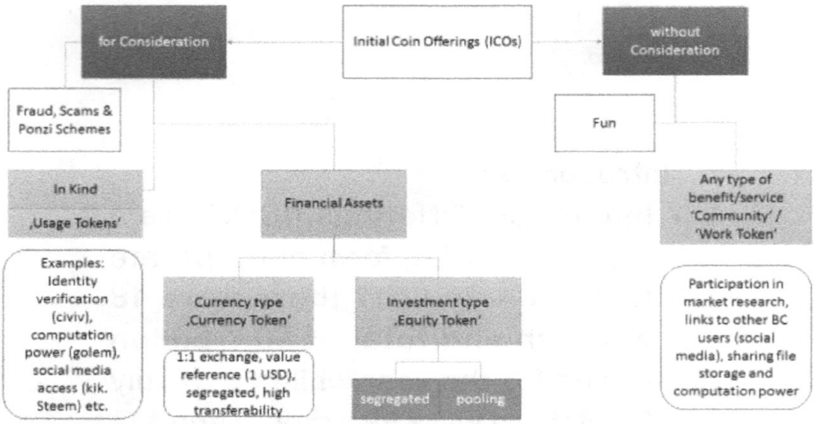

Figure 1: ICO Taxonomy by Token Reference

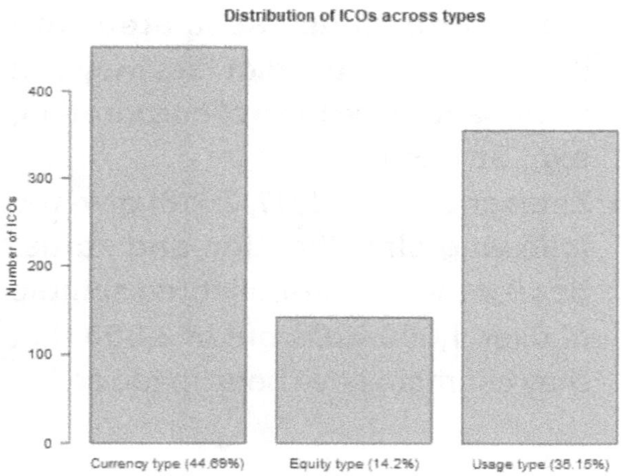

Figure 2: ICOs for Consideration by Reference Value

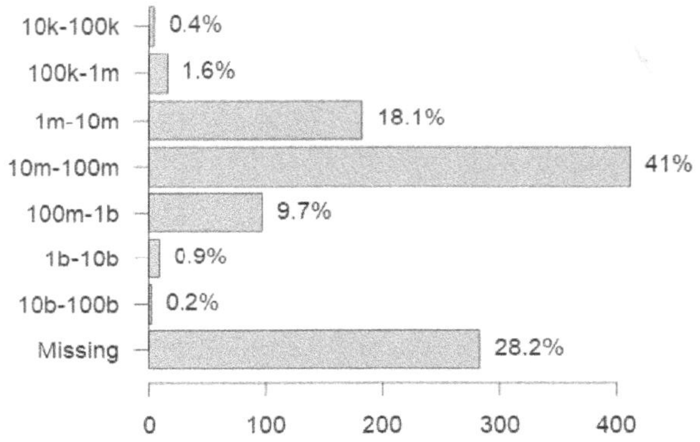

Figure 3: Distribution of ICOs by Market Cap.

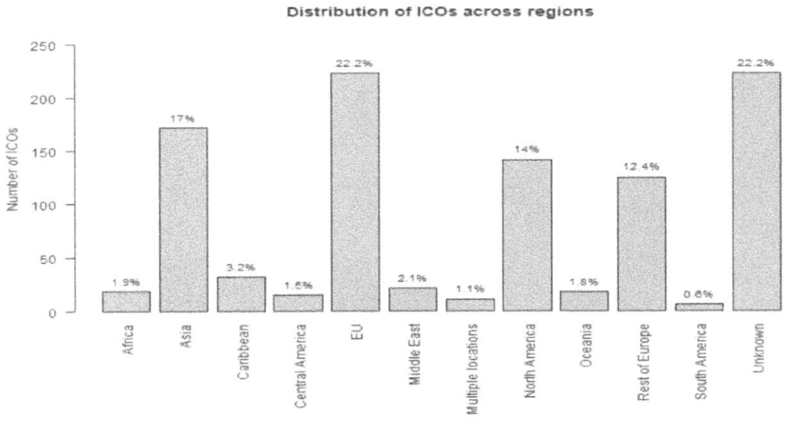

Figure 4: Geographical breakdown (by numbers of ICOs).

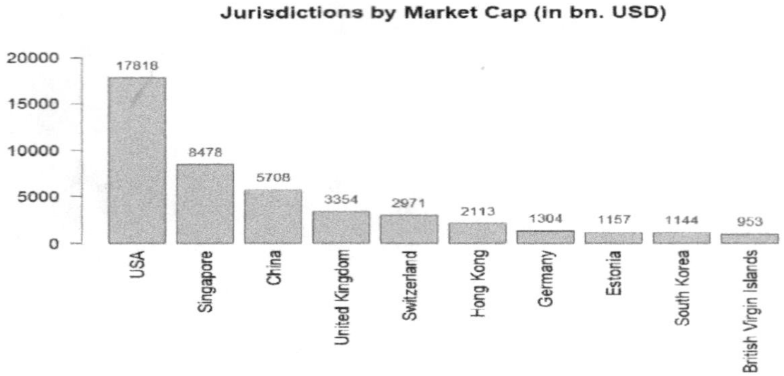

Figure 5: Top 10 ICO jurisdictions (by ICO market cap, at June 2018).

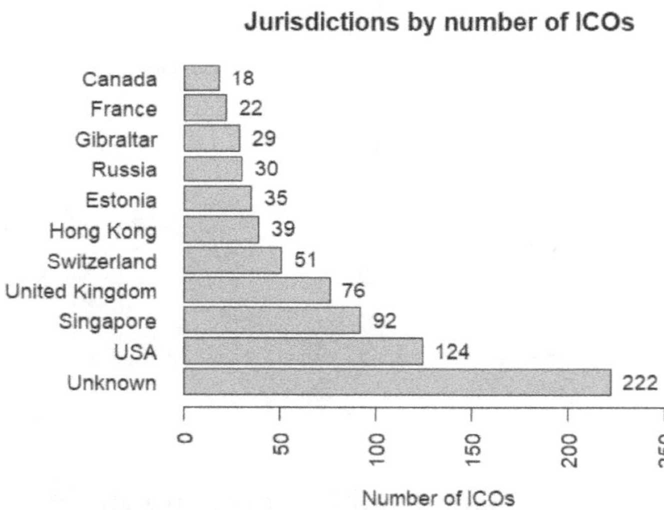

Figure 6: Top 10 ICO jurisdictions (by number).

Typical Sequence of Events with ICOs

- ICOs are done in a number of ways but a typical sequence of events is the following.
- The promoters making the ICO issue a "White Paper" — these take many different forms but usually describe the nature of the technology being funded and the uses the technology can be put to.
- Possible investors then have the opportunity to ask the promoters questions about the technology and the business that is being founded
- An initial sale of coins is made and the promoters use the funds to finish implementing the project.
- Coins can be used on the platform and bought and sold for conventional currencies on cryptocurrency exchanges.

Governance of ICOs

- Cohney *et al.* (2018) compare the governance of ICOs and protection of investors through computer code or what are known as "smart contracts" with traditional legal mechanisms in IPOs.
- They focus on three issues regarding promises made in the documentation and whether they were coded in the smart contracts.
  1. Did the promoters promise to restrict coin supply?
  2. Was the vesting of coins to promoters to provide incentives as promised?
  3. Did promoters retain the right to modify the code and was this disclosed?
- Cohney *et al.* found that ICO code and ICO disclosures often do not match.

Advantages and Disadvantages of ICOs

- Kaal (2018) points to several advantages of ICOs compared to conventional ways of raising capital.
  - ICOs enable borderless online sales with very few costs by enabling promoters to bypass the usual legal and jurisdictional hurdles by directly selling to a worldwide pool of investors.
  - They provide excellent liquidity because global cryptocurrency exchanges provide continuous access to trading ICO tokens from the early stages of the business.
  - ICOs provide liquidity to investors faster than other forms of capital formation — for example, venture capital funds can capitalize on existing profits early while avoiding long and complex processes leading up to an IPO or sale.
- The main disadvantage of ICOs is the lack of regulatory oversight and legal recourse to the promoters.

Example of a White Paper — Streamr

Unstoppable data for unstoppable apps: DATA coin by Streamr

Streamr

July 25th, 2017
Version 1.0

This whitepaper can be accessed via the following link and QR code: https://streamr.network/.

Streamr ICO

- The ICO raised 30 million CHF.
- There are a fixed number of DATAcoins.
- They are not mined but can be earned by selling data.
- More information can be accessed at the following:

https://token.streamr.com/
https://coinmarketcap.com/currencies/streamr-datacoin/

Returns on ICOs

- Many ICOs are scams but many are not.
- Benedetti and Kostovetsky (2018) find the following:
  - 179% average return from ICO price to the first day's opening market price on average 16 days later.
  - With –100% attributed to ICOs that don't list within 60 days the average return falls to 82%.
  - During the first 30 days of trading, the average buy and hold returns are 48%.

Economic Analysis of ICOs

- There have been a number of economic analyses of ICOS.
- A good example is Catalini and Gans (2018).
  - They develop a partial equilibrium model where an entrepreneur is raising funds for an innovative venture through an ICO and compare it with raising funds through a traditional equity offering.
  - The products of the firm are paid for with the coin that is issued.
  - Their main result is that issuing equity is superior to issuing coins because it can monetize the future equity return stream and so raise more money.
- How applicable is the analysis of Catalini and Gans (2018) to ICOs such as Streamr?
- The purpose of the Streamr project is to develop a trading platform or ecosystem for continuously available data.
- Prices in terms of DATAcoin are determined endogenously in a perfectly competitive environment.
- The platform is based on many nodes and ultimately will be fully autonomous with no human intervention — there is no stream of equity returns.
- The incentives to finish the platform are provided by the appreciation in the value of the DATAcoins.

Regulation of ICOs

- ICOs raise a whole set of interesting regulation issues.
- Often ICOs are structured to avoid regulation — in 51% of Zetzsche *et al.*'s (2017) sample, investors from certain countries were excluded from participation while 80% have no mention of the regulatory status of the ICO.
- Streamr website starts with:

By continuing you agree that you are not a citizen of the following countries: The United States of America, Japan, Finland, or any other jurisdiction in which it is not permissible to participate in token crowd contributions.

- Some examples of regulation in different countries.
    - Outright ban (e.g., China, South Korea).
    - In the US the Securities and Exchange Commission (SEC) in July 2017 released a Report of Investigation that found a blockchain-based token qualified as a security requiring registration under the Securities Act of 1933.
    - Regulatory warning (e.g., US, Singapore, Hong Kong, UK, Australia, Germany, EU's European Securities and Markets Authority (ESMA).
    - The UK's "Regulatory sandbox" approach is helpful for allowing Fintech innovations.
    - Switzerland provides a particularly good example of a regulatory system that encourages ICOs by being more permissive.

Switzerland's Swiss Financial Market Supervisory Authority (FINMA) Approach

- Selected excerpts from FINMA's website (see https://www.finma.ch/en/~/media/finma/dokumente/dokumentencenter/myfinma/4dokumentation/finma-aufsichtsmitteilungen/20170929-finma-aufsichtsmitteilung-04-2017.pdf?la=en).

FINMA recognises the innovative potential of distributed ledger/blockchain technology. It welcomes and supports all efforts to develop and implement blockchain solutions in the Swiss financial centre.

...

Swiss legislation on financial markets is principle-based; one such principle is technology neutrality.

Switzerland's Swiss Financial Market Supervisory Authority (FINMA) Approach (cont.)

...due to the underlying purpose and specific characteristics of ICOs, various links to current regulatory law may exist depending on the structure of the services provided. This concerns the following areas in particular:

- **Provisions on combating money laundering and terrorist financing: the Anti-Money Laundering Act applies where the creation of a token by an ICO vendor involves issuing a payment instrument. If this is the case, other supervisory issues may be effective for third parties, especially for professional cryptobrokers or trading platforms which carry out exchange transactions or transfers with tokens (secondary trading with tokens).**

...

A Suggestion for ICO Regulation

- The blockchain community in Zug has been fairly successful in developing innovative approaches and providing funds to successful firms like Streamr.
- However, preventing scams does seem an important thing to do but without preventing innovation.
- One possible approach is similar to the Rule 144A restrictions on private placements that have been quite successful in the US — ensure that only qualified investors (both in terms of computer science, the law and finance) can participate in ICOs.

Concluding remarks

- ICOs are becoming an increasingly important way of raising funds for innovative ventures.
- People with the combination of computer science, legal and finance skills needed to understand ICOs are rare.
- One particularly interesting aspect is the development of fully autonomous firms that operate without human intervention.
- Regulation should aim at excluding the unknowledgeable from ICOs while providing the knowledgeable with significant freedom to innovate.
- How should Singapore regulate ICOs going forward?

References

Beneditti, H. and L. Kostovetsky (2018). "Digital Tulips? Returns to Investors in Initial Coin Offerings," working paper, Boston College, SSRN-id3182169.

Cohney, S., D. Hoffman, J. Sklaroff and D. Wishnick (2018). "Coin-Operated Capitalism," working paper, University of Pennsylvania, SSRN-id3215345.

Catalina, C. and J. Gans (2018). "Initial Coin Offerings and the Value of Crypto Tokens," working paper, MIT, SSRN-id3137213.

Kaal, W. (2018). "Initial Coin Offerings: The Top 25 Jurisdictions and their Comparative Regulatory Responses," working paper, University of St.Thomas School of Law, SSRN-id3117224.

Zetzsche, D., R. Buckley, D. Arner and L. Fohr (2017, 2018). "The ICO Gold Rush: It's a Scam, it's a Bubble, it's a Super Challenge for Regulators," University of Luxemburg Law Working Paper 2017-011, SSRN-id3072298.

CHAPTER 15

Initial Coin Offerings
What, Why, How

Beatrice Weder di Mauro
INSEAD and CEPR

Singapore, 26-06-2018

Outline

1. What and why ICO
2. The good, the bad, the evil
3. Some stats
4. Regulating ICOs

1. The What
   - A new form of corporate finance.
   - A way of stimulating innovation in tech.
   - A new era of currency competition
   - Liberation from government and central banks.
   - Save the world with a blockchain.
   - A perfect scam.

Fighting World Hunger with Blockchain

Benevolent uses of secure technology with real human impact

1. The What: Mostly scams?

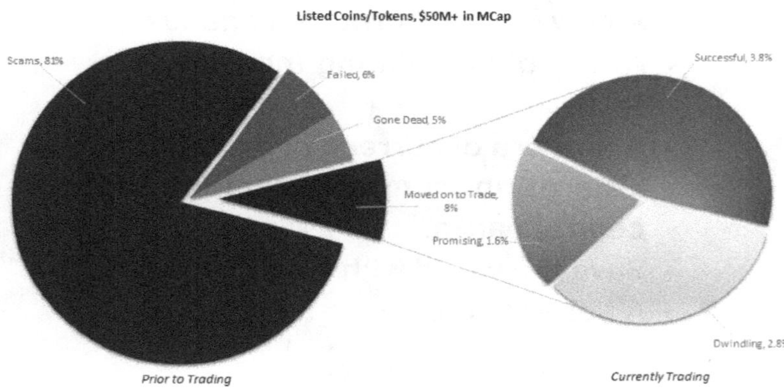

Source: https://news.bitcoin.com/80-of-icos-are-scams-only-8-reach-an-exchange/

1. The What

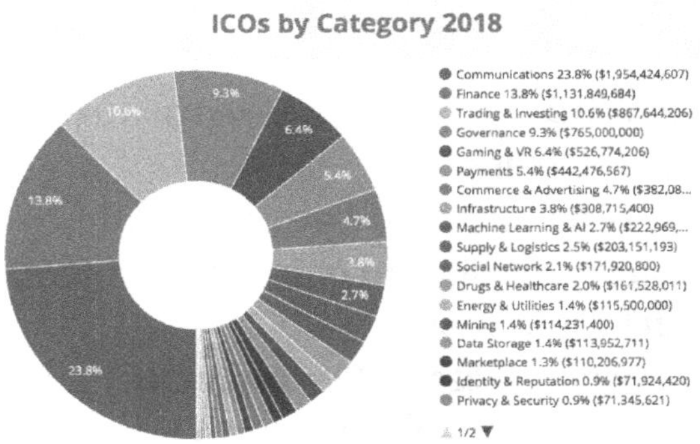

Source: https://www.coinschedule.com/stats.html?year=2018

- Types of projects.
  - Technology.
  - A lot more ...
- Types of coin.
  - Payments.
  - Equity like.
  - Utility tokens.

1. The What: Platforms with native (utility) tokens

Howell, Niessner and Yermak 2018

- Disintermediation of internet-based marketplaces:
  - Decentralize platform management.
  - value accrues to token holders.
- Token's value = value of the network:
  - token buyers fund the development,
  - token rewards network creators without giving them control.
  - token creates customer commitment since it's use is limited to the specific platform.

1. The Why : Economics
    - Completing markets?
    - Financing : Market failure in financing new venture.
        - — Arguments for public support of infant industries.
        - — Imperfections of venture capital (VC), private equity (PE), crowd-funding, seed funding,
        - — Expanding club funding.
    - Savers: Access to assets class.
    - All of the above?

2. The good the bad and the evil

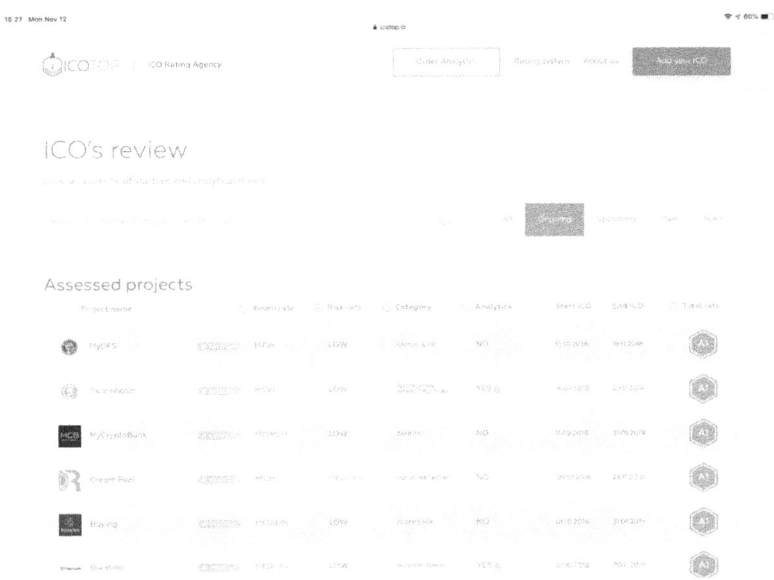

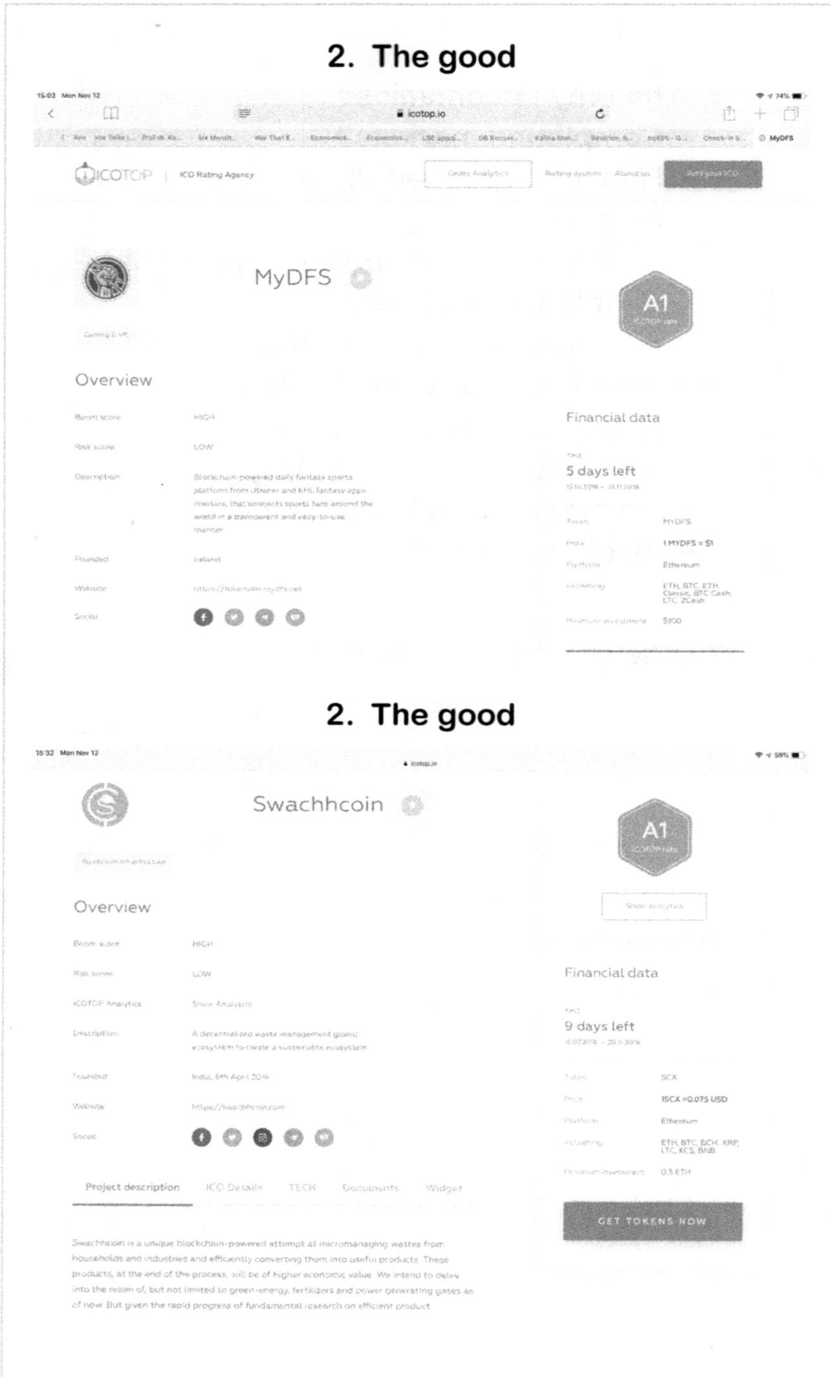
2. The good
icotop.io
ICOTOP
ICO Rating Agency
MyDFS
A1
Overview
Financial data
5 days left
1 MYDFS = $1
Ethereum
ETH, BTC, ETH Classic, BTC Cash, LTC, ZCash
$100
2. The good
Swachhcoin
A1
Overview
Financial data
9 days left
SCX
1SCX =0.075 USD
Ethereum
ETH, BTC, BCH, XRP, LTC, KCS, BNB
0.5 ETH
Project description
GET TOKENS NOW

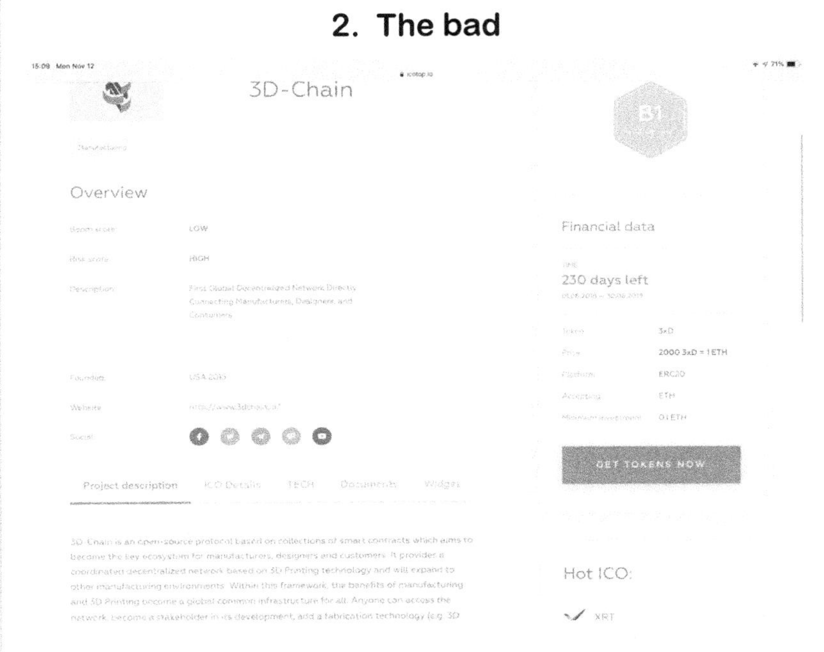
2. The bad
3D-Chain
Overview
LOW
HIGH
Financial data
230 days left
3xD
2000 3xD = 1 ETH
ERC20
ETH
0.1 ETH
GET TOKENS NOW
Project description
Hot ICO:
XRT

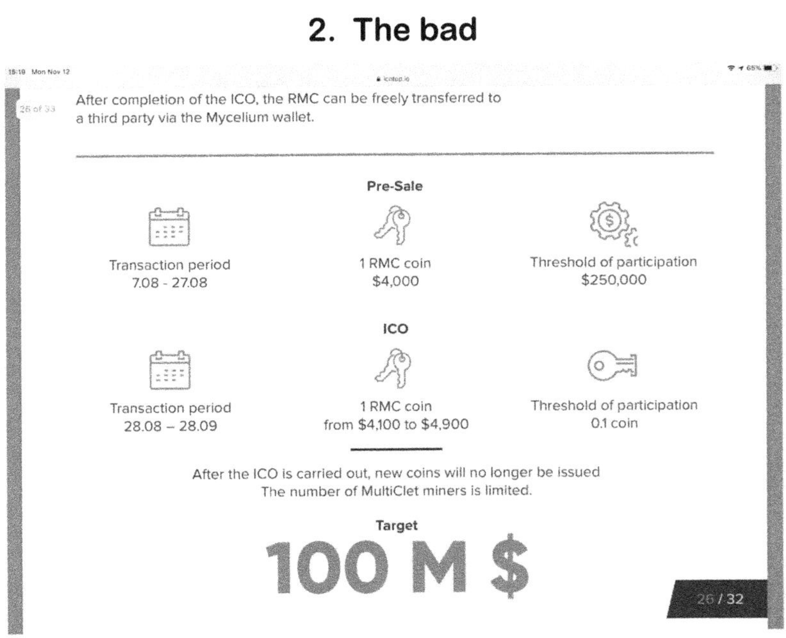
2. The bad
After completion of the ICO, the RMC can be freely transferred to a third party via the Mycelium wallet.
Pre-Sale
Transaction period
7.08 - 27.08
1 RMC coin
$4,000
Threshold of participation
$250,000
ICO
Transaction period
28.08 – 28.09
1 RMC coin
from $4,100 to $4,900
Threshold of participation
0.1 coin
After the ICO is carried out, new coins will no longer be issued
The number of MultiClet miners is limited.
Target
100 M $
26 / 32

2. The bad

"Surprisingly, in a community known for espousing a technolibertarian belief in the power of "trustless trust" built with carefully designed code, a significant fraction of issuers retained centralized control through previously undisclosed code permitting modification of the entities' governing structures" (Cohney *et al.* 2018)

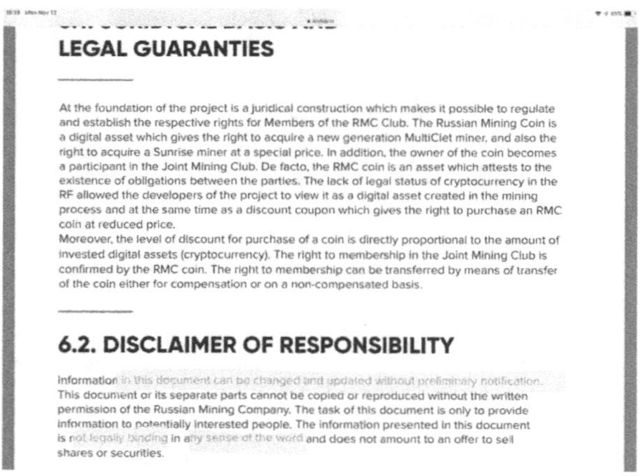

LEGAL GUARANTIES

At the foundation of the project is a juridical construction which makes it possible to regulate and establish the respective rights for Members of the RMC Club. The Russian Mining Coin is a digital asset which gives the right to acquire a new generation MultiClet miner, and also the right to acquire a Sunrise miner at a special price. In addition, the owner of the coin becomes a participant in the Joint Mining Club. De facto, the RMC coin is an asset which attests to the existence of obligations between the parties. The lack of legal status of cryptocurrency in the RF allowed the developers of the project to view it as a digital asset created in the mining process and at the same time as a discount coupon which gives the right to purchase an RMC coin at reduced price.
Moreover, the level of discount for purchase of a coin is directly proportional to the amount of invested digital assets (cryptocurrency). The right to membership in the Joint Mining Club is confirmed by the RMC coin. The right to membership can be transferred by means of transfer of the coin either for compensation or on a non-compensated basis.

6.2. DISCLAIMER OF RESPONSIBILITY

Information in this document can be changed and updated without preliminary notification. This document or its separate parts cannot be copied or reproduced without the written permission of the Russian Mining Company. The task of this document is only to provide information to potentially interested people. The information presented in this document is not legally binding in any sense of the word and does not amount to an offer to sell shares or securities.

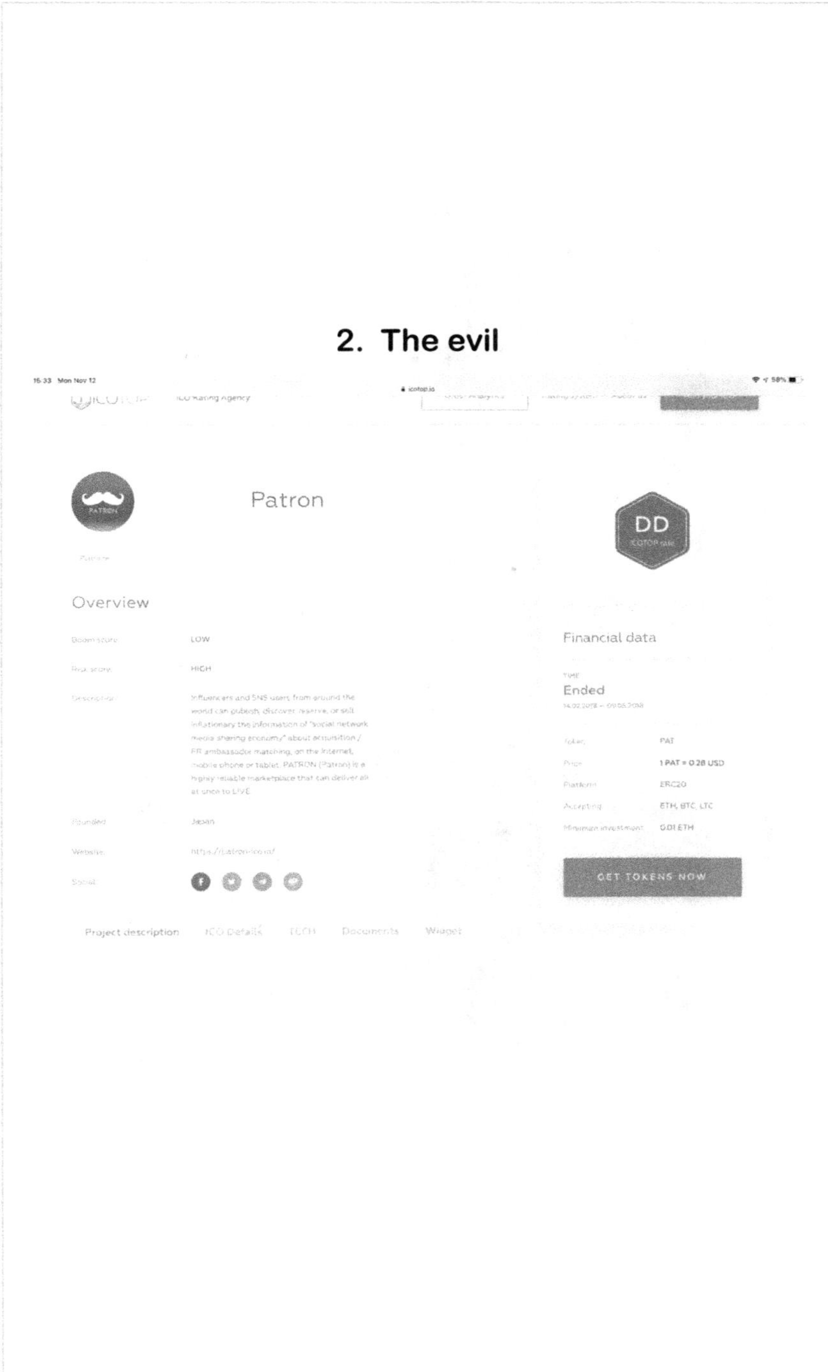
2. The evil
Patron
DD
Overview
LOW
HIGH
Japan
Financial data
Ended
PAT
1 PAT = 0.28 USD
ERC20
ETH, BTC, LTC
0.01 ETH
GET TOKENS NOW
Project description

2. The evil

Dead Coins
ADD A DEAD COIN
SIGN UP
Dead Coins
CURATED LIST
Of cryptocurrencies forgotten by this world....and more
Full List
Deceased
Hack
Scam
Parody
Detailed view
Search Entries:
Search
Clear
Coin Name
Coin Code
Summary
HPY
no connection with its product (an ugly as fuck wallet)
CAPX
This coin was a Ponzi scheme lending token promoted by ...
KMC
https://bitcointalk.org/index.php?topic=524216.0 "Comkort announced delist of KimoCoin, so, I think, this ...
bfdt
scam
XAX
Original Developers Abandoned the project after the appointed steering committee

3. The Stats
   - Properties of a new asset class (Hu, Parlor, Rajan 2018).
     Sample of 64 largest ICOs

— ICO First day returns (mean 4,7% median 115%).
— IPO first day return (mean 12.1%).

Secondary market
— Correlation with S&P (low 0.0045 (daily return)).
— Correlation with Gold (low 0.061).
— Correlation with Bitcoin (low 0.021).

3. The Stats

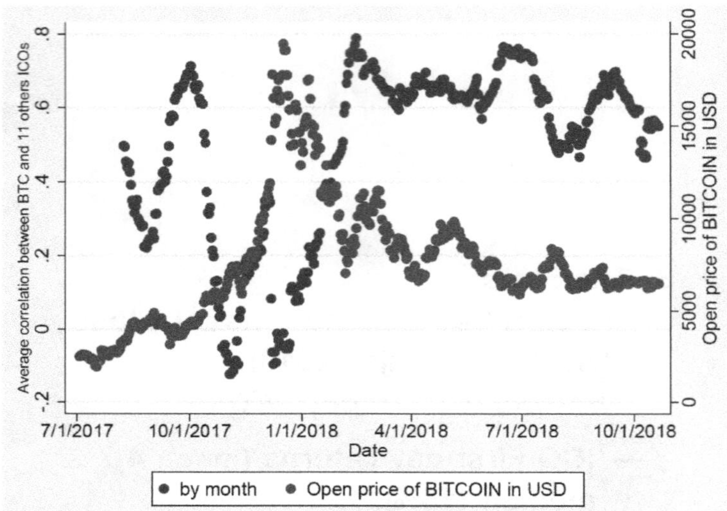

3. The Stats

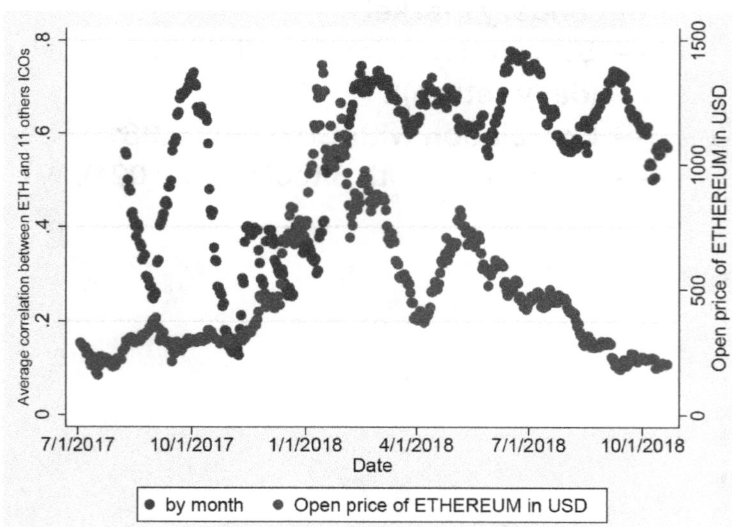

Globally, diverse ICO regulation is emerging – different approaches by geographies identified

Overview emerging regulation

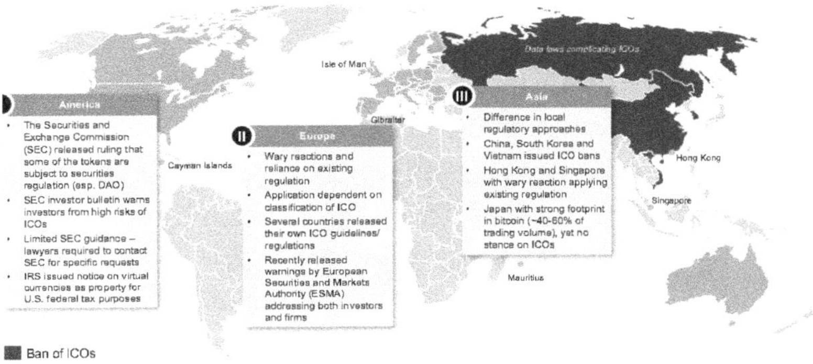

Most regulators did not determine the precise nature and asset class of cryptocurrencies as the basis for ICO regulation. The recent wave of ICOs might push regulators to act faster than planned on cryptocurrencies

***Source*: https://cryptovalley.swiss/wp-content/uploads/20171221_PwC-S-CVA-ICO-Report_December_final.pdf**

4. Regulation uncertainty

SEC statement on cryptocurrencies and ICOs (11 Dec 2017)

- Chairman Jay Clayton warns investors to put money into cryptocurrencies
- Trading cryptos and ICO activity may be in violation of federal security law
- Many platforms trading in cryptocurrencies may also be in violation of laws
- Calling a token a "utility" does not prevent token from being a security
- The disruptive potential of cryptocurrencies and blockchain is recognized

ICO ROAD MAP

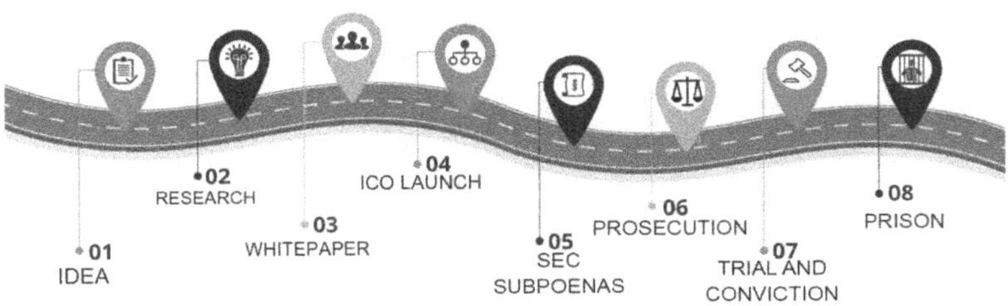

4. Regulation
    - On what grounds?
        - What benefits does the asset class provides (diversification, new venture financing (see point 1.)?
        - What costs/externalities (environment, social assistance, misallocation of resources)?
    - Protection of what/who?
        - Financial system stability.
        - Financial center competitiveness.
        - Investors protection.
    - On grounds of level playing field (Duck test).
        - Technologically neutral.
        - By type of token.
    - Investor protection ok, but how.
        - Prohibition.
        - Risk tolerance/knowledge.
        - Transparency.

Conclusions, what I would like to know

1. Why token financing?
2. What are the properties?
3. Why regulate?

Research & Policy Network @ CEPR
on Fintech and Digital Currency
Lead by Antonio Fatas

Thank you

CHAPTER 16

"Digital Currency Economics and Policy" — Conclusion

Bernard Yeung

President, ABFER
Stephen Riady Distinguished Professor
NUS Business School

- A big thank-you to the presenters, commentators, and all the participants.
- A big thank-you to MAS for jointly supporting and organizing the workshop.
- We have had an intellectual feast.
  - Covered more grounds than expected.
  - Heard first principle based analytics and insights.

- A proliferation of digital currencies.
  - Possibly a desire in some to have some freedom in carrying out transactions beyond using fiat money, beyond the reach of governments and dominant financial institutions.
  - Technological progress just came conveniently.

Two types of technological progress

- E-payment arrangements reduce transaction costs and facilitate more thorough record keeping than before.
    - Recently widely adopted in countries like China.
        - Use less cash.
- The block-chain type → bitcoin, cryptocurrencies.
    - Many related applications, beyond bitcoin.
        - Supply chain management, medical, ...
        - Decentralized, scalable, and resilient.

Block chain — Cryptocurrencies, a trustless decentralized system

- Facilitate out of the system transactions,
  - can be anonymous (and some transactions may be illegal)
  - may weaken capital flow management & monetary policy effectiveness.
  - limit seigniorage.
    - magnitude may be marginal.
- Consume high energy costs, transaction speed is slow, and expect forking.
- Traded, volatile price.
  - do not pass the test for being money — a unit of account, medium of exchange and storage of value.
  - cannot serve up the role of trusted lender of last resort.
  - or the decentralized system can make intelligent discretionary decisions to stabilize our economy.
- But, it is an alternative some like, seen as their economic freedom.

Immediate investment regulatory concerns

- Proliferation of private cryptocurrencies.
- Many enthusiastic souls see jackpots, e.g., buy cryptocurrency and invest in ICO.
    - ICO — Money for tokens, the money invested in finishing a platform, tokens used in the platform or traded on cryptocurrency exchanges.
- The irony: the technology promises reliable "trustless-ness" but generates traditional governance and investor protection concerns.
    - Some lead to jackpot returns, many fail.
    - Market solution may not be there yet — too few experts.
- Regulations.
    - Ban, Warn, Sandbox, Classify (e.g., duck test) and apply the relevant regulation.
- Government challenges.
    - Too much protection stifles innovation and risk taking.
    - Not having enough talent in the intersection of law, finance, and technology, etc.
    - Not knowing what we do not know!

Government will act

- To limit illegal activities, e.g., tax evasion, "black" activities, by-pass capital flow management.
- To protect seigniorage income and monetary policy effectiveness.
- Crypto-algorithm notwithstanding, we cannot let something we do not know well with no one accountable take too much space and responsibilities.
  - Anyway, people use less cash. E-arrangements for efficiency gains?
- Choices:
  - Regulate.
  - Embrace technology: simply going to all e-transactions to offering digital fiat currency.
    - limited access vs full fledge cashless digital arrangement, e.g., a debt-card for all.
- The choice ought to be grounded on the fundamental role of government — nurture the development of a stable and value enhancing system and a smooth transition path.

Positive considerations for offering a digital fiat money

- Raise efficiency, reduce transaction cost, especially in international payment.
- Constrain illegal transactions,
  - Note, however, we can do these without digitalization of the fiat currency.
- Digitalization relaxes the constraints of monetary policy at the zero lower bound, e.g., using negative interest rate.
- Critically, the government, through digitization, will acquire a lot more information than before.
  - stronger surveillance of transaction activities.
    - More policy angles and freedom, e.g.,
      - Better constrain illegal activities, better tax collections, etc.
      - More focused and effective policy, e.g., drone dropping of money (Rogoff's book), engineering stability, etc.

Negative considerations for offering a digital fiat money

- CBDC impacts on the private sector's financial institutions, affects economic behavior.
  - With a full fledge debit card type of CBDC, private sector financial institutions may have to focus purely on term structure and credit transformation.
  - The risk of fast run on banks
    - People can run to CBDC for safety by just pushing a button (but should note that a central bank can respond quickly too).
    - Nevertheless, private sector financial system's stability is a concern.

Really lots of unknowns, disruptions

- What is the implication on the cost of capital from investors' perspective in a full reserve system?
- What will the world be like if traditional financial institutions lose their transaction banking business and not rewarded for leveraging?
- Would CB have to hold more reserves if their liabilities include all current bank deposits?
- If non-residents have access to CBDC, what is the cross border ramification and externalities?
- Then, the cybercrime issues?
- Generically, how will our economy/financial sector function then?

What is the fundamental issue?

- Technological progress allows government or the private sector to have more records, thus, possibly more information.
  - Expands everyone's feasibility set.
- A system design problem: cash vs CBDC vs bitcoin is a centralized vs a decentralized system in generating (or not generating) the data and in allowing access of the data.
  - Should the government have all the transaction records.
    - Is this too big a temptation in developing an overbearing government?
  - Generically
    - How and what data should be generated and collated by whom?
    - Who should have access to the data?
    - Data are not information. Who should generate the information? With the right incentives?
    - Who should have what market power? Regulatory power? Political power?
      - Power corrupt people? Power breeds angels?

- We hope to nurture the development of research on digit currency economics.
  - ABFER organizes a special session and a master class on digital currency economics in our May 2019 workshop.
  - The 2019 AMPF features "digital currency" in its Policy Notes session.
  - Cooperating with CEBRA and CEPR and many central banks to have a research conference on digital currency economics on 18–20 July 2019 in NYC.

- Let me again thank you all for being here. Special thanks to the presenters and commentators.
- Thanks to Agustín Carstens, General Manager, BIS, Cecilia Skingsley, Deputy Governor, Sveriges Riksbank, and Ravi Menon, MD, MAS for a great panel.
- Thanks to Senior Minister Shanmugaratnam for attending yesterday's morning session.
- Thanks to MAS leaders, e.g., Jacqueline Loh, Andrew Khoo, Sing Chiong, and many others, for their support and being here in spite of a hectic week at MAS.
- Thanks to Ms Teo Swee Lian, Member of ABFER Advisory Council, for being here.

- Thanks to
  - Economic Policy Group organizers at MAS — Celina Sia, Xiongy Wei, Thasreen, Geraldine with assistance from Bernard wee and Choy Keen Meng.
  - The Corporate Support Department at MAS, the ABFFER team.
- Thanks to Dr Edward Robinson, my co-organizer and Chief Economist, MAS.
- Last but not the least, thanks to the participants for their great inputs which raised the workshop's intellectual intensity.

Index

CPSIA information can be obtained
at www.ICGtesting.com
Printed in the USA
BVHW040136081120
592233BV00018B/13

9 789811 22377